MW00780830

ALL ABOUT BONDS, BOND MUTUAL FUNDS, AND BOND ETFs

OTHER TITLES IN THE "ALL ABOUT..." SERIES

All About Stock Market Strategies
by David Brown and Kassandra Bentley

All About Technical Analysis
by Constance Brown

All About Derivatives
by Michael Durbin

All About Investing
by Esmé Faerber

All About Asset Allocation
by Richard A. Ferri

All About Index Funds
by Richard A. Ferri

All About Hedge Funds
by Robert A. Jaeger

All About Market Timing
by Les Masonson

All About Options, 3rd edition
by Thomas A. McCafferty

All About Dividend Investing
by Don Schreiber and Gary E. Stroik

All About Commodities
by Russell R. Wasendorf

All About Futures
by Russell R. Wasendorf

All About Stocks, 3rd edition
by Esmé Faerber

All About Exchange Traded Funds
by Archie Richards, Jr.

ALL ABOUT BONDS, BOND MUTUAL FUNDS, AND BOND ETFs

Third Edition

ESMÉ FAERBER

New York Chicago San Francisco Lisbon London
Madrid Mexico City Milan New Delhi San Juan
Seoul Singapore Sydney Toronto

Copyright © 2009 by Esmé Faerber. All rights reserved. Printed in the United States of America. Except as permitted under the United States Copyright Act of 1976, no part of this publication may be reproduced or distributed in any form or by any means, or stored in a database or retrieval system, without prior written permission of the publisher.

1 2 3 4 5 6 7 8 9 0   FGR/FGR   0 1 0 9 8

ISBN 978-0-07-183223-6

MHID: 0–07–154427–5

McGraw-Hill books are available at special discounts to use as premiums and sales promotions, or for use in corporate training programs. To contact a representative please visit the Contact Us pages at www.mhprofessional.com.

This publication is designed to provide accurate and authoritative information in regard to the subject matter covered. It is sold with the understanding that the publisher is not engaged in rendering legal, accounting or other professional service. If legal advice or other expert assistance is required, the services of a competent professional person should be sought.
                —From a Declaration of Principles Jointly Adopted by a Committee of the American Bar
                                Association and a Committee of Publishers and Associations

All investing concepts, ideas, strategies, methods, etc. in this book are intended for educational purposes only. They are not meant to recommend or promote any investing strategy or philosophy. You are advised to consult a financial professional before investing.

This book is printed on acid-free paper.

Library of Congress Cataloging-in-Publication Data

Faerber, Esmé
  All about bonds, bond mutual funds, and bond etfs / by Esmé Faerber. — 3rd ed.
    p. cm.
  Rev. ed. of: All about bonds and bond mutual funds. 2nd ed. c2000.

  1. Bonds. 2. Bond funds. 3. Exchange traded funds. 4. Investments. I. Faerber, Esmé. All about bonds and bond mutual funds. II. Title.

HG4651.F29 2009
332.63'23—dc22   2008031057

CONTENTS

PREFACE

This third edition includes information to assist bond investors to become more knowledgeable about their investments. Among the many changes to this edition are new chapters on foreign and emerging market debt, how to use duration and convexity concepts, and the inclusion of investing in bond exchange traded funds. Each chapter includes many new sections to provide both beginning and sophisticated bond investors with the tools to make more informed bond investments. Bond exchange traded funds are compared with bond mutual funds and investing in individual bonds.

The early chapters present information on the characteristics of bonds with the purpose of providing readers with an understanding of the workings of a bond, and their performance with regard to risk and return. The following chapters present the different types of bonds (Treasuries, government agency bonds, GNMA, FNMA, collateralized mortgage obligations, municipal bonds, corporate bonds, convertible bonds, zero coupon bonds, and foreign bonds) along with a comparison of the corresponding mutual funds and bond exchange traded funds. These chapters provide readers with the information to make their choices as to whether to invest in individual bonds, or bond mutual funds, or bond exchange traded funds. The last chapter provides the information to manage a bond portfolio.

As a more informed investor, it is easier for you to make better decisions regarding your bond investments.

ACKNOWLEDGMENTS

Many people facilitated the preparation of this book, and I am grateful for their assistance.

My husband, Eric, and our children, Jennifer and Michael, deserve a special note of thanks for their continued support and patience.

CHAPTER 1

What Bonds Can Do for You and Why You Should Consider Investing in Them

KEY CONCEPTS

- Reasons for investing in bonds
- What are bonds?
- Terminology of bonds
- How to buy and sell bonds

History provides not only insights into past returns from investing in the stock and bond markets, but also valuable lessons for investing in the future. Evaluating the performance of stocks and bonds can provide you with insights into planning your investments for the future. Advocates of stock investments quote historic returns over long periods of time, such as 20-, 50-, and 100-year periods because stocks have consistently outperformed bonds and other financial asset classes. However, when the time frame falls to shorter time periods (less than five years) the results can be markedly different, as Table 1-1 illustrates. The performance of bonds over two- to five-year periods has often outperformed the returns of stocks and money market securities (cash equivalents). Within these shorter time frames, there are at least two sets of circumstances where bonds outperform stocks. During recessions, bonds generally provide better returns than stocks, and when both interest rates and inflation are rising, short-term bonds (Treasury bills and money market equivalents) often outperform both long-term bonds and stocks.

TABLE 1-1

Historical Performance of Stocks, Bonds, and Treasury Bills

Time Period	Large-Cap Stocks	Corporate Bonds	Treasury Bills
1926–2004	9.37%	6.19%	3.5%
1980–2004	11.12%	10.84%	6.47%
1995–2004	14.00%	9.87%	3.92%
1999–2004	−0.7%	10.76%	2.7 %

An example illustrates the risk of loss from investing in only one asset class. If you had invested solely in stocks in the time period from March 1995 through March 2000 you would have earned spectacular returns, as the U.S. stock markets reached their all-time highs in March 2000. During that time period, other financial securities such as bonds and money market securities could not match the stellar stock market returns. However, for the following two and a half years, the broad stock market index fell by 50 percent, and technology stocks declined by roughly 80 percent, while bonds earned positive returns. For the next two and a half years through March 2005, the stock markets increased but they came no where near the highs of March 2000.

If you were clairvoyant you would have invested solely in stocks from 1995 to 1999, switched to bonds January 1, 2000, through 2002, and then switched back to stocks in 2003 through 2004, and your returns would have been hard to beat. The problem is that we do not know when we should be fully invested in stocks and when we should switch to bonds. The lessons that we can learn from this example are:

- It is virtually impossible to determine how the markets will perform in the future and so we should not have all our eggs in one basket, so to speak, by investing solely in stocks or bonds. We want to minimize the risk of loss.
- The key to minimizing the risk of loss is to invest in different classes of investments whose returns are not correlated—in other words, investing in asset classes

FIGURE 1-1

Historical Performance of Large-Cap Stocks, Long-Term
Corporate Bonds, and Treasury Bills from 1995 to 2004

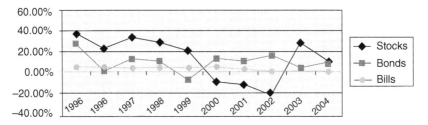

whose returns do not rise and fall together. When one
asset class declines in value, another asset class increases,
which minimizes portfolio losses and seeks positive
overall returns.

The concept of minimizing the risk of loss through asset allocation can be illustrated further by examining Figure 1-1. In the 10-year
period from 1995 to 2004, large-cap stocks earned on average 14 percent per year, but had negative returns for three of the years (2000
through 2002). Long-term corporate bonds had a negative return for
only one year in that same 10-year period.

As of March 2005, the Nasdaq composite index was still 60 percent lower than its highs of March 2000. A broadly diversified
portfolio of stocks, bonds, money market securities, and real estate
(real estate investment trusts [REITs] and not necessarily individual
properties) would have produced modest positive returns throughout the 10-year period, avoiding the pain caused by the negative
returns of stocks.

Figure 1-2 compares the returns of a balanced portfolio invested
with 50 percent in large-cap stocks and 50 percent invested in long-
term corporate bonds with large-cap stocks and long-term corporate
bonds over the 10-year period 1995 to 2004. This graph provides
a valuable lesson learned from many myopic investment strategies
pursued in the late 1990s through the early 2000s. Successful investing requires asset allocation (investing in different asset classes,
such as stocks, bonds, and money market securities) and diversification (selecting different investments within an investment class).

FIGURE 1 - 2

Historic Comparison of Stocks, Bonds, and a Balanced
Portfolio from 1995 to 2005

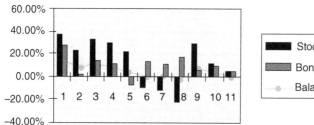 

A well-diversified portfolio is less likely to suffer the extreme ups
and downs within the markets.

Although the balanced portfolio (as shown by the line graph)
did not have the highs of both individual stock and individual bond
portfolios, it also did not produce the losses of the stock portfolio.

REASONS FOR INVESTING IN BONDS

- Investing in a diversified portfolio of stocks, bonds,
  money market securities, and other asset classes reduces
  the risk of loss and balances returns due to uncertainties in
  the markets. Bonds are like an anchor on a ship and act as
  a buffer when stocks decline.

- Investing in bonds provides financial security because
  bondholders are paid regular payments of interest
  and their principal is returned to them when their
  bonds mature.

- Certain types of bonds provide tax breaks. Municipal
  bonds are exempt from federal taxes, and may also be
  free from state and local taxes for taxpayers filing in the
  states and counties where the bonds are issued.

- Bonds can be sold before their maturity dates should
  bondholders need their money earlier than the stated
  maturity dates.

- Bonds are less risky than stocks. Treasury bonds are
  virtually free of credit and default risk, while bonds with

high credit ratings seldom default on their interest and principal payments.

- Bond investments preserve and increase capital, in addition to providing the opportunity for capital appreciation (and capital loss).

Despite these many reasons for investing in bonds, many investors overlook investing in bonds because they do not provide the capital appreciation of stocks. This is true—bonds are not stocks—but bonds can provide you with a lower risk approach to building a secure nest egg. Consequently, bonds should play a part in virtually every investor's portfolio.

WHAT PART SHOULD BONDS PLAY IN YOUR PORTFOLIO?

Bonds provide a predictable stream of income and preserve capital, making bonds less risky than stocks. Consequently, virtually every portfolio needs to be invested in bonds, and leads to the question, "How much of my portfolio should be invested in bonds?

ASSET ALLOCATION

The decision of how much to invest in each of the different investment classes of assets (stocks, bonds, real estate, futures, and cash) is an important decision that determines the return for the portfolio. This asset allocation decision has been shown to be the most important decision with regard to achieving an investor's financial goals. The reason is that each class of investment assets (stocks, bonds, money market securities, and real estate) has different levels of risk and return, and while one asset class may increase in value, another decreases or stays the same. If something goes wrong with one asset class, the other asset class may not be affected and could possibly compensate for the weak asset class.

One rule of thumb in determining your asset allocation is that the younger you are the more risk you can generally take, meaning that your investments can be geared more toward seeking capital appreciation than capital preservation. Investors close to retirement want to protect the value of their portfolios because a large decrease in the value of their holdings can affect their retirement lifestyles. It is your time horizon until you begin to draw down from your investments that determines your asset allocation. A long time horizon means that you will not need to draw down your assets and you can ride out the short-term market fluctuations of the stock market in order to grow your portfolio. Thus, with a long time horizon you can weather the risk of investing in stocks. Investors with a short time horizon would invest in assets with less overall risk, and the investments are weighted more toward bonds and money market securities. Figure 1-3 illustrates some portfolio asset allocation models for investors with different time horizons.

Another aspect to consider in determining your asset allocation is how long you will need your investments to last. Once you begin making withdrawals from your investments in retirement, the longer the retirement period, the greater will be the amount allocated to stocks. For example, a person retiring at age 55 years has a long retirement period ahead of him as compared with retiring at age 75. Depending on the size of the investment portfolio, the investor retiring at age 55 would need to grow investment assets so as not to outlive the funds.

FIGURE 1-3

Asset Allocation Models for Different Time Horizons

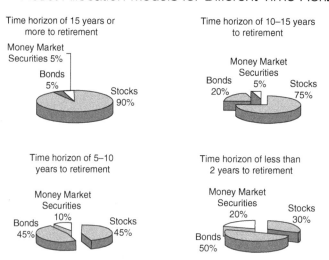

The amount of your financial wealth also determines your asset allocation. For example, a young couple with children might need to supplement their wages with investment income to meet their living expenses instead of investing for capital appreciation. Consequently, they would need to invest in bonds to provide them with a predictable stream of income.

Asset allocation is a means of balancing the growth in purchasing power of your investments and providing income while preserving your capital. The asset allocation plan that works for you depends on your time horizon to retirement, the length of time that you will withdraw from your investments, your risk tolerance, and the amount of your portfolio of investments. The asset allocation plans shown in Figure 1-3 are only suggestions, and you would need to determine what plan would work best for you. The general rule of thumb is that as you approach retirement more assets are transferred from stocks into bonds and money market securities.

DIVERSIFICATION

Once you have determined your asset allocation, it is important to diversify your investments within each asset class (stocks and bonds). Even though bonds are less volatile than stocks, they are not devoid of risk, such as inflation risk, interest rate risk, and credit risk. Figure 1-4 illustrates the 20-year performance of different bond types. In the years 1985 through 2004, junk bonds had the best year's return of close to 40 percent and the worst year's return of a 6 percent loss. The best year's return from investment-grade bonds was not as good as those for junk bonds or international bonds, but its worst year was less than those for junk bonds and international bonds. Money market securities preserved investment capital by not losing value while providing the lowest level of income.

Figure 1-4 shows the different risk and return characteristics of the four types of fixed income securities. Consequently, when choosing bonds for a portfolio, you want a selection of bonds that perform differently under changing conditions, namely market rates of interest, inflation, and credit quality. For example, if you have two years to retirement, you might consider bond types illustrated in Figure 1-5 to achieve a diversified bond portfolio.

FIGURE 1-4

Historical Performance of Bonds from 1985 through 2004

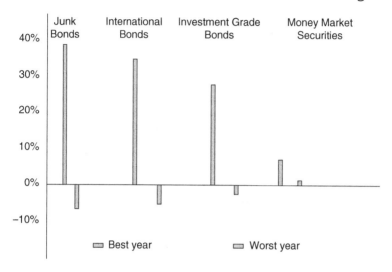

FIGURE 1-5

Example of a Diversified Bond Portfolio with 2 Years
to Retirement

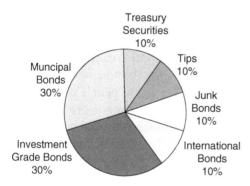

Treasury inflation protection securities (TIPS) and Treasury
securities issued by the U.S. Treasury have no credit or default risk.
The advantage of TIPS is that they protect against inflation by
adjusting the purchasing power of the bonds to the rate of inflation. Investment-grade bonds provide higher yields than Treasury

securities; consequently, when market rates of interest increase, investors in investment-grade bonds lose less of their principal in bond price fluctuations than they would for Treasury securities.

Junk bonds and international bonds have the potential for providing higher returns than those from Treasury securities and investment-grade bonds, but they also have the potential for producing the greatest risk of loss of principal. By understanding the characteristics of each class of bonds, you can control your exposure to inflation, credit risk, and changes in market rates of interest. By matching the maturities of your bonds to your financial needs for the use of the principal, you can reduce the risk of loss of principal.

Once you have determined your asset allocation and selected the individual securities within each asset type, you will want to revisit your asset allocation plan periodically to make sure that your portfolio is still in line with achieving your financial objectives. For example, as you get closer to retirement, your stock portfolio might have appreciated beyond your target allocation, requiring you to sell off a portion of your stocks and reinvest those proceeds into bonds and money market securities.

WHAT ARE BONDS?

A bond is similar to an IOU or savings account. When you deposit money in a savings account, you are lending the bank money and the bank pays you interest on the deposited amount. Similarly, if you buy bonds you are lending the issuer money in return for regular payments of interest. When the bonds mature (come due), you (the bondholder) receive the principal amount of the bonds back, as you would have, had you withdrawn the amount from a savings account. The major difference between a savings account and a bond is that bondholders can sell their bonds before they mature to other investors. Savings accounts with set maturities can only be redeemed by the issuing institution. A bond is a legal obligation by the issuer of the bond to pay the bondholder a predetermined rate of interest over the life of the bond and then repay the bondholder the principal (amount lent) at maturity. Figure 1-6 illustrates how a bond works.

FIGURE 1-6

How a Bond Works

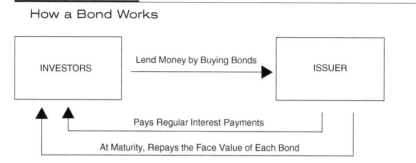

The three basic components of a bond are:

- The coupon rate
- The maturity date
- The price or yield

Coupon Rate

The coupon rate is the stated rate of interest that the issuer of the bond promises to pay the bondholder over the life of the bond unless it is a floating rate bond. If the coupon rate is 4 percent, the issuer of the bonds promises to pay $40 in interest on each bond per year (4% × $1,000). Many bonds pay interest semiannually. For a 4 percent coupon bond that pays interest semiannually, the bondholder receives $20 every six months for each bond held until maturity. Government National Mortgage Securities (GNMA bonds) pay interest on a monthly basis. Some bonds are issued with floating coupon rates of interest that are tied to a particular index. Consequently, the coupon payment fluctuates based on the movement of the underlying index. There are some bond types, such as zero-coupon bonds and Treasury bills, that do not pay periodic interest payments to their holders. Instead, these bonds pay their interest at maturity.

Maturity Date

The maturity date indicates the length of time until the bond comes due and the bondholder is repaid the face value of the bond. The maturity date also determines when bondholders receive their interest payments. For example, a bond with a maturity date of March 1, 2020, matures on that date and the issuer repays the bondholder $1,000, the par or face value of the bond, and also the last interest payment. If the bond pays interest on an annual basis, the bondholder of this particular bond receives interest on this date annually. If this bond pays interest semiannually, then bondholders receive their interest coupon payments on March 1 and six months later on September 1 of each year until maturity.

Price or Yield

The price or market value of a bond is determined by numerous factors, such as the relationship between the bond's coupon rate and market rates of interest, credit quality, and length of time to maturity. A bond's coupon rate remains fixed through the life of the bond (unless it is a variable or floating rate bond) but market rates of interest (or market yields of new and existing bonds) fluctuate, and changes in market rates of interest largely determine the price of the bond. For example, when the coupon rate is the same as market rates of interest (yields on comparable newly issued bonds), the price of the bond generally trades at par, which is $1,000. However, investors are willing to pay more for an existing bond with a higher coupon rate than for new bonds offered with lower coupon rates. Consequently, the price on the existing bond rises to compensate investors for the additional yield differential over the new bond. Similarly, when market yields on new bonds exceed market yields on existing bonds, prices of existing bonds fall because of their lower coupon yields.

There is an inverse relationship between market rates of interest and a bond's price: when market rates of interest rise, the prices of existing bonds decline, and when market rates of interest decline, prices of existing bonds increase. This relationship explains why a bond can trade at a premium price (above par value), at par value, or at a discount (below par value).

Bond investors are likely to be swayed by their expectation of interest rates in the economy. If they see a future decline in interest rates, they are more likely to invest in bonds, as prices of existing bonds will increase. On the other hand, if interest rates are expected to rise, investors are less likely to invest in bonds due to the decline in future bond prices.

Although other factors, such as length of time to maturity and the overall quality of the bond, also affect bond prices, this basic relationship of interest rates and bond price is a good starting point for an introductory discussion on bond price.

TERMINOLOGY OF BONDS
Par Value

Par value is also known as the face value of a bond, which is $1,000. Par value is the amount paid to the bondholder when the bond matures. For example, a bond purchased at issuance for $1,000 is acquired at its par value. At maturity, the holder receives $1,000 from the issuer of the bond.

Discount

Bonds trading below $1,000 trade at a discount. For example, Ford Credit Corporation bonds, with a coupon rate of 6 3/8 percent and maturity in 2008, traded at a discount on September 26, 2005, of $967.50 per bond.

Premium

Bonds trading above $1,000 trade at a premium. On September 26, 2005, IBM's 8 3/8 percent bonds maturing in the year 2019 traded at $1,328.75 per bond. This was a $328.75 premium per bond.

Coupon Interest Rate

The coupon rate is the interest rate that the issuer of the bond promises to pay the bondholder. If the coupon rate is 5 percent, the issuer of these bonds promises to pay $50 (5% × $1,000) in interest on each bond per year.

Many bonds pay interest semiannually. If a bond has a coupon rate of 5 percent paid semiannually, the bondholder receives $25 per bond every six months. Some bonds have adjustable or floating interest rates, which are tied to a particular index. This means that the coupon payment fluctuates based on the underlying index.

Maturity

The maturity of a bond is the length of time until the bond comes due when the bondholder receives the par value of the bond and the final interest payment (for coupon bonds).

Market Rates of Interest

Market rates of interest affect bond prices, which in turn affect bond yields. Put another way, bond prices are determined by the differences between their coupon rates and their yields. Suppose you bought a bond last year with a coupon rate of 5 percent when the coupon yields of comparable bonds' interest were 5 percent, and you paid $1,000 per bond. A year later, market rates of interest rise, causing new, comparable bonds to be issued with 6 percent coupons. What price would you get if you tried to sell your bond with a 5 percent coupon?

An investor would not want to buy your bond yielding 5 percent for $1,000 when new bonds with coupon rates of 6 percent could be bought for $1,000. The buyer would expect to get a yield of at least 6 percent, which means that your bond would sell at a discount (less than $1,000) in order to be competitive with current bonds.

Conversely, if market rates of interest fell below the coupon rate of 5 percent, investors would be willing to pay a premium (above $1,000) for a bond with a higher coupon rate than those of comparable new bonds being brought to the market. Thus, bond prices are vulnerable to market rates of interest as well as other factors, which are discussed in Chapter 2.

Call Provision

Some bonds have call provisions, which means that the issuer of the bonds can call or redeem the bonds at a specified price before their scheduled maturity. Issuers exercise the call provision when market rates of interest fall well below the coupon rate of the bonds.

Bid Price

Bond prices are quoted on a bid and ask basis. The bid price is the price at which owners of a bond can sell to dealers. For example, a bid price quote of $94^1/_2$ is translated as 94.50 percent of par value. The par value of a bond is $1,000, so an owner of this bond would be willing to sell this bond to a buyer/trader at $945.00.

Ask Price

The ask price is the price at which the public can buy a bond from a dealer or trader.

Spread

The spread is the difference between the bid and the ask price of the bond, part of which is a commission that goes to the broker/dealer. A large spread indicates that the bonds are inactively traded.

Basis Point

A basis point is one hundredth of a percentage point. For example, if the yield on a bond falls from 5.25 percent to 5.20 percent, then the yield has declined by 5 basis points. Basis points are used to measure the differences in bond yields.

HOW TO BUY AND SELL BONDS

There are many more complexities involved in buying and selling bonds than there are for other investments. Individual bonds are bought through brokerage firms like stocks, but there are significant differences in the pricing of bonds, which make them more costly to trade than stocks. In fact, most bonds trade infrequently and are available only at certain dealers (Braham, 2006).

Unlike stocks, individual bond buyers do not have ready access to bond price quotes. The reason for this is that bond prices are not quoted when they are traded on the Internet or any other central exchange. For the most actively traded bonds listed on the exchanges, investors might be able to find day-old prices in the financial newspapers. However, most bonds trade over the counter and are not listed on bond exchanges. The other problem is that brokers trade bonds from their inventory, and so the pricing for the same bond might vary significantly. One broker might sell, for example, a Ford Motor Corporation bond at $950, while it could be bought from another broker at $925 per bond. There are many reasons to account for this discrepancy in price: the brokers could have bought the bonds at different prices, or charged different markups, or had different sizes of those bonds in inventory. The commission on bonds is priced into the markup, so investors cannot separate out the markup from the cost of the bond (Braham, 2006).

Not all brokers charge markups. Many online brokers charge a flat commission to trade bonds (for example, $2 per bond or a minimum charge per trade, whichever is greater).

Investors should shop around at different brokerage firms to get the best prices before buying or selling individual bonds. When comparing bond prices, investors should compare the bid/ask prices because the difference, or spread, between the bid and ask price represents the commission. This spread varies from broker to broker and also varies for the different types of bonds. For example, the spread on government agency bonds and municipal bonds is wider than those for U.S. Treasury bonds, because the former two types are not as actively traded. Similarly, spreads are wider for thinly or inactively traded issues of all types. Large spreads might also indicate that the creditworthiness of the bond issuer is low.

The importance of the discussion so far is to highlight some of the reasons why bond prices vary so that investors know to shop around at different brokerage firms to get the best price when they buy or sell their individual bonds. Brokerage firms also do not carry the same bonds in inventory, which makes price comparisons difficult. Consequently, investors, who do not want to go through the difficulties in pricing individual bonds might consider investing in bond mutual funds or bond exchange-traded funds.

Bond Mutual Funds

A mutual fund pools money from investors and then uses it to make investments on behalf of those investors. The types of investments that the mutual fund invests in depend on the objectives of that particular fund. For example, if the objective of a mutual fund is to provide short-term income from money market securities, then this fund would invest in money market instruments. Similarly, there are stock mutual funds of various types and bond mutual funds of various types.

Mutual funds give investors the flexibility of investing in stocks, bonds, and/or money market investments without having to buy investments (stocks, bonds, and money market instruments) individually. Mutual funds are particularly popular with investors who do not have the expertise, knowledge, or time to research individual investment alternatives. Mutual funds are discussed in greater detail in each of the different types of bond chapters.

Bond Exchange-Traded Funds

Bond exchange-traded funds (ETFs) offer investors the opportunity to invest in bonds without having to be concerned with the lack of individual bond pricing transparency. ETFs track indexes and trade on the stock exchanges. Instead of investing in individual corporate bonds, for example, investors could choose the iShares iBoxx Investment Grade Corporate Bond Exchange fund traded on the stock market under the ticker symbol LQD. This ETF includes investments in a basket of investment grade bonds. Other bond ETFs track Treasury bonds, mortgage-backed bonds, and government bonds of various durations.

Bond ETFs offer investors diversified portfolios with low expense ratios and are tradable (listed on the stock exchange). Although expense ratios of ETFs might be lower than those of mutual funds, there is an added cost to investing in ETFs, which is brokerage commissions. Buying bond ETFs is no different from buying and selling stocks on the stock exchanges. The advantage of ETFs over mutual funds is that holders can buy or sell their ETFs at any time during the trading day at specified prices. Shares in mutual funds can only be traded at the end of the day at the closing prices of the mutual funds, which is not known until the end of the day.

The different types of bond ETFs are discussed in detail in the corresponding bond chapters. The saying on Wall Street that investors buy stocks to obtain wealth and buy bonds to keep their wealth aptly summarizes why bonds are an important part of investors' portfolios.

REFERENCE

Braham, Lewis, "Fixed Income at Your Fingertips," *Business Week*, November 13, 2006, pp. 124–125.

CHAPTER 2

Characteristics of Bonds

KEY CONCEPTS

- Bond issuer
- Length of time to maturity
- Bond provisions
- Taxes
- Characteristics of bond mutual funds
- Characteristics of exchange-traded funds (ETFS)

Although there are basic differences between the different types of bonds issued, bonds have similar characteristics:

- *Maturity date,* which is the date when the bond is paid off
- *Interest payments,* which the issuer promises to pay the lender in return for the use of the money loaned
- *Repayment of principal,* which the issuer promises to pay back at the maturity date
- *Bond indenture,* containing the information for the issue:
  - Amount of the bond issue.
  - Coupon rate.
  - Frequency of interest payments (annual or semiannual).
  - Maturity date.

- Call provision, if any. This provision allows the issuer of the bonds to call them in and repay them before maturity.
- Refunding provision, if any. This provision allows the issuer to obtain the proceeds with which to repay the bondholders when the issue matures by issuing new securities.
- Sinking fund provision, if any. This provision offers bondholders greater security in that the issuer sets aside earnings to retire the issue.
- Put option, if any. This provision allows bondholders to sell the bonds back to the issuer at par value.

Bonds provide a steady stream of income, and the investor's principal is returned when the bond matures. However, bonds with similar characteristics could experience wide fluctuations in price, making it important for you to be familiar with many of the differing characteristics before investing. For example, two bonds issued by different issuers with the same coupon rate, maturity, and credit rating could have wide fluctuations in price due to the credit risk of the issuer when interest rates in the economy change.

BOND ISSUER

Bond investors count on a steady stream of interest income, and if the bonds are held to maturity, investors receive the face value of the bonds back. Consequently, the financial stability of the issuer determines the assurance that investors are paid their interest and principal. Bonds issued by the U.S. Treasury are the most secure in that the risk of default (chance that the interest or principal might not be paid back) is negligible. The reasons are that the U.S. government can always raise additional revenue by increasing taxes, selling more bonds, and/or printing money. Consequently, Treasury securities are considered to be *risk free.*

Bonds issued by corporations do not have the same assurance as the U.S. Treasury that investors' obligations will be paid back. Companies issuing bonds need to be profitable in order to be able to pay their interest and principal. To compensate for this added credit risk and risk of default, corporate bonds offer higher yields than Treasury securities. Bond ratings by independent rating services, such as Moody's, Standard & Poor's (S&P), Fitch, and others, assist investors in determining a company's ability to pay its obligations (credit risk). Table 2-1 illustrates the bond ratings scales from Moody's and S&P.

Moody's and S&P's ratings are similar though not identical. The highest-quality bonds (lowest credit risk) are those with triple A ratings. Ratings of AAA, AA, A, and BBB from S&P are considered to be investment-grade quality. Bonds with ratings below BBB are considered to be junk bonds and are speculative. These junk bonds have lower ratings, which means that the issuers have a greater likelihood of default on their interest and principal repayments. Before buying a bond issue, investors should obtain the ratings on that issue.

A rule of thumb to ensure against sleepless nights is to stick to issues with ratings of BBB and above. These ratings, however, provide only a relative guide for investors, because the financial status

TABLE 2-1

Bond Ratings

Moody's	Standard & Poor's	Interpretation of Ratings
Aaa	AAA	Highest-quality obligations
Aa	AA	High-quality obligations
A	A	Bonds that have a strong capacity to repay principal and interest but may be impaired in the future
Baa	BBB	Medium-grade quality
Ba	BB	Interest and principal is neither highly protected nor poorly secured. Lower ratings in this category have some speculative characteristics.
	B	
B	CCC	Speculative bonds with great
Caa	CC	uncertainty
Ca	C	
C	DDD	In default
	DD	
	D	

of the issuer could deteriorate over time and result in the issue being downgraded to a lower rating. A downgrading usually causes a decline in the market price of the bond. The opposite occurs when a bond issue is upgraded. The same issuer with many different bond issues outstanding could have different ratings for each issue. For example, on May 1, 2007, S&P reduced its ratings on Leggett & Platt Inc.'s senior unsecured debt from A+ to A due to continued softness in the company's related business lines.

Investors need not be alarmed if their bonds are downgraded from AAA to A, for example, because this still indicates good quality. However, if the issue is downgraded below BBB, an investor should review whether to continue owning that bond. A case in point is the risky subprime mortgage loans made to consumers with troubled credit histories. Moody's and S&P downgraded many mortgage bond issues to junk bond status in a short period of time after the bonds were issued. This not only reflects poorly on the credit rating service's abilities to correctly assess the creditworthiness of the bonds, but also acts as a red flag to investors to pay attention to the financial condition of the issuers of their bond issues.

Even though different bond issues might have the same credit ratings, the issuer's creditworthiness might not be the same. U.S Treasury securities are superior to AAA-rated government agency securities for the reasons cited earlier. Similarly, AAA-rated state and local government debt might be considered to be more creditworthy than AAA-rated corporate bonds. Bond ratings are not cast in stone and only provide a guide as to the creditworthiness of the issuer. Enron bonds were rated good quality only a few years before the company ended up in bankruptcy and defaulted on its debt obligations.

LENGTH OF TIME TO MATURITY

A good starting point to lessening the risk of loss and improving returns from investing in bonds is to match bond maturities to the time needed for the principal. Maturities of bonds range from less than a year to longer than 50 years. Consequently, investors who have funds available to invest for six months would not want to invest in 30-year U.S. Treasury bonds because, if interest rates rise during that period, investors would lose a portion of their principal due to a decline in bond prices of existing issues. Similarly, if interest rates decline during that six-month period, investors would be able to sell those bonds at a profit, because prices of existing bonds would increase. By matching bond maturities to financial needs, investors can limit their losses due to market interest rate fluctuations.

Generally, bond issues with a longer time to maturity pay higher yields than issues with shorter maturities. This higher yield for investing in longer maturity bond issues compensates investors for future risk due to fluctuating interest rates, higher inflation, and any credit or default risk of the issuer. Choosing to invest in shorter maturity issues results in lower yields, but the risk of loss of principal is also limited. Bear in mind that there have been occasions when short-term interest rates have exceeded longer-term interest rates. The structure of interest rates, which determines the yield curve, varies according to economic conditions, which is discussed in Chapter 4.

SHORT-TERM MATURITIES

Many different short-term debt issues are negotiable and actively traded in the money market. The money market is a collection of markets consisting of brokers and dealers who trade in billions of dollars of short-term securities: Treasury bills, bankers' acceptances, negotiable certificates of deposit, and commercial paper, among others. There is a primary market for newly issued short-term securities and an active secondary market where issues that have already been issued trade.

The primary money market instruments are as follows:

- *Treasury bills* are sold by the U.S. Treasury to finance some of the federal government's expenditures. Their maturities are for 4, 13, and 26 weeks.
- *Bankers' acceptances* are promissory notes that are used mainly to finance international trade transactions. Their maturities are nine months or less.
- *Commercial paper* is issued by the most creditworthy companies as a source of short-term credit and is in essence an unsecured promissory note. Maturities are 270 days or less.

- *Negotiable certificates of deposit* are deposits of $100,000 or more deposited in commercial banks at a specific rate of interest. These can be bought and sold in the open market.
- *Repurchase agreements* are contracts that involve the sale of money market securities with the simultaneous agreement to buy the securities back at an agreed on price in the future.
- *Money market mutual funds* invest in a diversified portfolio of short-term securities such as those described above.

These short-term securities are relatively safe from default and are also fairly liquid due to the active secondary markets. Short-term debt instruments are discussed in greater detail in Chapter 5.

By tailoring your investment options to your financial needs you can build stability into your financial program. Short-term money should be matched with short-term securities, and longer-term funds should be invested in longer-term maturities.

Long-Term Securities

Long-term debt securities include notes and bonds with maturities longer than one year from the time that they are issued. Notes have maturities of 1 to 10 years, and bonds have maturities of greater than 10 years. These long-term securities are referred to as capital market securities. There is not always a clear distinction between short-term and long-term debt, because U. S. Treasury bonds and notes that are about to mature are considered to be money market securities.

Long-term debt securities that make regular interest payments include U.S. Treasury notes and bonds, U.S. agency issues, mortgage-backed bonds, municipal bond issues, and corporate issues. Zero coupon bonds and convertible bonds are hybrid debt securities. They have different characteristics but are also considered to be capital market securities.

The U.S. Treasury issues two types of long-term securities: *Treasury notes* and *Treasury bonds*. These debt issues pay stated coupon interest semiannually, and the interest is exempt from state and local taxes. Treasury debt issues are the most secure of all debt issues in that they have no credit or default risk.

U.S. governmental agencies sell long-term debt issues to finance various activities. Although they are not backed by the full credit of the U.S. government, U.S. agency issues are considered to be of good investment quality, but they have slightly more credit and default risk than Treasury securities. Because so many different agencies of the U.S. Government issue debt obligations, each issue should be analyzed with regard to its maturity, liquidity, and marketability.

State and local governments, counties, and cities issue *municipal bonds*. The main advantage of municipal bonds is their special tax treatment. Interest received from municipal bonds is exempt from federal income tax and exempt from state and/or local tax if issued in that state and county.

Corporate bonds are debt obligations of corporations and vary considerably in their features and their risk. Good-quality corporate bonds pay lower coupon interest than more speculative corporate bonds, also referred to as junk bonds.

Zero coupon bonds are hybrid issues in that they pay no periodic interest and are issued at a deep discount to their face value. At maturity, the bonds are redeemed at face value ($1,000). Another hybrid security is a *convertible bond*. Convertible bonds are issued by corporations, and the bonds can be exchanged for the common stock or preferred stock of the issuing company at the option of the bondholder.

Each of these types of long-term securities differs in risk, return, taxability, liquidity, and marketability. Investors should analyze the characteristics of the different types of bonds before investing.

Instead of investing in individual long-term bonds, investors have the choice of investing in bond mutual funds and bond ETFs. There are Treasury bond mutual funds, U.S. government agency mutual funds, corporate bond mutual funds, zero coupon mutual funds, and convertible bond mutual funds. The list of bond ETFs is expanding rapidly to give investors alternatives to specific bond mutual funds.

The advantages of investing in long-term maturities are the higher yields, and with a long time horizon the potential to ride out the price fluctuations.

BOND PROVISIONS

Investors should always check the provisions of a bond issue before investing. Corporate bond issues invariably contain a call provision, refunding provision, put provision, or sinking fund provision. These provisions can work for or against the investor; therefore, it is important to understand these specific characteristics. Investors should read and understand the details in these provisions before investing. For new bond issues, investors should obtain a final prospectus that contains the details of these provisions. A preliminary prospectus is often skimpy on details.

Call Provision

A call provision allows the issuer to call in the bonds before maturity. This feature is advantageous for the issuer because when interest rates fall below the coupon rate of the bond issue, the issuer is able to call in the bonds (pay them off before maturity) and issue new lower coupon interest bonds. The bond investor is disadvantaged because even though the principal is received early, reinvesting in new bonds means that the investor would receive a lower coupon interest rate.

The bond indenture spells out the details of the call provision such as when the bond can be called and the price at which the bond can be called. There are *freely callable* bonds that offer investors no protection, since issuers can call them anytime. *Deferred callable bonds* offer some protection because the bonds cannot be called until after a period of time (5, 10, or 15 years after issue). For example, a bond issued in 2007 could have 10 years of call protection, meaning that the bond issue becomes callable in 2017. To entice investors to invest in callable bonds, there might be a call premium of 5 percent over par. In such a case, if the bonds are called in the year 2017, the issuer will pay $1,050 per bond. Typically, however, a call premium declines toward par (face value) as the bond matures.

Noncallable bonds offer investors the most protection. Consequently, the price of callable bonds is lower than the price of comparable noncallable bonds. A call provision is important to investors who are purchasing bonds at a premium price (above $1,000) and if market rates of interest are at or near a peak.

Refunding Provision

A refunding provision does not allow the issuer to redeem a bond issue if the proceeds come from a new bond issue. In other words, if a bond issue has both a call and refunding provision, the issuer may call in the bonds, but the proceeds to repay bondholders only can come from cash, or from the sale of assets or common stock.

Bond issues with a refunding provision offer refunding protection, similar to call protection. If, for example, the call protection date and refunding protection date is the same (e.g., July 2010), and the call premium is 5 percent, the bonds can be called before July 2010, with the issuer paying $1,050 per bond, and the proceeds cannot come from the issuance of a new lower coupon bond issue. The proceeds can only come from "clean money"—cash, sale of assets, or common stock.

Put Provision

Bonds with put provisions are less common than bonds with call provisions, primarily because a put provision benefits the bondholder rather than the issuer. A put provision allows the bondholder to sell the bond back to the issuer at par (or a predetermined price). Thus, bondholders with a put provision are protected against inflation and rising interest rates (bond prices decrease when interest rates and inflation increase). Because a put provision is so advantageous to investors, many corporations issue bonds with a *one-time put provision*, which means that the bond can only be sold back on one date at a predetermined price.

A bond with a put provision generally sells for a higher price than a comparable bond without a put provision, and the flip side of the coin is that the yield of a putable bond is generally lower than that of a comparable bond without a put provision.

Sinking Fund Provision

A sinking fund in a bond's indenture allows an issuer to contribute to a fund from which the proceeds are used to retire bonds before maturity. The details, dates, and methods of retirement are described in the indenture. For example, the issuer can set specific dates for retirement or arbitrarily decide when to call in the bonds. When bonds are called for retirement, they no longer earn interest after the date of call.

There are two methods used to determine which bonds will be retired early. One method is to draw the bonds randomly, which means that some bondholders will not be affected. One complication of the use of this method is that it becomes difficult to value the bonds from this issue, because bondholders do not know when their bonds will be called in. The second method used to determine which bonds will be called is the pro rata method. With this method, all bondholders are affected equally. If the issuer decides for example to retire 5 percent of the issue, then all bondholders will have to retire 5 percent of their bond holdings. Valuation of the bonds when this method is used is not affected.

Even though a sinking fund provision like a call provision is disadvantageous to bond holders, there are two advantages to a sinking fund. The first is that the risk of default is reduced somewhat owing to the payments made by the issuer to the sinking fund. The second advantage is that a bond with a sinking fund offers a slightly higher yield than a comparable bond without a sinking fund provision.

Conversion Provision

Corporations issue bonds with a conversion provision that allow bondholders at their discretion to convert their bonds into the corporation's common stock. To complicate matters, most convertible bonds have call provisions, which give issuers the ability to force conversion when bond issues are called.

A reverse convertible issue gives the issuer control over whether the bondholder can receive common shares at conversion or the par value ($1,000) of the bond. The bondholder is denied the choice in the matter. Chapter 12 discusses convertible bonds in greater detail.

TAXES

Taxes diminish investors' returns, and so it becomes important to choose those investments that enhance investors' rates of return. Interest income from Treasury bonds, agency bonds, and corporate bonds is taxed at ordinary rates (the investor's marginal tax rate) at the federal level. Interest income from a municipal bond is generally exempt from federal taxes. Consequently, investors need to be able to compare returns from taxable bonds to tax-exempt bonds. The after-tax return of a taxable bond can be compared with the yield of a municipal (tax-exempt) bond. The after-tax return is calculated as follows:

$$\text{After-tax return of a taxable bond} =$$
$$(1 - \text{marginal tax rate})(\text{bond yield})$$

For example, an investor in the 35 percent marginal tax bracket who invests in a corporate bond yielding 6.8 percent has an after-tax return of 4.42 percent:

$$\text{After tax return} = (1 - .35)(.068)$$

$$= 4.42\%$$

This after-tax return can be compared with the rate of return of a municipal bond, which is tax free at the federal level. In many cases, taxes affect the choice of investments, and effective tax planning may reduce the level of taxes paid.

Interest income from Treasury securities is exempt from state and local taxes, and states generally do not tax interest income from municipal bonds issued in their states.

What you should know is that capital gains are taxed at lower marginal tax rates (as of 2008) if the securities are held for longer than one year. If the securities are held for less than one year before being sold, then any realized capital gains are taxed at the investor's marginal tax rate.

As taxes (federal, state, and possibly local) are levied on income and capital gains, the *after-tax return* of different bonds should be compared.

CHARACTERISTICS OF BOND MUTUAL FUNDS

Because bond mutual funds make investments on behalf of the fund's investors, mutual fund investors do not choose the individual bonds in the fund. However, investors in bond mutual funds should understand the characteristics of bond mutual funds in order to make the right investments.

Many investors choose to invest in bond mutual funds over individual bonds to avoid having to understand the complexities of individual bonds. Mutual funds have professional managers who make informed decisions on which bonds to buy, sell, and hold for the bond fund portfolio.

The basic differences between a bond mutual fund and an individual bond are:

- A bond mutual fund does not mature like an individual bond. When the bonds in the fund mature, the fund manager uses the proceeds to purchase new bonds. When individual bonds mature, holders receive their invested principal back in the form of the par value of the bond ($1,000 per bond).
- The amount of interest received by fund holders in the form of dividends varies, whereas individual bonds pay fixed coupon interest payments to bond holders.
- Bond mutual funds charge fees that diminish returns of mutual funds. Investors in individual bonds pay no fees other than the commissions to buy and sell the bonds.
- The quality, risk, and return of bond mutual funds change continually as bonds in the fund are bought and sold.

The advantages of investing in bond mutual funds are that they provide both convenience for investors who do not have the time, skill, or inclination to manage their own bond portfolios, and the opportunity to invest in a diversified bond portfolio without having to invest large amounts of money.

CHARACTERISTICS OF EXCHANGE-TRADED FUNDS

Bond ETFs are unique in that investors need not be concerned with the lack of pricing transparency of individual bonds. The reason is that ETFs are traded on the stock exchanges, and bond prices of the holdings of the ETF portfolio are reflected in the share price of the ETF. Shares of ETFs are traded during the hours that the stock market is open, whereas shares of mutual funds are only traded at the close of the day. Commissions incurred to buy shares of ETFs are lower than the transaction fees incurred to buy individual bonds. However, no-load mutual funds do not charge fees to buy and sell shares.

Bond ETFs share some characteristics with bond mutual funds, such as offering investors a share of a diversified bond portfolio and the convenience of not having to choose individual bonds to buy and sell or having to manage a bond portfolio. Fees charged for bond ETFs tend to be lower than those for bond mutual funds. Like mutual funds, ETFs pay interest received from bonds held in the portfolio in the form of dividends on a monthly basis.

The basic disadvantage of both bond ETFs and bond mutual funds is that the investor has no control over the amount of income or capital gains received. With an individual bond portfolio, an investor can choose higher-yielding bonds to receive greater income or hold bonds through maturity to avoid capital gains. Bond ETFs, however, give investors a flexible alternative to investing in individual bonds or bond mutual funds.

CHAPTER 3

Risks of Bonds

KEY CONCEPTS

- Interest rate risk
- Default or credit risk
- Call or sinking fund risk
- Purchasing power risk
- Reinvestment rate risk
- Currency or exchange rate risk
- Liquidity risk
- Prepayment risk
- Political risk
- Event risk
- Risk of bond mutual funds
- Risks of bond exchange-traded funds (ETFs)

The misconception many investors have about investing in bonds is that this class of investment carries no risk. When compared with investing in stocks, bond prices are less volatile than stock prices, but investing in bonds is not without risk. All bond instruments carry risk, but the degree of risk varies with the type of debt and the issuer. There is always the risk that if you try to sell a bond before maturity, you could lose money on it if market rates of interest have risen. Similarly, you could lose your entire investment if the bond issuer goes bankrupt. This does not mean that you should resort to stashing your money under the mattress, because that too involves a risk of loss. There are different types of risk, and you should be aware of how these affect your bond investments. Risk, therefore, can be defined as the possibility of losing money.

INTEREST RATE RISK

Suppose that you purchase a bond at issue for $1,000 that pays a coupon yield of 5 percent. A month later market rates of interest rise, and a new issue of bonds of comparable quality and maturity (to the issue that you purchased) sells for $1,000 per bond and pays a coupon of 5.25 percent. Investors wanting to purchase existing bonds would not offer to pay $1,000 for bonds from your issue because they can purchase similar bonds with a greater coupon rate (5.25 percent versus 5 percent). Consequently, to make the bonds of your issue more marketable, they would decline in price so that they are more marketable to entice investors to purchase them. Holders of that bond issue experience the effects of interest rate risk. When market rates of interest increase, prices of existing bonds decline. Similarly, when market rates of interest decline, prices of existing bonds increase. Figure 3-1 illustrates these relationships graphically.

Interest rate risk refers to changes in market rates of interest, which have a direct effect on bond investments. The price of fixed income securities changes inversely to the changes in interest rates. During periods of rising interest rates, investors holding fixed income securities will experience declines in the market prices of their bonds, because new investors in those bonds will want a competitive yield. Similarly, in periods of declining interest rates, prices of fixed income securities will rise. The longer the maturity and duration of the bond, the greater is the potential interest rate risk.

FIGURE 3-1

Market Interest Rates and Bond Prices

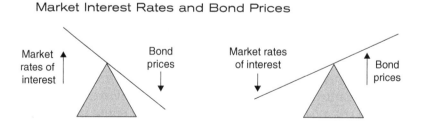

By reducing the maturities of bonds in a portfolio in addition to choosing bond issues with different maturities, an investor can lessen interest rate risk. Interest rate risk also is minimized if investors hold onto their bonds until maturity.

DEFAULT OR CREDIT RISK

Another risk involving bonds depends on the *creditworthiness* of the issuer of the debt. Creditworthiness is the ability of the issuer to make its scheduled interest payments and to repay principal when the bonds mature. Credit risk varies with bond issuers. An inability of an issuer to repay interest or principal may involve bankruptcy. However, issuers can experience financial difficulties, which could result in their bonds being downgraded by any of the major credit ratings agencies, such as Moody's, Standard & Poor's (S&P), or Fitch. The impact of a downgrade in ratings results in a decline in the price of a bond issue, even though the issuer may still be able to pay its interest obligations.

An analysis of the financial health of an organization determines the ability of an issuer to meet its financial obligations. Consequently, a rating of AAA by S&P indicates a strong likelihood that the issuer will meet its financial obligations. If the issuer's rating is downgraded from AAA to AA (owing to changes in the economy that might impact the issuer), there is still a strong likelihood that the issuer will not have any difficulty meeting its financial obligations. Bond investors should be cautious when their bonds are downgraded by more than two levels or drop from investment grade to below investment grade. Not only will the prices of their bonds fall significantly, but there is an increased credit or default risk. When bonds are downgraded by more than one level at a time, bondholders should evaluate their future holdings in that issue. Enron bond issues were downgraded over time until their bonds were in default.

U.S. Treasury issues carry virtually no risk of default. U.S. agency debt has slightly increased risks of default. Bonds issued by state and local governments depend on the financial health of the particular issuer and their ability to raise revenue. For corporate issuers, credit risks are linked to their balance sheets, income statements, and earnings capacities.

Credit risks can be minimized by buying bonds with investment-grade ratings (A and above by S&P), which have a reduced likelihood of default, and by diversifying investments. In other words, instead of investing all your money in the bonds of one issuer, buy bonds of different issuers.

CALL OR SINKING FUND RISK

Bonds with call and sinking fund provisions have early redemption risk. Many corporate, municipal, mortgage-backed, and agency bond issues are issued with call provisions. The risk facing holders of the bonds is that issuers can repurchase their bonds at a specified (call) price before maturity, which is beneficial to issuers and detrimental to investors. Issuers call bonds early when interest rates drop below the bond issues' coupon rate and then issue new bonds with lower coupon rates.

Call risk poses a potential loss of principal when the bonds are purchased at a premium and the call price is less than the premium price. Call risk can be anticipated by estimating the level to which the interest rates must fall before the issuer would find it worthwhile to call the issue. As will be explained in a later chapter, the call provision of a bond makes the duration of the bond uncertain.

To minimize call risks, examine the call provisions of the bond and choose bonds that are unlikely to be called. This is particularly important if you are contemplating the purchase of bonds that are trading above their par values (at a premium). However, not all bond issues with call or sinking fund provisions are called before maturity. If market rates of interest are higher than bond coupon rates, it would be disadvantageous for issuers to call them in.

PURCHASING POWER RISK

Purchasing power risk affects all bond issues because the amount of bond coupon interest and principal received are fixed; consequently, the value of the payments is affected by inflation. When the rate of inflation rises, bond prices tend to fall because the purchasing power of the coupon payments is reduced. Thus, to say the least, bonds are not a good hedge against inflation. Bond prices react favorably to low rates of inflation as long as the coupon rate exceeds the rate of inflation. For example, when monthly announcements of the consumer price index or producer price index (measures of inflation in the economy) are less than anticipated, bond prices rise.

To combat purchasing power risk, invest in bonds whose rates of return exceed that of anticipated inflation. If you anticipate inflation in the future, invest in floating rate bonds whose coupon rate adjusts up and down with market interest rates.

REINVESTMENT RATE RISK

Returns from bonds are composed from two components: interest receipts, and the market value of the bond received when sold or the par value of the bond when held to maturity. Interest receipts from bonds are either reinvested or spent. *Reinvestment rate risk* is defined as the risk of reinvesting interest receipts at a lower rate of interest than the original coupon rate of the bond issue. All coupon bonds are subject to reinvestment rate risk. Zero coupon bonds that make no periodic interest payments have no reinvestment risk.

Market interest rates fluctuate over time, so it is likely that over the life of a bond, interest payments received will be reinvested at different rates from the coupon rate of the issue. If market rates of interest are higher than the coupon rate of the bond, the returns from reinvesting interest receipts will be higher than the original coupon rate. Reinvestment rate risk prevails when interest payments received are reinvested at lower rates than the original coupon rate of the bond issue. Thus, reinvestment rate risk will be greater for longer-maturity bonds than shorter-maturity bonds.

EXCHANGE OR FOREIGN CURRENCY RISK

Bonds denominated in foreign currencies have uncertain dollar cash flows owing to fluctuations in foreign exchange rates. For example, if an investor purchases a euro-denominated bond, and the euro depreciates relative to the dollar, then the interest received in dollars will be lower. The opposite is also true: if the euro appreciates relative to the dollar, the interest receipts will be greater. Currency rate risk also affects the proceeds from the bond at maturity or if sold before maturity. Foreign exchange rate risk is an additional risk over and above all the other risks of domestic bonds that bondholders face when they invest in foreign bonds.

It is evident that risk cannot be avoided even with the most conservative investments, such as savings accounts and Treasury bills—even stashing money under the mattress entails risks. However, through diversification, which is investing in different types of bonds rather than investing completely in one bond issue, certain levels of risk can be minimized. By understanding and recognizing the different levels of risk for each type of bond, the total risk can be better managed in the construction of a bond portfolio.

LIQUIDITY RISK

Liquidity risk is the risk that a bond cannot be bought or sold without a significant price concession. Because most bonds trade over the counter, there may not be a ready buyer or seller on the other end of your trade for a bond resulting in a large price concession. Consequently, thinly traded bonds are highly illiquid.

By their nature, bonds are less liquid than stocks because of the lack of pricing transparency for bonds. The bid and ask spread is generally not easily found for bonds, and many brokers mark up their bonds to include a profit. Another factor that adds to the illiquidity of bonds is that the commissions or markups to buy and sell bonds in odd lots (less than 1,000 bonds) are larger than when trading in round lot sizes.

PREPAYMENT RISK

Prepayment risk affects bondholders of mortgage-backed bonds (also called pass-through certificates) and collateralized mortgage obligations. Prepayment risk occurs when market rates of interest decline and mortgage owners pay off their old mortgages and refinance their homes with new lower interest mortgages. Mortgages that are part of a pool of mortgages are packaged and sold to investors. Consequently, when owners of mortgages refinance, investors in the pool of mortgages have their principal returned to them.

A similar risk occurs when mortgage owners make additional principal payments on their loans, resulting in investors in the pool receiving their principal faster, which is then reinvested at lower rates of return.

POLITICAL RISK

Political risk affects bondholders of foreign government and corporate debt. This category of risk includes civil unrest, military coups, nationalization of assets, inflation, currency devaluation, or any other factors that affect the receipt of interest and principal. To entice investors to invest in these higher-risk foreign bonds, issuers pay higher coupon rates to compensate for the risk. Another consideration when investing in foreign bonds is to determine how well regulated the markets are and the types of protection afforded foreign bondholders.

EVENT RISK

Event risk occurs when a company is merged or bought using large amounts of debt to finance the purchase (known as *leveraged buyouts*). The increased debt of the combined companies can result in a downgrade of the company's bonds, causing bond prices to fall and increasing the likelihood of default.

RISKS OF BOND MUTUAL FUNDS

Bond mutual funds, like individual bonds, are exposed to various types of risk. The major risk with bond mutual funds is the risk of loss of principal invested due to a decline in net asset value. The longer the maturity of the bond fund, the greater is the possibility of a decline in the net asset value due primarily to interest rate risk. An increase in market rates of interest results in the decline in bond prices and, consequently, net asset values of bond funds. Similarly, when interest rates decline, bond prices and net asset values of bond funds appreciate.

Credit risk affects those funds that invest in speculative bonds such as junk bonds. Nervousness about bond defaults can provoke a major sell-off in the junk bond market that results in steep declines in junk bond prices and, consequently, net asset values of related bond funds. However, credit risk may not be as significant for bond funds as it is for individual bonds, because funds are large and diversified, holding many different bond issues. The loss from the default of one or two issues would have a small impact on the price of a fund.

The risk of insolvency of mutual funds, especially in light of some of the bank failures in the past, may be of concern to investors. Although there is always the risk that a mutual fund could go under, the likelihood of this happening is small. The key distinction between banks and mutual funds is the manner in which mutual funds are set up, which reduces the risks of failure and loss due to fraud. Typically, mutual funds are corporations owned by share-holders. A separate management company is contracted to run the fund's daily operations. The management company oversees the investments of the fund, but it does not have possession of the investments (assets). The investments are held by a custodian such as a bank. If the management company gets into financial trouble, it cannot get access to the investments in the fund.

Another safeguard is that shareholders' accounts are main-tained by a transfer agent. The transfer agent keeps track of pur-chases and redemptions of shareholders. In addition, management companies carry fidelity bonds, which are a form of insurance to protect the investments of the funds against malfeasance or fraud perpetrated by their employees. Besides these safeguards, there are two other factors that differentiate mutual funds from banks and savings and loan associations:

1. Mutual funds must be able to redeem shares on demand, which means that a portion of the investment assets must be liquid.
2. Mutual funds must be able to price their investments at the end of each day, known as *marking to market*.

Hence, mutual funds cannot hide their financial difficulties as easily as banks and savings and loans.

In addition to these checks and balances, mutual funds are reg-ulated by the Securities and Exchange Commission. Therefore, the risk is small that investors in mutual funds will have to worry about losing money due to the financial collapse through fraud. However, investors should be aware that they can lose money by purchasing a fund whose investments perform poorly in the markets. The major risk of bond mutual funds is the potential for the fund to underperform the comparable index. Research has shown that most bond funds underperform their comparable indexes post expenses.

RISKS OF EXCHANGE-TRADED FUNDS

Like mutual funds, the major risk of bond ETFs is that they can lose part of a shareholder's investment. Bond ETFs are subject to market risk in that their share prices fluctuate in value as a result of supply of and demand for the shares in addition to fundamental and market factors.

Bond ETFs are subject also to interest rate risk (inverse relationship between the movement of share prices and market rates of interest), credit and default risk, inflation risk, and the risk of underperforming the relevant bond index after expenses.

CHAPTER 4

Yield and Price

KEY CONCEPTS

- Yield
- Coupon yield
- Current yield
- Yield to maturity
- Yield to call
- Yield curve
- Valuation of bonds
- Why bonds fluctuate in price

There is a direct correlation between risk and return, and therefore bond yields and prices. The greater the risk of an investment, the greater is the potential return to entice investors. However, in most cases investing in bonds with the greatest rate of return and therefore the greatest risk can lead to financial ruin, if the odds do not pan out and something goes wrong with the investment. The return on a bond depends on the amount of the coupon interest payment, market rates of interest, the length of time to maturity, and the amount of the principal received when the bond is sold or matures. The determination of the risk of a bond is the relative certainty of the ability of the issuer to make the interest and principal payments.

YIELD

Yield is a measure of return to a bond investor. If you are interested in investing in a 10-year Treasury bond, you would want to know what your earnings would be from the bond. As of June 12, 2007, the 10-year Treasury yielded 5.249 percent, providing you with a yardstick for your potential return from such an investment. By comparison, the yield on a AAA-rated corporate bond with the same maturity (on the same day) was 6.18 percent.

A relationship exists between bond yields and price, as illustrated in Figure 4-1. When bond yields increase, prices of existing bonds decrease. Similarly, when bond yields decrease, prices of existing bonds increase. This relationship is explored in greater detail in this chapter. Four basic types of yields exist.

Coupon Yield

The coupon yield is the stated yield of the bond issue and is determined when the bond is issued. The coupon yield is the specified amount of interest that the issuer of the bond promises to pay to the bondholder each year. This amount of interest may be stated as a percentage of the par value of the bond or as a dollar amount. For instance, a bond with a par value of $1,000 that pays $35 of annual interest has a 3.5 percent coupon yield. Some bonds pay coupon interest semiannually. For example, a bondholder of a 5 percent coupon bond that pays semiannually receives two payments of $25 per year. The coupon yield is fixed throughout the lifetime of a bond issue unless it is a variable-interest coupon, which fluctuates throughout the lifetime of the bond. If market rates of interest are equal to the coupon rate of a bond, the bond price is

FIGURE 4-1

Bond Prices and Yields

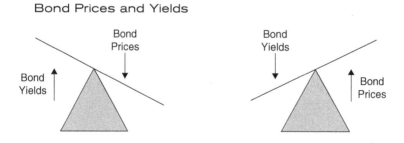

$1,000 (par value). If the coupon rate is lower than market rates of interest, the bond will trade at a discount (below $1,000). Similarly, when market rates of interest are lower than the coupon rate, the bond will trade at a premium price (above $1,000).

Current Yield

The current yield is the annual rate of return from a bond based on the income received in relation to the purchase price of the bond. It is calculated by dividing the bond's coupon by the purchase price or market price of the bond:

$$\text{Current yield} = \frac{\text{Coupon interest amount}}{\text{Purchase price of the bond}}$$

For example, if a bond is purchased at par, $1,000, and the coupon is 4 percent (interest paid is $40 per year), then the current yield is 4 percent (same as the coupon yield). However, on the secondary market most bonds trade above or below par. For a bond purchased at $1,100 with a 4 percent coupon, the current yield is 3.63 percent (40/1,100).

A relationship exists between bond prices, current yields, and coupon yields. Bonds trading at a discount to their par values have current yields that are higher than their coupon rates. Similarly, bonds trading at a premium to their par values have current yields that are lower than their coupon rates. Table 4-1 summarizes these relationships. The current yield is a useful measure of return for investors who are looking for bond investments with high current income.

TABLE 4-1

Relationships Between Bond Prices, Current Yield, and Coupon Yield

Bond Price			
Discount	Current yield	>	coupon yield
Par	Current yield	=	coupon yield
Premium	Current yield	<	coupon yield

Yield to Maturity

The *yield to maturity* is the annual (discounted) rate of return earned on a bond held to maturity. The yield to maturity is the discount rate calculated by mathematically equaling the cash flows of the interest payments and principal received with the purchase price of the bond. This term is also referred to as the internal rate of return or expected rate of return of the bond and is the yield most investors in a bond are interested in. Table 4-2 illustrates how to calculate the yield to maturity of a bond using Microsoft Excel software.

The yield to maturity is 8.5 percent. If you do not have Microsoft Excel software on your computer you can use the

TABLE 4-2

Calculating the Yield to Maturity of a Bond using Microsoft Excel

The yield-to-maturity of a bond that was purchased for $770.36 that pays a coupon of 5 percent ($50 annually) with a maturity of 10 years can be solved as follows:

Click on "*f*," which is on the top row of the toolbar in the Excel spreadsheet program. A list of functions pops up. Highlight "financial" in the box on the left and "rate" in the box on the right, and then click "OK". A box with five rows in it is displayed:

Nper		Enter the total number of payments
PMT		Enter the interest payments
PV		Enter the purchase price of the bond
FV		Enter the par value of the bond
Type		Enter 0 for payment received at the end of a period

Nper	10
PMT	50
PV	−770.31
FV	1000
Type	0
Formula result = 0.085	

following approximation formula to determine the yield to maturity (YTM) for the same example:

$$\text{YTM} = \frac{(\text{Coupon payment} + 1{,}000 - \text{Purchase price}/\text{Years to maturity})}{(1{,}000 + \text{Purchase price}/2)}$$

$$= \frac{(50 + (1{,}000 - 770.36/10))}{(1{,}000 + 770.36/2)}$$

$$= 8.24\%$$

Using the approximation formula, the 8.24 percent yield understates the true yield to maturity calculated with a computer. The reason is that the approximation formula does not use the time value of money for compounding of the coupon payments.

The yield to maturity hinges on two assumptions:

1. The bonds are held to maturity.
2. The interest payments received are reinvested at the same yield as the yield to maturity.

If the bond is not held to maturity, you can calculate the internal rate of return of the bond by substituting the sale price of the bond for the maturity value and the period held to the sale date for the period to maturity.

The yield to maturity rate assumes that the bondholder reinvests the interest received at the same yield to maturity. If this does not occur, the holder's rate of return will differ from the quoted yield-to-maturity rate. For example, if the interest received is spent and not reinvested, the interest does not earn interest; the investor earns much less than the stated yield to maturity. Similarly, if the stated yield to maturity is 8 percent and the investor reinvests the interest at lesser (or greater) rates, the 8 percent is not achieved. In reality, matching the yield-to-maturity rate for the interest received is difficult because interest rates are changing constantly. The interest received is usually reinvested at different rates from the stated yield-to-maturity rate.

The yield to maturity is useful, however, in comparing and evaluating different bonds of varying quality with different coupon rates and prices. For example, by comparing the yield to

TABLE 4-3

Relationships Between Coupon Yield, Current Yield, and Yield-to-Maturity

Bond Price						
Discount	Coupon yield	<	Current yield	<	Yield to maturity
Face	Coupon yield	=	Current yield	=	Yield to maturity
Premium	Coupon yield	>	Current yield	>	Yield to maturity

maturity of an AAA-rated bond with a BBB-rated bond, you can easily see how much the increment in yield would be in choosing the lower rated bond. You can also see the yield differential between bonds with different maturities.

The relationship between the coupon yield, current yield, yield to maturity, and bond price is summarized in Table 4-3.

Table 4-3 Relationship between Coupon Yield, Current Yield and Yield-to- Maturity

Yield to Call

The *yield to call* is the annual rate of return a bondholder receives to the date on which the bond is called. When a bond has a call feature, the bondholder can calculate the yield to call by substituting the call price for the maturity price in the equation discussed in the yield to maturity section. Both the yield to call and the yield to maturity should be determined because if the bond is called, the yield to call is the yearly total return that the bondholder receives on the bond.

The Yield Curve

The yield curve shows the relationship between bond yields and the term to maturity of bonds with the same level of risk. Figure 4-2 shows the yield curve for U.S. Treasury securities as of June 21, 2000, June 19, 2003, December 31, 2004, and June 15, 2007. Yields for the 3-month, 6-month, 2-year, 5-year, 10-year, and 30-year Treasury securities were plotted. The graph illustrates the relationship between bond yields and maturities on each of these 4 days. Table 4-4 lists the bond yield data for the different Treasury securities on the 4 days.

An examination of a yield curve on any particular day gives you a snapshot of the different yields of various maturities for a bond security. Figure 4-2 shows the yield curve for Treasuries, but you can create a yield curve for other bond types, such as municipal bonds, corporate bonds, and agency bonds.

Note the shape of the yield curve for June 21, 2000. It has an upward slope from 3 months to 2 years, and then a declining curve for longer maturities through 30 years. This inverted curve is generally atypical. An inverted yield curve indicates that by extending maturities, investors are taking greater risks for smaller returns. The most common type is the rising yield curve, as depicted on June 19, 2003, and December 31, 2004. You might expect an upward-sloping curve because the longer the maturity, the greater is the bondholder's

FIGURE 4-2

Treasury Yield Curve

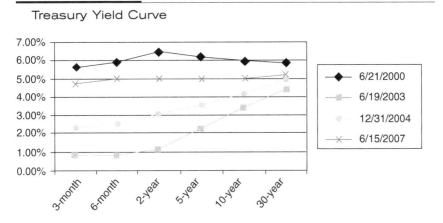

TABLE 4-4

Bond Yield Data

	June 21, 2000	June 19, 2003	December 31, 2004	June 15, 2007
3-month Treasury bill	5.63%	0.82%	2.28%	4.773%
6-month Treasury bill	5.92%	0.83%	2.56%	4.96%
2-year Treasury note	6.43%	1.17%	3.04%	4.98%
5-year Treasury note	6.20%	2.28%	3.58%	4.98%
10-year Treasury note	6.02%	3.37%	4.21%	5.02%
30-year Treasury bond	5.89%	4.42%	5.00%	5.25%

exposure to risk. For this reason, bond issuers tend to pay more to compensate investors for the risk involved with longer maturities. With interest rates at a 45-year low, this steeply positive yield curve points to higher future rates. The December 31, 2004, yield curve shows how yields increased during the 18 months from June 2003.

Note the relatively flat yield curve of June 15, 2007, indicating that short-term yields were almost equal to long-term yields. The Federal Reserve Bank raised short-term interest rates between December 2004 and June 2007, resulting in the rise of short-term yields while long-term yields also rose but remained level with short-term yields. A flat yield curve is an unusual phenomenon and generally indicates a recession. Depending on economic conditions, a flat yield curve will either change to an upward slope or a downward slope.

On a few occasions, the yield curve has had a downward slope where short-term yields exceed long-term yields; yields decline as maturities increase. Such a situation occurred in 1979, 1981, and 1982. A downward sloping yield curve may indicate an economic recession, but it also gives an outlook on inflation. Investors expect declining future long-term interest rates and benign inflation due to fears of recession; consequently, they are willing to invest in long-term bonds to lock into those yields.

The shape of the yield curve changes daily with changes in yield because of fluctuations in market rates of interest. The yield curve can assist you in choosing which maturities of bonds to buy. The yield curve provides a comparison of bond yields of different maturities, enabling you to determine the incremental yield of where to invest on the yield curve. Table 4-5 illustrates how to use the Internet to obtain information to graph a yield curve.

TABLE 4-5

How to Obtain Bond Yields to Construct a Yield Curve

Using the Internet, obtain yields for the different maturities of Treasury securities to construct a yield curve. Based on the shape of the yield curve, decide whether you would invest in long-term or short-term maturity bonds. You can obtain information from www.tradebonds.com. On its home page is a ticker tape that posts the daily prices and yields of Treasury securities.

Keep in mind the following generalities about yield curves:

- Most of the time the yield curve is upward sloping where yields on long-term securities are greater than the yields of short-term securities.
- Changes in the yield curve generally take the form of shifts up and down over time. When short-term yields increase, generally long-term yields also rise. Similarly when short-term yields decline, long-term yields also fall.
- During a recession, short-term yields fall faster than long-term yields; during a period of economic expansion, short-term yields rise faster than long-term yields.

The yield curve is an excellent tool for forecasting interest rates, the direction and state of the economy, and the yields and prices of bonds.

VALUATION OF BONDS

Bond prices fluctuate because of the relationship between coupon rates, market rates of interest (required rate of return), the bond's creditworthiness, and length of time to maturity. Figure 4-3 illustrates the factors that affect the price of a bond. The characteristics and the investor's risk assessment of a bond affect the investor's

FIGURE 4-3

Factors that Affect the Value of a Bond

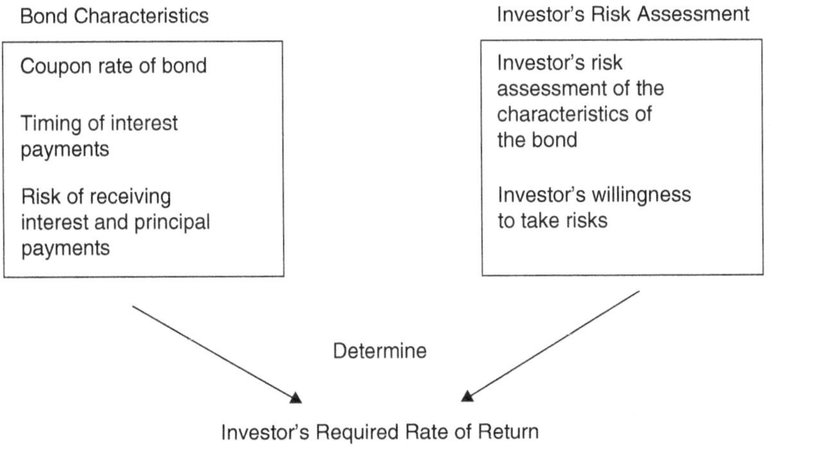

Bond Characteristics

Coupon rate of bond

Timing of interest payments

Risk of receiving interest and principal payments

Investor's Risk Assessment

Investor's risk assessment of the characteristics of the bond

Investor's willingness to take risks

Determine

Investor's Required Rate of Return

required rate of return, which then determines the price of the bond. An investor who perceives one bond to be riskier than another is more inclined to pay less for the riskier bond. As a result, speculative (junk) bonds have higher coupon rates than investment-grade bonds in order to entice investors to buy them. Thus, an investor's required rate of return for a junk bond is higher than that for an investment-grade bond or Treasury bond.

After bonds are issued, they rarely trade at their par values ($1,000) in the secondary markets because interest rates are always changing. Certain bonds sell at premium prices and others sell at discounted prices.

The market price of a bond is determined using the bond's coupon payments, the principal repayment, and the investor's required rate of return, as illustrated in Figure 4-4. Using the time value of money, this stream of future interest payments and principal repayment is discounted at the investor's required rate of return or the market rate of interest to its present value in today's dollars. For example, the cash flows from a bond with three years to maturity, paying a coupon of $30 at the end of each year with the return of the par value, $1,000, at maturity would be discounted at the investor's required rate of return to equal the purchase price.

Most corporate bonds pay interest semiannually, which means that the coupon rate is halved and the length of time to

FIGURE 4-4

Market Price of a Bond

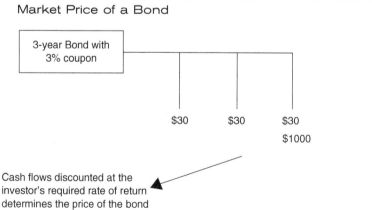

maturity is multiplied by 2 to convert to 6-month periods. Using these modifications, the price of a bond is easily determined using Microsoft Excel.

What is the price of a bond that has a 3 percent coupon rate, pays interest semiannually, and matures in three years' time? The investor's required rate of return for this bond is 6 percent.

A 3 percent coupon payable semiannually results in a coupon payment of $15 per six-month period, and the 6 percent annual investor's required rate of return is halved to 3 percent for six semiannual periods until maturity.

Using Excel to find the price of a bond, click on f* and then highlight PV and enter the data as illustrated in the following list:

Rate	0.03
Nper	6
PMT	15
FV	1,000
Type	0

Formula result = 918.742

The price of the bond is linked to its coupon payment, market rates of interest or investor's required rate of return, risk of the bond, and the length of time to maturity. If you compare the price of a U.S. Treasury note with the same coupon rate and maturity as that of a corporate bond, you notice that they have different prices. The Treasury note trades at a higher price than that of the corporate bond because a greater risk of default exists with the corporate bond; the price is therefore calculated with a higher discount rate (or yield to maturity). You then require a greater coupon yield (and required rate of return) on the corporate bond for assuming a greater risk of default. This description confirms why a AAA-rated corporate bond trades at a higher price than a BBB-rated corporate bond if the coupon and maturity are the same. The difference in yield between the AAA- and BBB-rated bonds is referred to as the *excess yield*, which issuers must pay for the extra grade of credit risk. Bond prices fluctuate depending on investors' assessments of the bond's risk. The relationships can be summarized this way: the greater the risk of a bond, the greater its yield, and the lower its market price.

WHY BONDS FLUCTUATE IN PRICE

Several factors account directly for fluctuations in bond prices. These factors include the relationships between bond prices, coupon rates, market yields, maturities (Malkiel, 1962), and risk assessment. The following axioms illustrate these relationships:

- *The coupon rate relative to market rates of interest.* When market rates of interest rise and exceed the coupon rate of a bond, the price of the bond declines in order to relate the current yield to the market rate of interest. When interest rates decline, the price of the bond rises. The smaller the coupon rate of the bond, the greater is the fluctuation in price.
- *The length of time to maturity.* The longer the maturity, the more volatile is the bond's price fluctuation.
- *For a given change in a bond's yield.* The longer the maturity of the bond, the greater is the magnitude of change in the bond's price.
- *For a given change in a bond's yield.* The size of the change in the bond's price increases at a diminishing rate the longer the maturity of the bond.
- *For a given change in the bond's yield.* The magnitude of the bond's price is inversely related to the bond's yield.
- *For a given change in a bond's yield.* The magnitude of the price increase caused by a decrease in yield is greater than the price decrease caused by an increase in yield.
- *Changes in risk assessment by the market.* The lesser the quality of the bond, the lower is the price. The greater the quality of the bond, the higher is the price. The greater the risk of the bond, the more volatile is the bond's price fluctuation.

Interest Rates and Bond Prices

The first reason that bond prices fluctuate has to do with the inverse relationship between bond prices and market rates of interest. When market rates of interest rise, the prices of existing bonds fall; when interest rates fall, prices of existing bonds rise. The extent of this change in bond prices is determined by the coupon rates of the bonds. This relationship between interest rates and the coupon rates of bonds determines whether bonds trade at a discount or at a premium price:

- *Discount.* Bonds trade at a discount when their coupon rates are lower than market rates of interest.
- *Discount.* When the yield to maturity of the bond (ask yield or bid yield) is greater than the coupon rate, the bond generally trades at a discount.
- *Premium.* A bond trades at a premium when its coupon rate is higher than market rates of interest.
- *Premium.* A bond generally trades at a premium when its yield to maturity is lower than its coupon rate.

Interest Rates and Maturity

A second reason for the fluctuations in bond prices is the relationship between interest rates and the length of time to maturity. Some bonds are more sensitive to changes in interest rates than other bonds because of their different maturities. For example, two bonds with the same coupon rate but different maturities react differently to changes in interest rates. Not only is the longer-maturity bond more volatile than the shorter- maturity bond, but the magnitude of price changes is also greater for bonds with longer maturities.

REFERENCE

Malkiel, Burton C., "Expectations, Bond Prices and the Term Structure of Interest Rates," *Quarterly Journal of Economics,* May 1962, pp. 197-218.

CHAPTER 5

DURATION AND CONVEXITY

KEY CONCEPTS

- Duration
- Modified duration
- Convexity

DURATION

Bonds, as discussed in previous chapters of this book, are subject to the following major risks:

- Risk of default by the issuer
- Loss of purchasing power through inflation
- Fluctuations in market rates of interest

Investors can lessen the risk of default by investing in a diversified portfolio of bonds. In other words, investors should not put all their money into the bonds of one issue or a few issues, and should buy better quality bond issues. There is not much that investors can do to reduce inflation in the economy, but investors can purchase bonds with yields that exceed current and expected future rates of inflation. Similarly, investors may be able to lessen the impact of interest rate risk through the concept of duration.

Duration is defined as the average time that it takes for a bond-holder to be repaid the price of the bond by the bond's total cash flows (interest and principal). It is the point in time in the life of the bond where the bond's return remains the same or unchanged despite the movement of market rates of interest. Understanding the cash flow payments of a bond explains the concept of duration. For example, a bond with a maturity of five years that pays a 5 percent annual coupon has the following cash payments: $50 per year for five years and $1,000 at the end of five years. The total cash flow over the life of this bond is $1,250 (5 × $50 + $1,000). In the second year of this bond, the total remaining cash flow is $1,200, and so on until the final year (maturity), when the total cash payment is $1,050. Frederick Macauley, the originator of the concept, weighted these average cash flows by the time period in which they were received to indicate the length of time for an investor to be paid off for the amount of the bond. These weighted average payments were discounted using the time value of money to equal the present value of the cash flows, summed the total discounted cash flows, and then divided this sum by the price of the bond to equal the duration of the bond.

Macauley's duration concept is illustrated in Table 5-1 using a bond with a coupon of 6 percent maturing in three years with a

TABLE 5-1

How to Calculate Duration

Time Period of Payment		Payment Amount (Coupon & Principal)		Present Value (Interest Factor 7%)		Present Value of Time Weighted Payments
1	×	$60	×	0.9346	=	$56.08
2	×	60	×	0.8734	=	$104.80
3	×	1060	×	0.8163	=	$2595.83
Total present value of time-weighted payments						$2756.71

$$\text{Duration} = \frac{\text{Summation of Present Value of Time-Weighted Payments}}{\text{Market Price of the Bond}}$$

$$= \frac{\$2,756.71}{\$973.44}$$

$$= 2.83 \text{ years/periods}$$

market price of $973.44 and current market rates of interest of 7 percent.

Duration is a time-weighted average of the summation of the present values of the coupon and interest payments multiplied by the time periods of the payments, which is then divided by the market price of the bond. The present value is the opposite of the future or compound value in the time value of money concept. A dollar today is worth more in the future because of its earnings potential. Similarly, a dollar in the future can be discounted to today's value and is worth less now than in the future. A 2.83 duration means that this bondholder will collect the average of the coupon interest and principal payments for this bond in 2.83 years.

A simpler method for calculating the duration on a $1,000 face value bond with a coupon of 6 percent, maturing in three years with a market price of $973.44 and current market rates of interest of 7 percent, is to use the duration formula:

$$\text{Duration} = \frac{(1+y)}{y} - \frac{(1+y) + n(c-y)}{(c[1+y]^n - 1] + y)}$$

where c = coupon rate

y = yield to maturity

n = number of years to maturity

Substituting the figures in the example:

$$\text{Duration} = \frac{(1+.07)}{0.07} - \frac{(1+.07) + 3(.06 - .07)}{.06[(1+.07)^3 - 1] + .07)}$$

$$= 2.83 \text{ years}$$

For bonds that pay regular coupon interest, duration is always less than the maturity. For zero coupon bonds whose entire cash flow is paid at maturity, the duration is equal to the bond's maturity. Bonds with different maturities and different coupons have different durations. Bonds with higher durations experience greater price volatility as market rates of interest change and bonds with lower durations have lower price volatility. Different bonds with the same durations have similar price fluctuations to changes in market rates of interest. This concept of the same coupon rate but different maturities is explained in Table 5-2, which shows the bond prices when market rates of interest change.

When market rates of interest decline below the coupon rate (of 6 percent) to 5 percent, the price of the bond increases above par value. Correspondingly, as maturities increase from 2 years to 20 years, so do the prices of the bond. The opposite is true when market rates of interest rise to 7 percent (greater than the coupon rate of 6 percent), as illustrated in Table 5-2. Bond prices fall below par and decline further as maturities extend into the future.

Following are the generalizations for bonds with which duration can be better explained:

- The longer the maturity of a bond, the greater the price volatility.
- There is an inverse relationship between bond prices and market rates of interest: when market rates of interest rise, bond prices fall, and when market rates of interest decline, bond prices increase.

Consequently, a bondholder with a coupon of 6 percent and a maturity of 30 years faces greater price volatility than a similar coupon bond with a shorter maturity. A lower coupon bond (for example, 4 percent) with a long maturity will experience even greater price volatility with changes in market rates of interest than a shorter maturity bond. This is true because the bondholder with

TABLE 5-2

Impact of Market Fluctuations in Interest Rates on the Price of a Bond with a Coupon Rate of 6% with Different Maturities

Maturity	Market Rate of Interest	
	5%	7%
2 years	$1,018.56	$981.88
5 years	$1,042.27	$959.01
10 years	$1,077.21	$929.72
20 years	$1,124.63	$894.04

the lower coupon bond receives smaller cash flows ($40 per year through maturity versus $60 per year), which when reinvested produces lower future values. The longer the maturity of the bond, the longer the bondholder has to wait to receive the face or par value of the bond. Hence, the present value of the par value of the bond is discounted to a lesser amount than the present value of the par value of a bond maturing earlier.

Duration accounts for this reinvestment rate risk, the coupon rate, and the term to maturity of a bond as follows:

- The lower the coupon, the higher the duration.
- The higher the coupon, the lower the duration.
- The longer the term to maturity, the higher the duration.
- The shorter the term to maturity, the lower the duration.
- The smaller the duration, the smaller the price volatility of the bond.
- The greater the duration, the greater the price volatility of the bond.

Duration explains why a zero coupon bond has the same duration as its term to maturity. With a zero coupon bond, there are no coupon payments and only the principal is received at maturity. Thus, except for zero coupon bonds, the duration for all coupon interest bonds is always less than the terms to maturity.

Duration is a tool that can be used to manage interest rate risk and the maturity of the bonds with the timing of the investor's needs for the funds. By matching the duration of bonds with the timing of the funds, investors can lessen their risks of loss on their bonds. Table 5-3 illustrates how duration can assist an investor in lessening the effects of price losses due to interest rate changes.

MODIFIED DURATION

Modified duration is a concept that measures the price sensitivity of a bond to changes in interest rates. For example, two bonds with the same duration but different maturities will not react in the same way to changes in interest rates. Modified duration allows you to determine which bond will rise or fall more in price when interest rates change. The following equation measures the changes in price of a bond when the yield to maturity (interest rates) changes.

$$\text{Change in price} = \frac{-(\text{Duration} \times \text{Change in yield})}{(1 + \text{Yield to maturity})} \times \text{price}$$

For example, a bond with a coupon rate of 6 percent, maturing in three years with a market price of $973.44 and a yield to maturity of 7 percent (required rate of return), has a duration of 2.83. What will the bond's price be if the yield to maturity increases to 7.1 percent?

$$\text{Change in price} = \frac{-(\text{Duration} \times \text{Change in yield})}{(1 + \text{Yield to maturity})} \times \text{price}$$

$$= \frac{-(2.83 \times 0.001)}{(1.07)} \times 973.44$$

$$= -\$2.57$$

An increase in yield of one basis point (1/100 of a percent or 0.1 percent) results in a decrease of $2.57 in the price of the bond.

TABLE 5-3

The Damage to Bond Prices from Rising Interest Rates

Bond prices rose over the three-year period 2000 to 2003 due to declining interest rates. The rise in bond prices resulted in increased total returns for bondholders. Bondholders who sold their bonds at higher prices than the purchase prices received capital gains in addition to the regular interest payments received from their bonds. Brokerage firms, traders, and individual investors were invested in bonds based on their belief that interest rates would continue to fall. According to Moody's Investors Service, banks increased their holdings of U.S. government bonds by 46 percent to $355 billion during the 28 months through June 2003 (Zuckerman, 2003). However, interest rates had tumbled to 45-year lows, indicating that they could not fall much further. Rising interest rates would result in whopping losses for bond investors. How much damage would this cause? That would depend on the coupon rates of the bonds, the change in interest rates, and the maturity of the bonds. Consider the changes in price that would occur if interest rates increased by 1 and 2 percentage points for the following Treasury notes (bonds issued at $1,000):

	2-Year 1.5% Coupon Note	5-Year 2.75% Coupon Note	10 Year 3.5% Coupon Note	30-Year 4.57% Coupon Note
Interest Rate				
1% rise	$980	$955.16	$920.87	$855.78
2% rise	962	912.81	849.25	740.71

A 1 percent increase in interest rates has the least effect on the 2-year note, whereas the loss on the 30-year maturity is the greatest. An increase in interest rates of 2 percentage points results in even greater losses on the longest maturity bonds. Thus, even including the coupon interest payments, bond-holders would receive negative total returns for all the maturities listed above if interest rates rose by 2 percentage points. However, if bondholders held their 10-year notes and rein-vested the interest payments that they received at the higher interest rates of 6.57%, they would be able to recoup some of their losses in the price of the bond. In fact, if bondholders held this note for 6.92 years, they would not lose any money on this note. This is the note's duration. Duration would also apply if interest rates declined. This is because bondholders would reinvest their interest payments at lower rates of interest. Thus, duration is the point in a bond's life where changes in interest rates would have no effect on the bond's return.

With interest rates at historically such a low level, it is likely that interest rates will rise in the future. The reasons for the rise could be many: an increase in inflation, increased budget deficits, Federal Reserve decision to tighten the money supply, or a falling dollar.

CONVEXITY

Convexity is a measure of the curvature of the price-yield relation-ship of a bond. Duration is a useful concept when market rates of interest change in small increments. However, when changes in interest rates are large, estimates made using the concept of modified duration are not accurate due to the fact that the relationships are not linear. The concept of convexity can help reduce the errors when the changes in interest rates are large.

Convexity is a measure of the curvature of the relationship between bond prices and the different yields to maturity. When bond yields decline, bond prices rise at an increasing rate. Similarly, bond prices fall at a decreasing rate when yields rise. In other words, bond prices do not move up and down at the same rate. Bond prices rise faster than they decline, which means that the price yield curve has a positive convexity curve. This is a property of all non-callable bonds. The meaning for bond investors is that they can make more money when interest rates decline than they will lose when interest rates increase. The amounts of money that can be made or lost resulting from changes in bond yields depend on duration and convexity (characteristics of the bond).

Table 5-4 shows the price yield relationships for three bonds and Figure 5-1 illustrates the convexity of these three bonds with their different coupon yields and maturities.

TABLE 5-4

Relationship Between Yields to Maturity and Bond Prices

Bond A 13%, 3-Year Bond		Bond B 8%, 10-Year Bond		Bond C Zero-Coupon, 30-Year Bond	
Yield to Maturity	Bond Price	Yield to Maturity	Bond Price	Yield to Maturity	Bond Price
1%	$1,352.93	1%	$1,663.00	1%	$742.90
2%	1,316.92	2%	1,538.64	2%	552.00
3%	1,282.56	3%	1,426.64	3%	412.00
4%	1,249.75	4%	1,324.88	4%	308.00
5%	1,217.82	5%	1,231.64	5%	231.40
6%	1,187.09	6%	1,147.21	6%	174.10
7%	1,157.46	7%	1,070.19	7%	131.40
8%	1,128.82	8%	1,000.00	8%	99.40
9%	1,101.27	9%	935.82	9%	75.40
10%	1,074.60	10%	877.07	10%	57.30
11%	1,048.88	11%	824.14	11%	43.70
12%	1,024.03	12%	774.02	12%	33.40
13%	1,000.00	13%	731.56	13%	25.60

FIGURE 5-1

Bond Convexity

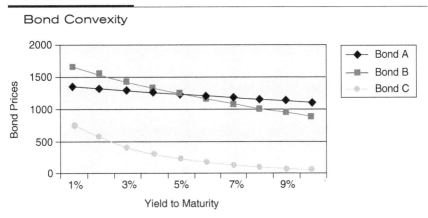

Yield to Maturity

Bond A in Figure 5-1 with the highest coupon rate and the shortest maturity (13 percent coupon maturing in three years) has an almost flat curve with very little convexity, whereas Bond B with an 8 percent coupon and 10-year maturity has a more convex line. Bond C with a zero percent coupon and 30-year maturity has the greatest convexity of the bonds shown. What these curves show is that the greatest change in yield to maturity has the greatest impact on the prices of bonds with the greater convexities. In general, the relationships regarding convexity are as follows:

- The greater the yield to maturity, the lower the convexity.
- The lower the coupon rate, the higher the convexity.

Figure 5-2 shows the relationships between duration and convexity when there are changes in yield. The convexity of Bond A is shown along with the duration lines at two different points on the bond curve. These lines indicate the slope or duration at the points where they touch the bond curve. As the yield declines on the graph, the slope of the line gets steeper. Similarly, as the yield increases, the slope of the line gets flatter.

In general, the relationships between yield and duration are as follows:

- When yield to maturity decreases, the duration of the bond increases.

FIGURE 5-2

Relationship Between Duration and Convexity

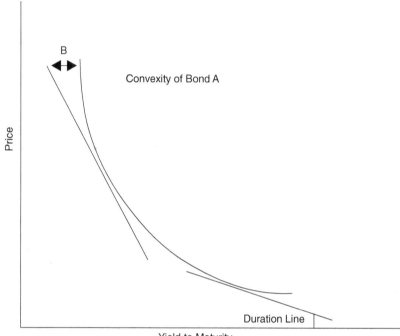

- When yield to maturity increases, the duration (slope) of the bond falls.

Duration is fairly accurate in determining the price of a bond when the change in yield is small. However, with large changes in yield, duration estimates the price of the bond at less than the actual price, as shown by arrow B in Figure 5-2. Duration uses a linear measure rather than the actual curvilinear relationship used for convexity.

WHAT IS THE VALUE OF CONVEXITY FOR INVESTORS?

Investors can use the concept of convexity to determine which bonds to buy. For example, when faced with a choice between two bonds, both with the same duration and yield, the convexity of the bonds can assist in the decision-making process. Figure 5-3 illustrates the different convexities of two bonds, Bond 1 and Bond 2, which are trading at the same price, yield, and duration. It doesn't matter what happens to interest rates because Bond 1 will always trade at higher prices than Bond 2. This is because Bond 1 has a higher convexity than Bond 2.

The question is how much more would you be willing to pay for Bond 1 over Bond 2 at different yields? The answer lies in the expected changes in interest rates. If interest rates are expected to change very little into the future, then the advantages of the changes in bond prices of Bond 1 over those of Bond 2 will not be that significant. In other words, investors might not be willing to

F I G U R E   5 - 3

Convexity of Two Bonds

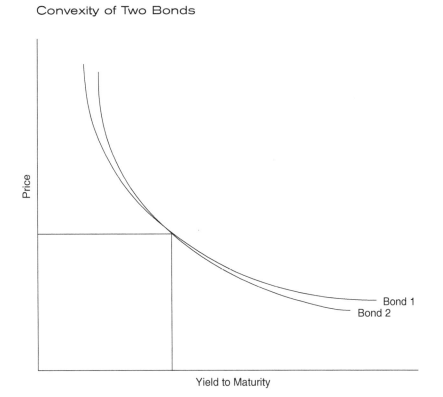

pay premium prices for Bond 1 over Bond 2. However, if interest rates are expected to be quite volatile, then investors may be more willing to pay the premium prices for Bond 1 over those of Bond 2.

REFERENCE

Zuckerman, Gregory, "Wall Street Wins with Bonds ... for Now," *Wall Street Journal,* June 30, 2003, pp. C1, C3.

CHAPTER 6

The Economy and the Bond Markets

KEY CONCEPTS

- The relationships between the economy and the bond markets
- Economic terms: gross domestic product (GDP), industrial production, inflation, deflation, unemployment, and housing starts
- The effects of monetary policy on the bond markets
- How changes in fiscal policy affect the financial markets
- Relationships between the dollar and the financial markets

The easy years of earning double-digit returns on bonds (1980s to early 1990s, and in the year 2001 to 2002) are over. Returns on these investments are reverting back to the normal annual levels of around 5 percent for bonds. Investors now have to be more careful in the selection of their investments. By understanding the relationships between the economy and the financial markets, you can make more informed decisions as to the types of investments for your portfolio.

This chapter examines the many positive and ambiguous economic relationships between the financial markets and the macroeconomic environment. The hallmark of economic analysis, as many of you know, is the basic disagreement by leading economists about the prescriptions for the economy. Yet within these disagreements is enough of a consensus for investors to use in their investment decision making. This chapter begins with an examination of the economy, monetary policy, and fiscal policy, followed by a description of the implications of the relative strength or weakness of the dollar on the bond markets.

THE RELATIONSHIPS BETWEEN THE ECONOMY AND THE BOND MARKETS

Encouraging economic news causes the stock market to rally in the short term, and in most cases causes the bond market to decline. Mixed economic signals also have ramifications for the financial markets in general, and for stock and bond investors in particular. Weak economic news generally causes the bond market to rally. An examination of the forces that drove the stock market down during the January 2001 through November 2002 period may make the relationships between the movement of the stock and bond markets and the economy clearer.

After the "irrational exuberance" experienced during the stock market bubble of the late 1990s through 2000, breakdowns in corporate governance and excessive stock valuations caused the stock market to decline during 2001. These negative forces on the market prevailed despite the economic gains in productivity during the same period. Corporate malfeasance created a crisis of confidence among investors. Enron declared bankruptcy in December 2001, followed by revelations of auditing fraud and corporate sleaze at World-Com, Tyco, Adelphia, and Global Crossing. These occurrences exacerbated the decline in the stock market, even when quality company stock prices became cheap by historical standards. Stock investors stayed away from the stock market and put money into bonds. While the stock market declined over the three-year period 2000 through 2002, the bond market saw double-digit gains.

On July 19, 2006, the Federal Reserve Chairman, Ben Bernanke, testified to Congress that economic growth would slow and inflation would decline, which laid the groundwork for a bond market rally for the rest of 2006. Bond yields declined and bond prices rose as demand remained strong for bonds. The fall in interest rates sparked a rally in both the housing market and the stock market. The economic factors that could end this bond market rally are many. For example, oil and commodity prices rising to higher levels could cause inflation. Such a scenario would prompt bond investors to seek higher yields, resulting in a decline in bond prices.

Is the stock market a better predictor of the economy than the bond market? A closer look at the state of the economy provides some clues. When the economy is in recession, the Federal Reserve generally lowers interest rates to encourage economic growth. Both bond and stock markets rise when interest rates fall. Similarly, when the economy overheats, causing fears of inflation, interest rates rise, resulting in both stock and bond market declines. Consequently, it is the direction of interest rates and the availability of capital, which are linked more to the bond market than the stock market, that seem to provide more clues to the state of the economy. The relationship between the availability of capital and bonds through interest rates is strong.

The yield curve shows the relationship between short- and long-term interest rates. Historically, when the yield curve is inverted (short-term rates exceed long-term rates), this is a precursor for the economy to go into recession. The bond market through the yield curve has correctly predicted most of the recessions in the United States. A reason is that bankers do not like to lend money on a long-term basis when they can obtain higher yields from short-term maturities, and so, long-term credit becomes tight.

The flip side of the coin is when long-term interest rates exceed short-term interest rates, which provides greater incentives for bankers to lend money. The yield curve becomes steeper, indicating an accelerating economy. Therefore, by following the bond market and yield spreads, clues are provided as to the direction of the economy.

The clearest picture of the economy and financial markets is gained through hindsight, but after-the-fact information is too late for investment decisions. By interpreting economic and financial market indicators, investors are looking for early signs of changes in the direction of the stock and bond markets. On the other hand, the astute reader will observe that if economists and financial analysts can't agree on the state of the economy, how is the lay individual to come up with any more definitive answers?

For individual investors, it is not important if the forecasted numbers from economists are not in agreement because, after all, economists and analysts all base their forecasts on the same information. What is important, however, is to be able to use either their range of forecasts or the key statistical indicators to predict changes in the direction of the economy and the financial markets. An understanding of the economic indicators can help you make timely decisions in the stock and bond markets.

WHAT IS THE STATE OF THE ECONOMY?

Investors are better equipped to plan their investment strategies if they are able to understand and forecast the state of the economy. A wealth of new economic information is released on a weekly basis that shapes perceptions of where the economy is headed. This section outlines the effects of the most common economic indicators, which can be used to identify trends in the economy.

Gross domestic product (GDP) is a measure in dollar value of the economy's total production of goods and services. Comparing the current GDP with previous periods indicates the economy's rate of growth or decline. An increasing GDP indicates that the economy is expanding and companies have greater opportunities to increase their sales and earnings. Inflation distorts the accuracy of this measurement of growth, so there is a measure of the real growth of an economy's output, referred to as "real" GDP. *Real GDP* is adjusted for price level changes and measures each period's goods and services using prices that prevailed in a selected base year. A comparison of real GDP figures with those of prior periods provides a more accurate measurement of the real rate of growth. GDP is therefore a measure of the economic health of a country. Inflation in the United States has been low recently and has not significantly detracted from real GDP. Figure 6-1 illustrates the quarterly real GDP for a 7-year period. Real GDP has been positive every quarter since the third quarter of 2001.

The performances of both the stock and bond markets were positive in 2006 and the first half of 2007, indicating a positive correlation with GDP growth. A closer scrutiny of the performance of the bond market relative to GDP growth indicates that when GDP is negative, the bond market reacts favorably because of the expectation of

FIGURE 6-1

Real Domestic Gross Product

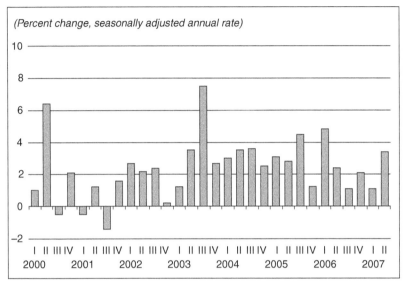

U.S. Bureau of Economic Analysis

future interest rate declines to spur the economy. Bear in mind that a general definition of a recession is when GDP is negative for two consecutive quarters. Even though GDP growth was positive from the second quarter in 2006 to early 2007, the yield curve also was inverted, predicting an economic recession. At the other extreme, the bond market does not react favorably to high, accelerating rates of growth in GPD because of the fear of inflation. To ascertain the state of the economy, you would need to look at more indicators than GDP performance.

A more narrowly focused measure of a nation's output is the monthly *industrial production* report, which measures the nation's manufacturing output of its factories, mines, and utilities. The manufacturing sector generally leads the economy's short-term swings. Figure 6-2 shows industrial production and capacity utilization in the United States from 1970 through 2005. Industrial production increased steadily over this period, whereas over the five-year period from 2000 to 2005 production leveled off and was consistent when compared with real GDP growth during the same period.

FIGURE 6-2

Industrial Production and Capacity Utilization

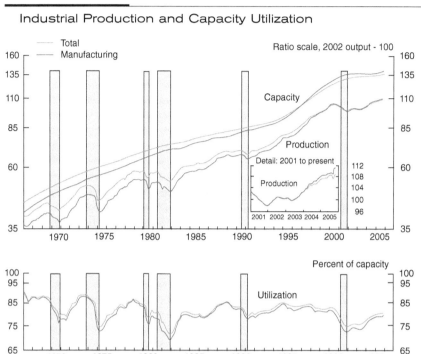

Notes: The shaded areas are periods of business recession as defined by the National Bureau of Economic Research (NBER).

When an economy is in recovery, the *manufacturing capacity utilization rate* is a key indicator to watch (the second graph in Figure 6-2). This indicator measures how much of the economy's factory potential is being used. Economists worry about inflation when the nation's factory capacity rises above 85 percent. For example, when a recovery is robust and the economy is growing rapidly, with interest rates remaining low, there will be a decline in unemployment, which will give rise to increasing wage pressures and increasing prices of goods. For April through July 2007, the manufacturing capacity utilization rate ranged from 81.4 to 81.9 percent.

The vertical lines in the graphs in Figure 6-2 indicate the recessions in the economy. Industrial production and capacity utilization decreased during each recession and then grew consistently in the recovery periods.

The *unemployment rate* is the percentage of the nation's labor force that is out of work, and it is another indicator of the economy's strength (or lack of it). An unemployment rate of 4 to 6 percent is considered to be healthy in an economy. Lower rates than these are considered to be inflationary because of rising salaries, whereas higher rates have the potential to be a downside to consumer spending in the economy. As of May 2007, the unemployment rate was 4.5 percent, and as shown by the graph in Figure 6-3 has been on a declining trend over the past seven years. Rising unemployment rates lead to recessions (indicated by the vertical lines), and following recessions, unemployment rates fall. Generally, a growing economy and a low unemployment rate in combination have traditionally fueled inflation. Concern arises when rates for labor rise faster than productivity gains. It is for this reason that the bond and stock markets pay so much attention to the speeches by the Federal Reserve Chairman to Congress about interest rates. When there is even a hint of inflation on the horizon, the Federal Reserve reacts by raising short-term interest rates, thereby depressing prices of existing bonds.

FIGURE 6-3

Civilian Unemployment Rate

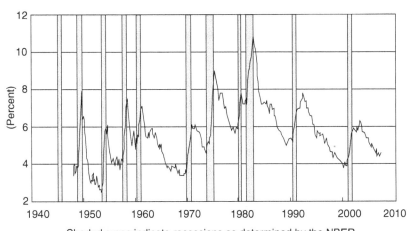

Shaded areas indicate recessions as determined by the NBER.
2007 Federal Reserve Bank of St. Louis: research.stlouisfed.org

Source: U.S. Department of Labor, Bureau of Labor Statistics

The other side of the coin is a high unemployment rate. Governments become concerned when the unemployment rate rises above a certain level (about 7 percent) and the action is to stimulate the economy (through fiscal and monetary policies) in order to reduce the unemployment rate. These actions also are inflationary. A government's approach is to aim for nearly full employment without increasing inflation.

Inflation is defined as the rate at which prices for goods and services rise in an economy over a period of time. Inflation is also defined as an increase in the supply of money and credit. Inflation often characterizes a growing economy in which the demand for goods and services outstrips production, in turn leading to rising prices. Looked at another way, there is too much money chasing too few goods and services. As of August 2007, the inflation rate was relatively low at 2.1 percent. Some economists expect the rate to go below 2 percent, while others argue that inflation is far from being dead.

The *consumer price index* (CPI) is one measure of inflation. The Bureau of Labor Statistics calculates the CPI monthly. The Bureau monitors the changes in prices of items (such as food, clothing, housing, transportation, medical care, entertainment) in the CPI. It is a gauge of the level of inflation and is more meaningful when it is compared to the CPIs of previous periods.

Many economists believe that the CPI fuels inflation, similar to a cat chasing its tail. Social Security payments and many cost-of-living increases in employment contracts are tied to increases in the CPI. The CPI may, in fact, exacerbate the level of inflation.

When the level of inflation is high (relative to previous periods), government pursues restrictive economic policies to attempt to reduce the level of inflation. Figure 6-4 illustrates the relatively low rates of inflation as measured by the CPI over the 17-year period from 1990 to 2007.

The *producer price index* (PPI) is announced monthly and monitors the costs of raw materials used to produce products. The PPI is a better predictor of inflation than the CPI, because when prices of raw materials increase, there is a time lag before consumers experience the price increases.

Another key indicator is the Commodity Research Bureau's *commodity price index*, which is a measure of raw material prices. When this index rises significantly over a six-month period, it is a warning that inflation is on the horizon.

FIGURE 6-4

U.S. Inflation

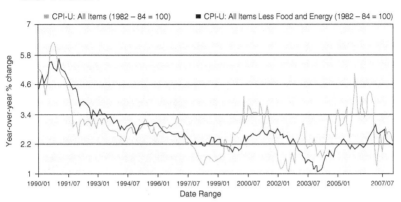

Source: Federal Reserve Bank of Cleveland

The *leading inflation index*, developed by Columbia University's Center for Business Cycle Research, is an index that anticipates cyclical turns in consumer price inflation. When it moves up with commodity prices, it is a clear signal that inflation is ahead.

Inflation has a detrimental effect on both the bond and stock market as well as on the economy. When the level of inflation increases, real GDP falls (in 1980 in the United States). Similarly, when inflation declines, there is a real increase in GDP. This inverse relationship does not always hold up, as evidenced by the economy during the mid 1990s. Despite lower levels of inflation, real GDP showed insignificant growth, which translated into the economy taking a long time to move out of recession.

Deflation is the opposite of inflation. A simplistic definition of deflation is a general decrease in prices over a period of time. Deflation, broadly defined, is a contraction in the supply of money and credit. This difference is illustrated using the following example. In the 2002 economic environment, companies had a lack of pricing power (falling prices), yet at the same time in the third quarter of 2002, productivity increased by 5.1 percent on an annual basis. This was a bullish signal for the economy because with the same labor pool there was an increase of 5.1 percent in productivity. If price declines are less than productivity gains, there is no deflation.

Housing starts are released monthly and show the relative strength in housing production. Housing starts are the number of permits issued for the construction of new homes. An increase in

FIGURE 6-5

New Housing Units Started in the United States
(Seasonally Adjusted Annual Rate)

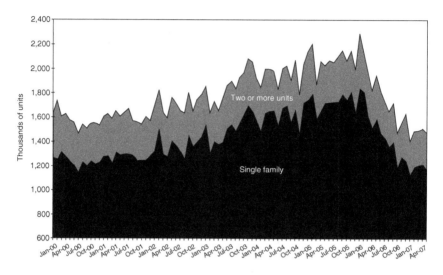

housing starts relative to previous months indicates optimism about the economy as more people are buying homes. Thus, strength in housing starts shows consumer confidence in the economy. Figure 6-5 indicates the relative strength and weakness of housing starts for single-family homes during the period January 2000 through April 2007.

Housing starts declined beginning in January 2006 through July 2007. The cause of the decline was a record housing building boom in 2005, which resulted in a decline in house prices, and coupled with the subprime mortgage crisis of 2007, caused a recession in the housing sector of the economy. Resulting job losses in the construction industry muted economic growth in the economy, and consequently has led many economists to predict an economic recession.

Table 6-1 lists some Web sites that provide economic information. These indicators are some of the pieces to the overall economic picture. By examining such indicators and statistics, investors may be better able to fine tune their opinions and forecasts of the economy. This brief overview of the economy highlights the complexities of the economy. This does not mean that the investor should throw in the towel and discount the economy. Instead, by using a consensus of economic forecasts, investors are better prepared in deciding how to invest their funds.

TABLE 6-1

How to keep up with the State of the Economy.

> News and analysis of the state of the economy is available on a daily basis from newspapers, business magazines, and from various websites on the Internet:
>
> www.businessweek.com
>
> www.wsj.com
>
> www.federalreserve.gov
>
> www.economics.about.com

Point of Interest: Whither the Economy? Is the Glass Half Empty or Half Full?

Is the economy headed back into recession or surging ahead into a period of sustained economic growth? Both pessimistic and optimistic views can be found on where the economy is headed. Additionally, there is a slew of economic data that can be used to substantiate both points of view on the economy. Cogent arguments can be made for both future anemic annual economic growth of 1 percent and for future annual robust growth of 4 percent. There are many uncertainties that confront the economy, such as terrorism, war, and a loss of consumer confidence. These all have a telling effect on business investment, consumer spending, and the state of the economy, which affect both the stock and bond markets.

This is a perplexing situation for investors trying to forecast where the economy is going. Ignoring the economy is tantamount to burying one's head in the sand, which ultimately leads to poor returns. Discounting the economy is not an option for serious investors. Instead, by using a consensus of economic forecasts, investors are better prepared in deciding how to invest their funds. The actions from Wall Street illustrate this point. Within the same week, two brokerage firms changed their suggested asset allocation plans for investors. One firm expecting a return to recession reduced their exposure to stocks by 5 percent, while the other firm's outlook on the economy was positive, and they increased their exposure to stocks.

THE EFFECTS OF THE ECONOMY ON THE BOND MARKET

There is a strong correlation between the performance of the bond market and interest rates. When interest rates in the economy decline, bond markets rally (prices of existing bonds rise). Interest rates generally decline when the economy enters a recession. During this time period investors in bonds benefit from holding bonds in their portfolios, and lengthening the time of the maturities of the bonds that they hold as interest rates decline.

During a recession, there is normally a shift to higher quality bonds due to credit and default concerns. Consequently, the spread in credit yield between good quality bonds and speculative bonds widens. Investors buy Treasuries, which drives prices up and lowers the yield, while speculative bonds are sold, which decreases their prices and increases their yields.

The opposite occurs in a period of economic recovery. The Federal Reserve Bank (the Fed) raises interest rates to combat any fears of inflation and the economy growing too quickly. This action results in bond prices declining and bond yields rising. Yields of both speculative and good quality (AAA-rated) bonds rise, and as a result, the credit spread is narrowed. When interest rates are rising in an economy, investors in bonds are likely to buy or hold shorter maturity bonds, which will experience smaller price concessions in their holdings. Patient investors will wait until they think that interest rates in the economy have reached their peak before committing funds to new bonds.

MONETARY POLICY AND THE FINANCIAL MARKETS

Monetary policy impacts the economy and the financial markets. The Federal Reserve Bank is the central bank of the United States and works with the government to maintain financial stability and to devise and implement monetary policy. In addition, the Federal Reserve regulates the nation's banks and provides financial services to the U.S. government. The stability of the monetary system depends on the supply of money in the economy. By regulating the supply of money and credit in the economy, the Federal Reserve Bank affects the country's economic growth, inflation, unemployment, production, long-term interest rates, and ultimately the stock and bond markets.

THE IMPACT OF THE FEDERAL RESERVE ON CHANGES TO THE MONEY SUPPLY AND INTEREST RATES

The Federal Reserve Bank can increase or decrease the nation's money supply to provide a stable currency value, a reasonable level for interest rates, and sufficient money to fund transactions in the economy. The principal tools used by the Federal Reserve Bank to change the supply of money are:

- Open market operations
- Reserve requirements
- Discount rate

Open Market Operations

Open market operations involve the Federal Reserve buying and selling securities (mostly U.S. Treasury bills and repurchase agreements) in the open market to increase or decrease the money supply and the reserves of commercial banks. The T-accounts in Figure 6-6 illustrate the debits and credits when the Federal Reserve expands the money supply by buying securities on the open market. The Federal Reserve purchases securities on the open market, which expands the Fed's inventory of securities. Payment is made within three days by depositing a check in a commercial bank, thereby expanding the bank's deposits. This action increases the reserves of the commercial banks and the reserves of the commercial banks at the Federal Reserve. Banks can lend more money, expanding the nation's credit and money supply.

FIGURE 6-6

Transactions when the Federal Reserve buys Securities on the Open Market

Federal Reserve Bank		Commercial Banks	
Inventory of securities increases when the Fed buys securities	Reserves of the commercial banks held at the Federal Reserve bank increase	Reserves of the banks increase which allows banks to issue more credit	Demand deposits increase when the Fed pays the sellers of securities

FIGURE 6-7

Transactions when the Federal Reserve sells Securities on the Open Market

Federal Reserve Bank		Commercial Banks	
Inventory of securities decreases when the Fed sells securities	Reserves of the commercial banks held at the Federal Reserve bank decrease	Reserves of the banks decrease which reduces banks' abilities to issue credit	Demand deposits decrease when the Fed is paid by the buyers of the securities

To contract the money supply, the Federal Reserve sells securities from its portfolio in the open market. This action has the effect of siphoning off money from the nation's money supply. The reserves of the commercial banks are reduced, thereby reducing the banks' capabilities to lend money. Figure 6-7 illustrates the effects of the Federal Reserve Bank's and the commercial banks' T accounts when the Fed sells securities to contract the money supply.

These open market operations are conducted by the Federal Open Market Committee (FOMC), composed of the president of the Federal Reserve Bank of New York, the board of governors, and the presidents of the other Federal Reserve Banks on a rotating basis. This committee meets every two weeks, and the minutes of its meetings are released to the public six weeks after each meeting. Bond traders are acutely aware of the Fed's actions in regard to buying, selling, or refraining from open market transactions because of the impact on interest rates, which affect bond prices.

Open market operations have a direct impact on interest rates. When the Fed expands the money supply by buying securities, it bids up the prices of Treasury bills to entice investors to sell their securities. This action lowers the yields of Treasury bills, leading to lower interest rates. The opposite is true when the Fed contracts the money supply.

Reserve Requirements

The reserve requirement is the percentage of deposits that banks must hold as vault cash or on deposit at the Federal Reserve Bank. The reserve requirement was 10 percent on transaction deposits as of 2006. The Fed changes the reserve requirement infrequently.

The Fed can increase the money supply by reducing the reserve requirement: banks then need to keep less in reserve and can therefore increase their lending. The reverse is true when the Fed increases the reserve requirements: upward pressure is exerted on interest rates. Changes in the reserve requirements not only increase or decrease the money supply, but also have a multiplier effect on the money supply.

A simple example illustrates this concept. Suppose you deposit $100 in Bank X and the reserve requirement is 10 percent. Bank X now has $100 on deposit, of which $10 is kept on reserve and $90 is lent to Corporation A. Corporation A deposits this $90 check in its bank, Bank A. Bank A keeps $9 on reserve and lends the remaining $81. This process is repeated, which shows how the original $100 is increased through the banking system to expand the money supply. Figure 6-8 illustrates the multiplier process graphically.

The Fed can stimulate the multiplier effect by lowering reserve requirements, which correspondingly increases banks' capacities to lend. In reality, a strong connection does not exist between the reserve requirement and money creation because the reserve requirement applies to only transaction deposits, which are a narrow measure of the money supply (M1). Time deposits or savings accounts, which are components of M2 and M3, have no reserve requirements. (See the next main section, "Defining the Money Supply," for a discussion of M1, M2, and M3.) Thus, reserve requirements play a relatively limited role in the creation of money.

FIGURE 6-8

The Multiplier Process

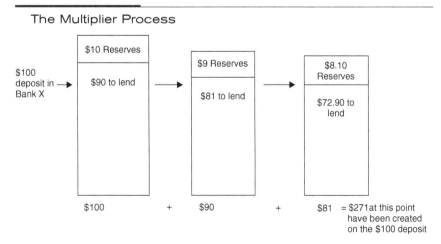

The Fed does not pay interest on the banks' reserves. Banks with excess reserves lend to other banks that need to add to their reserves. These funds, called federal funds, are provided mostly on a short-term (one-day) unsecured basis, although they are occasionally for longer terms. The Fed can alter the money supply by changing the federal funds rate. Changes to the federal funds rate and reserve requirements are widely reported in the newspapers and financial Web sites.

The target federal funds rate has declined from 5 percent on May 10, 2007, to 2.25 percent on March 18, 2008. Over a 10-year period from 1998 through March 2008, federal funds target rates ranged from a high of 6.5 percent in 2000 to a low of 1 percent in 2003. Changes in the federal funds rate have implications for money market and bond securities. Yields on money market securities such as Treasury bills are compared with the federal funds rate and generally move in tandem with any changes to the federal funds rate. The federal funds rate also affects yields on long-term notes and bonds.

Discount Rate

The discount rate is the Fed's third tool. The discount rate is the rate at which banks borrow from the Federal Reserve. When the discount rate is too high, banks are discouraged from borrowing reserves from the Fed. When the discount rate is low or lowered, banks are encouraged to borrow. By changing the discount rate, the Fed can therefore expand or contract the money supply. Changes in the discount rate are reported in the newspapers and financial Web sites. The discount rate is set every 14 days by the board of directors of the Fed.

By monitoring changes in open market transactions, reserve requirements, federal funds, and discount rates, investors can get a better feeling for the direction of future interest rates.

DEFINING THE MONEY SUPPLY

Before looking at the relationship between the money supply and the financial markets, it is important to define the different measures of the money supply. The process of defining the money supply can be likened to measuring your own personal money supply, although that is somewhat more finite by comparison! How much cash do you have? You have the cash in your pockets, in your wallet, under the mattress, and in your checking account. Savings accounts, money market funds, and some investments can be converted easily into cash. A sum of these sources gives you the amount of your money supply.

The narrowest measure of the nation's money supply is referred to as M–1, a broader definition is M–2, and the broadest category is M–3.

- *M–1* consists of the nation's cash, coins, travelers' checks, checking accounts (NOW accounts, which are interest-bearing checking accounts, are included), and demand deposits.
- *M–2* includes the elements of M–1 in addition to savings and time deposit accounts (for example, certificates of deposit [CDs] and money market deposit accounts of less than $100,000).
- *M–3* includes M–1 and M–2 in addition to time deposits and financial securities of large financial institutions.

Which is the best measure of the economy's money supply? Economists continue to debate this question. The Federal Reserve Bank's preferred measure is M–2, which is America's broad money supply.

Interest rate changes explain any discrepancies between the measures of the money supply. When short-term interest rates decline, investors move their savings from low-yielding bank deposits (included in M–2) to higher-yielding bonds, because long-term rates are higher than short-term rates. Economists argue that portfolio shifts make the definitions of the money supply unreliable as indicators of the state of the economy. For example, you can see that M–1 can increase without affecting M–2 when people transfer money from savings accounts to checking accounts. Discrepancies occur between the classifications of the money supply from week to week, but investors should be more concerned with the overall changes over time so that they can see a trend. By monitoring the Fed's open market transactions, changes in the reserve requirements and the discount rate, and the rate of growth or decline in the money supply, investors can make their investment decisions.

In short, evidence suggests that changes in the money supply have an influence on nominal economic activity, although their influence on real economic growth is still hotly contested.

IMPACT ON THE FINANCIAL MARKETS

When the Fed pursues a restrictive monetary policy, it can sell securities on the open market to siphon money from the money supply, or raise the reserve requirement, or both. These actions reduce the banks' capacities to lend money, and raise the discount rate to discourage banks from borrowing money.

These changes in monetary conditions have an effect on corporate earnings. When the money supply is decreased, interest rates rise, making it more costly for companies and individuals to borrow money. This situation causes them to delay purchases and leads to lower sales. With a decrease in sales and higher credit costs, companies have reduced earnings, which translate into lower stock prices and lower prices of existing bonds.

When interest rates are rising, investors earn more by investing in fixed-income securities and money market instruments. Therefore, many investors take their money out of the stock markets and invest in liquid short-term securities and longer-term debt securities, which exert more downward pressure on stock prices. Higher interest rates also translate into higher borrowing costs for margin investors. These investors move their money to debt securities to receive higher regular streams of income to justify their higher borrowing costs.

Monetary policy has a direct effect on interest rates, and interest rates and the stock market are strongly correlated. Rising interest rates tend to depress stock market prices, and falling interest rates have the opposite effect. There have been occasional inconsistencies to these relationships, such as during the 2000 to 2002 period when interest rates fell to their historic lows while at the same time the stock market declined.

Stock market investors generally move into bonds when interest rates go up and out of bonds when interest rates go down. Rising interest rates are favorable for investors moving into bonds, but not very good for investors holding bonds. The reason is that an inverse relationship exists between market rates of interest and bond prices. During periods of rising interest rates, investors holding fixed income securities find that the market prices of their bonds decline, because new investors in these bonds want a competitive yield. Similarly, in periods of declining interest rates, prices of existing bonds rise.

The open market operations of the Fed have a direct impact on interest rates and bond markets. When the Fed buys Treasury securities on the open market, it competes with other buyers, thus driving up prices and causing a decrease in Treasury yields. This situation creates a rate discrepancy between the yields on government debt and corporate debt. As a result, investors purchase corporate debt, causing prices to increase and yields to decrease. The reverse is true when the Fed sells government securities on the open market.

This discussion suggests that if investors anticipate changes in monetary policy they can make the appropriate changes to their investment strategies.

FISCAL POLICY AND THE MARKETS

Fiscal policy is the government's use of taxation, government spending, and debt management to stimulate or restrain the economy. The government uses both monetary and fiscal policy to pursue the same goals: full employment, economic growth, and price stability. Changes in fiscal policy can also affect the financial markets.

The federal government uses *taxation* to raise revenue and to reduce the amount of money in the economy. Taxation policies can stimulate or depress the economy and the financial markets. When taxes are increased, consumers have less money to invest and spend on goods and services, and corporations have reduced earnings, which leads to lower stock prices.

Tax cuts, however, have the opposite effect. Individuals have more money to spend and invest, and corporations experience the benefits of greater consumer spending along with lower corporate taxes, which generally leads to higher sales and earnings, and higher stock prices.

Government Spending

A tax cut has a favorable effect on savings and investments, whereas government spending has a greater effect on the goods and services produced in the economy. Government spending can also be used as a tool to stimulate or restrain the economy.

Debt Management

When the government's revenues are less than its expenditures, it runs a deficit. Deficit spending can have a significant effect on the financial markets in general and the stock and bond markets in particular. The government can finance its deficit by, borrowing in the financial markets, or by increasing the money supply.

By borrowing in the financial markets, the government drives up yields on the bond market, which depresses the stock market. By selling securities on the market, prices of government securities decline, which increases their yields. To counter the rate differential (between corporate and government securities), investors invest in government securities rather than in corporate securities, which reduces the prices of corporate bonds, which leads to increased yields on corporate bonds. When the government borrows in the market, bond prices become depressed and interest rates increase. The opposite is true when the government is buying securities in the market. Bond prices are pushed up and interest rates are lowered.

When a government is faced with financing an increasing deficit, it has to pay high rates of interest to attract buyers to invest in its securities. This action leads to higher interest rates in the economy, which has a depressing effect on stock prices and tends to drive up yields. The announced reduction in the budget deficit in 1998, for example, had the effect of a downward pressure on bond yields and increasing bond prices and stock prices. This trend in the stock and bond markets followed through to the year 2000 as the deficits turned into budget surpluses.

Increasing the Money Supply

If the government increases the money supply, inflation can raise its ugly head. Inflation has a negative effect on the economy, particularly the bond and stock markets.

When a government cannot reduce the growth of its deficit spending, it has an effect on the bond and stock markets. When a government can reduce its deficit spending, it can reduce its borrowing and pay down its debt, which lowers interest rates in the economy. Investors continually look for policies or budgets that can effectively change the direction of growth of a deficit or surplus.

Increased government spending can be inflationary and can bring an immediate response from bondholders. Because of computerized global trading, bondholders can unload millions of dollars of U.S. Treasuries within minutes and can send bond prices plummeting and long-term yields soaring. This statement is especially true for the U.S. Treasury bond market, which attracts a large amount of foreign investment because of the perception of the dollar as a safe haven currency. This instant access to information is exhibited in the increased volatility in the stock markets worldwide. Traders and large institutional stock investors can unload their positions quite quickly, causing stock markets to reverse their directions within minutes.

Fiscal policies affect the securities markets. By anticipating changes in these policies, you can better formulate your investment strategy.

THE DOLLAR AND THE FINANCIAL MARKETS

A relationship exists between the relative value of the dollar and the financial markets. The value of the dollar at the end of 2007 relative to other major currencies, such as the euro and British pound, had fallen to its lowest levels since 2000. The fall in the dollar was caused largely by economic factors and more specifically by the geopolitical risk that has dogged the United States. The war in Iraq and historically high oil, gas, commodity, wheat, corn, and soybean prices have had negative consequences on the value of the dollar.

The relative weakness of the dollar, however, is not all bad news for the economy. A weaker dollar makes U.S. exports less expensive around the world, giving U.S. exporting companies an advantage over their foreign competitors. This advantage should, theoretically at least, increase U.S. exports of goods and reduce

imports of goods (as they become more expensive), thereby narrowing or eliminating the U.S. trade deficit. However, the other
side of the coin is that foreigners might not be inclined to invest in
the United States when the value of their investments decline in
value because of the falling dollar.

The value of one currency is measured against the value of
other currencies through the forces of supply and demand. When
a great demand for a currency exists, it appreciates in value relative to other currencies. With low demand, the currency loses
value. Prices of currencies are determined on the foreign exchange
markets, which are composed of international banks and exchange
traders.

Inflation and interest rates are important economic factors,
which influence a currency's value.

Inflation

High inflation in a country causes the currency in that country to
depreciate. For example, if inflation were to rise to 6 percent in the
United States, the price of goods that originally cost $100 increases
to $106. As a result, American consumers might prefer to buy
imported goods for the equivalent of $100. Demand for foreign cur-
rencies is increased, which puts downward pressure on the dollar.
The *theory of purchasing power parity* addresses this issue. If the
prices of goods go up in one country relative to another, the currency (in the country with inflation) must depreciate to keep parity
in prices of goods between the two countries.

Inflation also has a detrimental effect on foreign investments,
because foreigners do not invest in financial assets that will potentially lose value. Therefore, higher inflation puts upward pressure
on interest rates to attract foreign investors.

Rising interest rates exert downward pressure on the bond
markets, because investors sell their long-term bonds and invest in
shorter-term securities whose yields increase as interest rates go up.

Interest Rates

When interest rates are higher in one country relative to another,
foreigners then invest in that country's Treasury bills, CDs, and
other higher yielding investments. These investments create a

greater demand for that country's currency, theoretically an appreciation in value of that currency. The opposite holds true for low interest rates and lower rates of inflation. The relationships between interest rates, inflation, and the value of the currency all add an important dimension to international investments.

This discussion points to the overall relationship between economic activity and the financial markets. Generally, if companies are experiencing greater earnings, an expanding economy might be accompanied by a booming stock market. Economic expansion can also spook the bond markets, however, which react to fears of inflation. These relationships, however, should not be oversimplified. A declining bond market can have a detrimental effect on the stock market during economic expansion because of fears of inflation and the anticipation of higher interest rates. Similarly, a declining economy can be associated with a rising bond market because of lower interest rates, which would have a positive effect on stock markets. By forecasting the direction of the economy, investors can anticipate the direction of the bond and stock markets.

CHAPTER 7

Money Market Securities

KEY CONCEPTS

- Money market mutual funds
- Treasury bills
- Commercial paper
- Bankers' acceptances
- Repurchase agreements

Money market securities are liquid, marketable, safe investments that have maturities of one year or less. They are typically used for the investment of emergency funds and short-term cash. Examples of these types of investments are certificates of deposit (CDs), money market mutual funds, Treasury bills, commercial paper, bankers' acceptances, and repurchase agreements. These investments are also used as temporary, short-term cash substitutes.

The money market is a subsector of the bond market and includes debt securities with maturities of one year or less. The money market is not located in one place but consists of banks and dealers throughout the United States that are connected by telephones and computers. The advantage of investing in money market securities is that idle cash earns a return until more permanent uses for this cash is found. The characteristics of these short-term investments are low risk of default, high liquidity, and marketability. However, many

TABLE 7-1

Features of Money Market Securities

Investment Objectives	Characteristics	Advantages	Disadvantages
Payment of income	Liquid	Provides a return for idle cash and emergency funds	Low yields that might not cover inflation
Preservation of principal	Marketable	Temporary parking place for funds between investments	Many individual money market securities require large investment amounts
Access to funds	Low-risk	High-credit quality	

money market securities trade in large denominations, precluding their investment by many individual investors. Table 7-1 summarizes some of the features of money market securities.

Money market mutual funds are convenient ways for individual investors to invest their short-term funds in money market securities. Despite the ease of investing in money market funds, investors should understand the characteristics of the different individual short-term investments, such as Treasury bills, commercial paper, bankers' acceptances, and repurchase agreements for two reasons:

1. Money market mutual funds invest their pooled funds in these individual short-term fixed-income securities. Understanding how these securities work enables you to assess the risks and returns of the different money market mutual funds.
2. There are times when these individual securities offer greater advantages and returns than using a money market mutual fund.

MONEY MARKET MUTUAL FUNDS

Money market funds compete directly with bank deposit accounts, and over the years money market funds have grown considerably at the expense of bank accounts. Banks, brokerage firms, and investment companies offer money market funds. However, many of the brokerage house mutual funds have higher fees and sales commissions (loads). Brokers and financial advisors are motivated to move your funds away from the investment companies' money market mutual funds to their own products, where they are compensated through sales commissions, also called loads. For example, persuading you to invest in a short-term bond fund yielding 4 percent annually rather than in a money market fund with a yield of $3^1/2$ percent annually might look like a better alternative at face value. However, a short-term bond fund is not the same as a money market fund, because the net asset value of the bond fund fluctuates, whereas the net asset value of a money market mutual fund has a fixed value of $1 per share. Table 7-2 shows the effects of a short-term bond fund with a load charge versus a no-load money market mutual fund. With a no-load fund the entire principal is invested. In addition, operating expenses for brokerage funds might be higher than investment company funds. It could take several years for a bond fund to recoup the load fee just to equal the amount of the funds invested in the no-load money market fund.

Investment companies offer the majority of money market mutual funds, which provide for an alternative parking place for cash and short-term money than higher risk stock and bond investments. Investment companies managing money market funds pool investors' money and issue shares to investors. Then the fund managers invest the money in short-term securities such as Treasury bills, commercial paper, bankers' acceptances, CDs, Euro-dollars, repurchase agreements, and government agency obligations.

TABLE 7-2

Load versus a No-load Fund

Load Fund of 2%	versus	No- Load Fund	
Amount Invested	$10,000	Amount Invested	$10,000
3% Load charge	($200)	No-Load	0
Funds Available	$9,800	Funds Available	$10,000

There are three types of money market funds:

1. *General purpose funds,* which invest in a wide range of money market securities such as Treasury bills, commercial paper, bankers' acceptances, CDs, repurchase agreements, and short-term off-shore securities.

2. *U.S. government funds,* which invest in short-term Treasury securities and U.S. agency obligations.

3. *Tax-exempt money market funds,* which invest in short-term municipal securities. The income from these securities is exempt from federal income taxes.

HOW SAFE ARE MONEY MARKET FUNDS?

Money market mutual funds do not carry the Federal Deposit Insurance Corporation (FDIC, an independent agency of the U.S. government) insurance carried by bank money market deposit accounts, but they are relatively safe because:

1. The investments are in securities issued by the government and its agencies, and large corporations.

2. The maturities of these securities are short-term, lowering the risk.

The safest money market funds invest only in U.S. Treasuries, which carry the full faith and credit backing of the U.S. government. All money market funds are relatively safe because large institutional issuers of short-term securities are unlikely to default on their obligations, and prices of short-term securities do not fluctuate widely, which accounts for the constant share price of $1 per share for money market funds.

Before investing in a money market fund, read the prospectus, which lists the types of securities that the money market mutual fund invests in. Historically, the risk of default has been low for Treasury bills, CDs, bankers' acceptances, and commercial paper. A few companies have defaulted on their commercial paper, which affected money market funds holding those issues. However, the investment companies running those funds absorbed the losses instead of the shareholders of the fund.

The subprime mortgage market financial crisis of 2007 exerted the stresses in the commercial paper market. Two mortgage investment companies filed for bankruptcy protection due to bad mortgage loans. These companies then extended the maturities of their extendible asset-backed commercial paper. Asset-backed commercial paper accounted for roughly half of the commercial paper outstanding in the United States in July 2007 (Saha-Bubna, 2007).

Higher-yielding, high-risk, short-term securities do exist, and some aggressive money market funds invest in these to raise their yields. The prospectus of a fund outlines the investment restrictions for that fund. Examine your money market fund for their holdings of extendible asset-backed commercial paper and other higher-yielding risky money market assets.

Another concern for shareholders is fraud. What if someone in the fund steals or embezzles shareholders' savings from their accounts? This, of course, could happen with all investments, but there are certain safeguards with money market funds:

- The investment company does not physically handle the funds. A custodial bank is appointed to record the deposits into and transfers from shareholders' accounts.
- The custodial bank has insurance as well as being bonded in the event of theft or loss due to embezzlement or fraud.

Thus, money market funds have the same safeguards against fraud as other short-term investments, such as in savings accounts, and investors' fears should be allayed.

HOW TO INVEST IN MONEY MARKET FUNDS

The constant share price of money market mutual funds offers investors the advantage of being able to add and withdraw funds from these accounts without incurring any tax consequences. By comparison, short-term mutual bond funds do not have constant share prices, with the result that when shares are sold, there are capital gains or losses when the purchase and sale share prices differ. For this reason, you do not want to invest your short-term funds in a short-term bond fund rather than a money market mutual fund.

To invest in a money market fund, call the fund company (most have toll-free telephone numbers), or download the prospectus and application form from the fund's Web site. The Internet provides a comprehensive list of all the mutual fund families. One of these Web sites is www.moneymarketmutualfunds.com. Mutual fund companies are required by the Securities and Exchange Commission (SEC) to send the prospectus either by mail or through the Internet to new investors. The prospectus includes information about the fund, such as:

- The minimum dollar investment necessary to open an account
- How the investor can withdraw funds from the account
- The fund's investment objectives and policies as well as the investment restrictions
- Who manages the fund, fees charged by the management company, and an outline of the operating expenses and other fees
- The fund's financial statements

Read the prospectus before filling out the application form. The completed form can be sent back with a check to open the account or using the Internet with the money transferred electronically. Investors receive monthly statements showing the number of shares in their accounts, and their deposits, withdrawals, and dividend income. Most funds have a minimum amount (usually $100) for additional investments.

Money can be withdrawn in a number of ways:

- Through check writing.
- Wire transfers from the fund to your bank account.
- Check written by the fund and mailed to your account in response to a written withdrawal request.
- Transfer of money to other funds within the same investment company's family of funds.
- A systematic withdrawal plan (SWP) can be set up whereby the fund sends a periodic check to you, your bank account, or a third party.

Caveats

- Choose a money market fund from an investment company that has a wide range of different funds, allowing you greater flexibility in your transfers to other types of investment funds.
- Avoid funds that have sales charges, redemption fees, and high management and expense ratios.
- Avoid keeping too much money in money market funds, as over the long term real rates of return from money market funds are unlikely to exceed the rate of inflation.
- Avoid choosing short-term bond funds over money market mutual funds as a parking place for your cash for short periods of time. You could experience losses in principal if the share price falls below the purchase price with short-term bond funds.

TREASURY BILLS

Treasury bills (T-bills) are short-term (with maturities of one year or less) debt securities, issued by the U.S. government, that are sold at a discount from their face value. Although T-bills are slightly more difficult to purchase directly than money market funds, many people prefer to invest directly in T-bills rather than indirectly, through money market funds. T-bills are the most popular of the short-term individual investments, after money market mutual funds.

T-bills are issued by the U.S. Treasury and fully backed by the U.S. government (no credit or default risk). Consequently, returns from T-bills tend to be lower than those from other money market securities. Spreads between T-bills and other money market securities increase or decrease with changes in economic conditions.

T-bills are negotiable, non-interest-bearing securities with maturities of 4 weeks, 13 weeks, 26 weeks, and 52-weeks. These securities are available in minimum denominations of $100 and multiples of $100. Table 7-3 describes T-bill issues.

A T-bill is issued at a discount from its face value. The amount of the discount depends on the prices that are bid in T-bill auctions. At maturity, the bills are redeemed at full face value. The difference

T A B L E   7 - 3

Auction details of Treasury bills

Term	Minimum	Multiples	Auction	Day of Auction
4 week	$100	$100	Weekly	Tuesday
13 week	$100	$100	Weekly	Monday
26 week	$100	$100	Weekly	Monday
52 week	$100	$100	4 weeks	

T A B L E   7 - 4

Determining the Yield and Price of Treasury Bills

Because T-bills have no stated rate of interest, the yield on T-bills is determined using the following equation:

$$\text{Yield} = \frac{(\text{Face value} - \text{Price paid})}{\text{Price Paid}} \times \frac{(365)}{\text{Days to Maturity}}$$

A 26-week Treasury bill purchased for $980 and redeemed at face value has a 4.081% annual yield:

$$\text{Yield} = \frac{(\$1,000 - 980)}{980} \times \frac{(365)}{182.5}$$
$$= 4.081\%$$

To make matters more complex, however, bids submitted to a Federal Reserve Bank are not quoted on an annual basis, as shown in the preceding example, but rather, on a bank discount basis.

Yield on a Bank Discount Basis

$$\text{Yield} = \frac{(\text{Face value} - \text{Price paid})}{100^*} \times \frac{(360\dagger)}{\text{Days to Maturity}}$$

Using the same example, the discount is $2 for the T-bill selling at $98 per $100 face value with a 6-month maturity. The bank discount yield is shown in this example:

$$= \frac{100 - 98}{100} \times \frac{360}{180}$$
$$= 4\%$$

The bank discount yield is always less than the annual yield.

* The yield is quoted for each $100 of face value.

† Note the use of 360 rather than 365 days.

TABLE 7-5

Determining the Price of Treasury Bills

T-bills are sold at a discount, which is less than the $1,000 par or face amount, and then redeemed at par at maturity. This difference between the price paid and the amount received is attributed to interest income. The price for a T-bill with a 4.10% bid discount (the price that dealers are willing to pay for this bill on that day), and a 4.08% ask discount (the price that dealers are willing to sell this security on that day), with a maturity of 180 days is determined as follows:

The *dealer's selling price*, which is the price at which an investor would buy, is calculated as follows:

$$= \text{Par value} - \text{Par value (Ask discount)} \times \frac{[\text{Days to Maturity}]}{360}$$

$$= \$100 - 100\,(0.0408) \times \frac{[180]}{360}$$

$$= \$97.96 \ \text{ or } \ \$979.60 \text{ per T-bill}$$

The *dealer's purchase price* (the price at which an investor would sell) is calculated as follows:

$$= \text{Par value} - \text{Par value (Bid discount)} \times \frac{[\text{Days to Maturity}]}{360}$$

$$= \$100 - 100\,(0.0410) \times \frac{[180]}{360}$$

$$= \$97.95 \ \text{ or } \ \$979.50 \text{ per T-bill}$$

---

in the amount between the discount value and the face value is treated as interest income. For example if you buy a 26-week $1,000 T-bill at $985 and hold it until maturity, the interest you earn is $15. Tables 7-4 and 7-5 discuss the determination of T-bill yields and prices, describe how to buy and sell T-bills, and outline the differences between competitive and noncompetitive bids.

BUYING AND SELLING TREASURY BILLS

New issues of T-bills can be bought directly from any of the Federal Reserve Banks in the primary market with no commissions or fees charged. New issues of T-bills can also be bought indirectly through banks and brokerage firms, which charge commissions for their services. Investors buy and sell existing T-bill securities on the secondary markets through banks and brokerage firms.

Direct Purchase

Buying directly from the Treasury involves opening an account and then submitting a tender form. See Figures 7-1 and 7-2 for a copy of a new account request form and a tender form for a T-bill, respectively.

The first step is to fill out the new account request form (Figure 7-1) to establish an account with the Department of the Treasury. The nine-digit routing number on the form is the identifying number of your financial institution. The routing number is found in front of your account number on the bottom line of your check or deposit slip.

Submit this form to the Federal Reserve Bank or branch (you can submit it online, at www.publicdebt.treas.gov). You then receive confirmation that the account has been established along with your account number. Your purchases of Treasury securities are recorded in this account, which is free up to the amount of $100,000 of securities. When you invest more than this amount, the Federal Reserve charges $25 to maintain the account.

Fill in the tender form to buy T-bills directly from the Federal Reserve Bank. See Figure 7-2 for a sample tender form.

The Federal Reserve Bank auctions new issues of T-bills weekly and you can submit bids on either a competitive or noncompetitive basis.

T-bills purchased directly through Federal Reserve Banks are held in the Treasury direct book-entry system, designed primarily for investors who intend to hold their securities to maturity. Investors who decide to sell T-bills before maturity would have to fill out a transfer request form (PD 5179), which transfers their accounts to the commercial book-entry system. Then, the T-bills can be sold through a broker before maturity. The commercial book-entry system records those Treasuries bought through financial institutions and government securities dealers. Information on T-bills can be found on the U.S. government's Web site (www.publicdebt.treas.gov).

Competitive Bids

A *competitive bid* is a bid to the U.S. Treasury to buy Treasury securities at a particular yield. A competitive bid is submitted with a

FIGURE 7-1

New Account Request Form

PD F 5182 E
Department of the Treasury
Bureau of the Public Debt
(Revised March 2006)

www.treasurydirect.gov
1-800-722-2678

 Legacy Treasury Direct ®

OMB NO. 1535-0069

NEW ACCOUNT REQUEST

SEE INSTRUCTIONS - TYPE OR PRINT IN INK ONLY - NO ALTERATIONS OR CORRECTIONS

1. Legacy Treasury Direct ACCOUNT INFORMATION

ACCOUNT NAME

_____

_____

_____

ADDRESS

_____

_____

_____

City _____ State _____ ZIP Code

FOR DEPARTMENT USE

DOCUMENT AUTHORITY

APPROVED BY

DATE APPROVED

EXT REQ ☐

FOREIGN ☐

BACKUP ☐

REVIEW ☐

2. TAXPAYER IDENTIFICATION NUMBER

1st Named Owner _____ Social Security Number OR _____ Employer Identification Number

CLASS ☐

3. TELEPHONE NUMBERS

_____ Work _____ Home

4. PAYMENT INFORMATION

ROUTING NUMBER _____

FINANCIAL INSTITUTION _____
(Limited to 30 characters/spaces)

NAME ON ACCOUNT _____
(Limited to 22 characters/spaces)

ACCOUNT NUMBER _____   ☐ Checking   ☐ Savings   (Check One)

5. AUTHORIZATION I submit this request pursuant to the provisions of Department of the Treasury Circulars, Public Debt Series Nos. 2-86 (31 CFR Part 357), and 1-93 (31 CFR Part 356).

Under penalties of perjury, I certify that:
1. The number shown on this form is my correct taxpayer identification number (or I am waiting for a number to be issued to me), and
2. I am not subject to backup withholding because: (a) I am exempt from backup withholding, or (b) I have not been notified by the Internal Revenue Service (IRS) that I am subject to backup withholding as a result of a failure to report all interest or dividends, or (c) the IRS has notified me that I am no longer subject to backup withholding, and
3. I am a U.S. person (including a U.S. resident alien).

Instructions. You must cross out item 2 above if you have been notified by the IRS that you are currently subject to backup withholding because you have failed to report all interest and dividends on your tax return.

I further certify that all other information provided on this form is true, correct and complete.

_____   _____
Signature   Date

SEE INSTRUCTIONS FOR PRIVACY ACT AND PAPERWORK REDUCTION ACT NOTICE.   (OVER)

FIGURE 7-2

Treasury Marketable Securities Tender Form

PD F 5381 E
Department of the Treasury
Bureau of the Public Debt
(Revised May 2007)

www.treasurydirect.gov
1-800-722-2678

Legacy Treasury Direct®

OMB No. 1535-0069

TREASURY MARKETABLE SECURITIES TENDER

For Noncompetitive Purchases in Legacy Treasury Direct

TYPE OR PRINT IN INK ONLY – TENDERS WILL NOT BE ACCEPTED WITH ALTERATIONS OR CORRECTIONS

| 1. NONCOMPETITIVE BID INFORMATION *(Must Be Completed)*
 Par Amount:

 $ _____
 (Sold in units of $1,000) | 2. Legacy Treasury Direct ACCOUNT NUMBER
 (If NOT furnished, a new account will be opened.)

 _____ | DEPARTMENT USE
 TENDER NO.

 RECEIVED BY/DATE |

3. TAXPAYER ID NUMBER *(Must Be Completed)*

Social Security Number (First-Named Owner) _____   OR   Employer ID Number _____

| 4. TERM SELECTION *(Fill in One)*
 (Must Be Completed)

 Bill   Select the number of
        reinvestments
 ○ 13-Week ....

 ○ 26-Week ....

 Note
 ○ 2-Year Note
 ○ 5-Year Note
 ○ 10-Year Note

 TIPS
 ○ 5-Year
 ○ 10-Year | 5. ACCOUNT NAME *(Must Be Completed)*

 _____

 _____

 6. ADDRESS *(For new account or changes to existing accounts.)*   ○ New Address?

 _____

 _____
           City   State   ZIP Code |

ENTERED BY

APPROVED BY

ISSUE DATE

CUSIP 912795-

CUSIP 912828-

FOREIGN ☐

BACKUP ☐

REVIEW ☐

| 7. TELEPHONE NUMBERS *(For new account or changes to existing accounts.)*
 ○ New Phone Number?

 Home _____   Alternate _____

 8. PAYMENT INFORMATION *(For new account only.)*   Changes? Submit PD F 5178.

 Routing Number _____

 Financial Institution Name _____

 Financial Institution Account Number _____

 Name on Account _____

 Account Type: *(Fill in One)*   ○ Checking   ○ Savings | 9. PURCHASE METHOD
 (Must Be Completed)
 ○ Pay Direct® *
 (Existing Legacy Treasury Direct Account Only)

 ○ Checks: $ _____
   Make checks payable to Legacy Treasury Direct. $ _____
   Personal checks are acceptable ONLY for notes and TIPS $ _____

 ○ Other $ _____
 Total Payment Attached: $ _____
 CHECKS ARE DEPOSITED IMMEDIATELY |

CHECK #

10. AUTHORIZATION *(Must Be Completed – Original Signature Required)* **Tender Submission:** I submit this tender pursuant to the provisions of Department of the Treasury Circulars, Public Debt Series Nos. 2-86 (31 CFR Part 357) and 1-93 (31 CFR Part 356), and the applicable offering announcement. As the first-named owner and under penalties of perjury, I certify that: 1) The number shown on this form is my correct taxpayer identification number (or I am waiting for a number to be issued to me), and 2) I am not subject to backup withholding because: (a) I am exempt from backup withholding, or (b) I have not been notified by the Internal Revenue Service (IRS) that I am subject to backup withholding as a result of a failure to report all interest or dividends, or (c) the IRS has notified me that I am no longer subject to backup withholding, and 3) I am a U.S. person (including a U.S. resident alien). I further certify that all other information provided on this form is true, correct, and complete.

Certification Instructions: You must cross out item 2 above if you have been notified by the IRS that you are currently subject to backup withholding because you have failed to report all interest and dividends on your tax return.

Pay Direct. * (If using this purchase method.) I authorize a debit to my account at the financial institution I designated in Legacy Treasury Direct to pay for this security. I understand that the purchase price will be charged to my account on or after the settlement date. I also understand that if this transaction cannot be successfully completed, my tender can be rejected, the transaction canceled, and a 1% penalty assessed. If there is a dispute, a copy of this authorization may be provided to my financial institution.

_____   _____

Signature(s)   Date

yield (to two decimal places) on a bank discount basis. For example, if you want to buy $100,000 of six-month T-bills and pay $98,000, the competitive bid you submit to the Federal Reserve Bank is 4.00 percent. Until 1998, the Federal Reserve accepted the bids that had the lowest discount rates (the highest prices) from all bids received. The accepted bids had a range of yields, from the lowest to the highest. The highest yield (the lowest price) accepted for new Treasury securities issued in a Treasury auction is known as the *stop-out yield*. Investors who had their bids accepted at the "stop-out yield" or close to it received greater returns than those received for bids at the lowest accepted yields. This concept is referred to as the winner's curse. However, all Treasury auctions now use the *single price or Dutch auction*, in which all the winning bids that are lower than the stop-out yield are accepted, thereby eliminating the winner's curse. For example, if the range of accepted yields is 3.99 to 4.12 percent, all bidders receive 4.12 percent.

The yields bid depend upon money market yields being offered by competing short-term instruments as well as expectations of what short-term rates for T-bills would be. By studying these rates, an investor has a better chance of submitting a bid that will be accepted. With competitive bidding, investors face the risk of not having their bids accepted if their bids are above the stop-out yields. The advantage of placing a competitive bid is that an investor can bid for larger dollar amounts in an auction than a noncompetitive bidder.

Noncompetitive Bids

A *noncompetitive bid* is a method of purchasing U.S. Treasury securities without having to submit a price or yield. Noncompetitive bids allow you to buy T-bills at the average accepted competitive bid in the auction. Generally, all noncompetitive bids of up to $1 million per investor per auction for T-bills and $5 million for Treasury notes are accepted, which means that investors are assured of their purchases.

The two disadvantages of submitting a competitive bid are: a bid must be calculated, which is difficult for inexperienced investors, and there is a risk that the competitive bid might not be accepted (fall out of the range of accepted bids).

You can send tender forms to submit bids through the mail, electronically, or in person to the Federal Reserve Banks and branches before the close of the auction. Competitive bids must be received by the time designated in the offering circular. Non-competitive bids that are mailed must be postmarked by no later than midnight the day before the auction and received on or before the issue date of the securities. Payment must accompany the tender form.

After your bid is accepted, you receive a confirmation receipt from the Federal Reserve and a payment, which is the difference between the tender amount submitted and the discounted price of the T-bills. You can stipulate on the tender form whether you want the Federal Reserve to reinvest the T-bills when they mature. If you do not choose the reinvestment option, the Federal Reserve credits your account for the face value of the T-bills at maturity. The advantage of buying T-bills directly and holding them to maturity is that you avoid paying commissions or fees.

When you submit a competitive bid, you always run the risk that your bid will not be accepted because of unanticipated fluctuations of money market interest rates on the day of the auction.

Certificates of Deposit

A *certificate of deposit* (CD) is a time deposit in a financial institution that has a maturity date. Money invested in CDs earns interest at a stated rate for the specified period. When the CD matures, the investor receives interest plus the return of principal. For example, you might decide to invest $500 in a six-month CD that pays interest of 4 percent per annum. The $500 is deposited in the bank, and in six months' time the bank promises to pay you $510 (principal plus interest) at maturity. CDs are not marketable, in that if you need the funds before maturity, there is no market of buyers for your security. You would have to go to the issuing financial institution and pay the early redemption penalty (for example, forfeiting the interest for a quarter) to cash in your CD before maturity.

Negotiable certificates of deposit are marketable in that they are traded in a secondary market. A negotiable CD is a large denomination (over $100,000) CD with a specific maturity date and rate of interest, which can be bought and sold in the open market before maturity. A round lot for a trade in the market is $1 million or greater. Rates and maturities are individually negotiated between lenders and financial institutions. Rates on negotiable CDs are generally comparable to other money market securities such as T-bills and commercial paper.

Banks that are members of the FDIC provide insurance of up to $100,000 per ownership of accounts in a bank. Many investors use CDs as their investment vehicles for their short-term funds because of the insurance provided by the FDIC. Internet banks offer the highest rates online, but some of these banks may be less creditworthy, so you should check that these banks do carry insurance from the FDIC.

Commercial Paper

Commercial paper is difficult for individual investors to buy, but it is a widely held indirect investment by money market funds. Understanding what commercial paper is enables you to be able to assess the risks of your money market funds. *Commercial paper* is an unsecured, short-term promissory note (IOU) issued by the largest and most creditworthy financial and nonfinancial corporations as a source of credit. Commercial paper is sold at a discount from its face value, with maturities typically ranging from a few days to 270 days. Denominations for commercial paper are large, ranging from $5,000 to $5,000,000.

Commercial paper is sold either through dealers or directly by issuers to investors. Dealers buy commercial paper and then immediately resell the paper in large amounts to institutional investors, charging relatively small margins (1/8 of 1 percent per annum) (Stigum and Fabozzi, 1987). Even if individual investors have large amounts ($150,000) to invest, dealers will not sell commercial paper to individual investors, because the SEC states that commercial paper should only be sold to sophisticated investors, and dealers consider all individual investors to be unsophisticated. Consequently, individual investors buy dealer paper through brokers who offer the paper in smaller amounts ($25,000 and over) and charge commissions, which can be significant on small purchases (Stigum and Fabozzi, 1987).

Individual investors might buy commercial paper directly from issuers in relatively small amounts ($25,000). By telephoning or writing to well-known finance companies such as General Motors Acceptance Corp. (GMAC), Chrysler Financial Corp., Sears, etc., you can find out their terms, rates, and maturities.

Commercial paper may also be bought through a bank, for which the bank charges a fee for its efforts. Purchase good quality commercial paper with top-tier ratings even if you can obtain higher rates from lower quality paper, as the additional credit risk is not worth the additional return from lower rated paper.

Asset-backed commercial paper is a short-term debt instrument secured by a pool of assets. Some basic differences between regular commercial paper and asset-backed commercial paper are: companies issue commercial paper to obtain funding for their daily operations, and money market mutual funds and large institutional investors invest in (buy) this debt. Asset-backed commercial paper is used by financial companies to obtain cash to buy mortgages, car loans, credit card, and trade receivables. Some of this commercial paper is backed by subprime loans (loans issued to borrowers with poor credit). The subprime meltdown in 2007 was caused by defaults from subprime borrowers, which in turn resulted in many issuers and hedge funds that had invested in asset-backed commercial paper losing money.

By its nature, asset-backed commercial paper involves greater default and credit risk than regular commercial paper. Consequently, before investing your money in a money market fund, you should examine the amount and quality of the fund's investments in asset-backed commercial paper.

Structured Investment Vehicles

Related to the subprime loan crisis in 2007 are structured investment vehicles (SIVs) and commercial paper. SIVs are fixed-income funds that borrow money using commercial paper and then use the money to invest in mortgages (asset-backed bonds). The interest rate received on the asset-backed securities is greater than the rate paid on the commercial paper, which represents profit for the SIV. However, when commercial paper spreads widened to 100 basis points in September 2007, investors did not roll over their commercial paper, but demanded their money back. This action forced many SIVs to sell their bonds when they were losing much of their value. The resulting lack of liquidity caused some SIVs to fail and other SIVs to obtain financial support from their bank sponsors. The important fact that emerged from these complex financial investments is that commercial paper investors have not lost any money.

Bankers' Acceptances

Bankers' acceptances are the least understood of all the short-term money market investments, yet they are good investments for individual investors. Bankers' acceptances are negotiable time drafts commonly issued for import-export transactions. For example, if importers want to pay for goods when they are received, not when they are shipped, they arrange a time draft with a local bank to pay for the goods when they arrive three or six months later. If the exporter does not want to wait for payment, the draft can be taken to the firm's bank for payment. The firm's bank can sell the draft to investors, who buy this bankers' acceptance at a discount from its face value and then receive the face value at maturity (when the importer pays the bank). Due to the large amounts of money involved in bankers' acceptances, the predominant investors are central banks, not individual investors. Yields on bankers' acceptances are generally slightly lower than those of commercial paper and CDs.

Individual investors can approach large commercial banks and dealers who deal in bankers' acceptances to see what bankers' acceptances are available for investment. The amounts that can be invested typically range from $25,000 to $1,000,000. Bankers group bankers' acceptances into packages at these higher denominations. Individual investors mostly hold bankers' acceptances indirectly through their investments in money market mutual funds.

REPURCHASE AGREEMENTS

A repurchase agreement (repo) is a contract whereby one party sells securities to another party and simultaneously executes an agreement to buy them back at a contracted price in the future. U.S. government securities are the major type of securities used. The length of the holding period is tailored to the needs of the parties in the transaction, but most repos are transacted for only a few days.

The interest is the difference between the selling and the repurchase price of the repo. Interest is taxed at the federal, state, and local levels of government. There are no regular published repo rates, as they are determined through direct negotiations between buyers and sellers. However, repo rates are closely related to T-bill and federal funds rates. Repo rates may be lower than the federal funds rate because of the security provided by the securities in the repo. This does not mean that repos are devoid of risk. In 1982, Drysdale Securities, a brokerage company, defaulted on close to $4 billion of repos. Since a repo is a loan with security, investors still need to pay attention to:

- The borrower's ability to be able to repay the loan.
- Not paying more than the securities are worth, because if the seller defaults, the buyer will lose money.

Why, then would an investor or institution want to buy a repo instead of buying the securities?

- The first advantage is that the maturity of a repo can be tailored to the length of time that the short-term money is needed.
- A repo removes the risk of loss due to market fluctuations of the underlying securities in the transaction. Sellers could, of course, sell their securities when they need the cash, but there is a drawback to this action. If the price of the securities falls below the original purchase price, there is a capital loss. The buyer of the repo avoids this risk, because the securities are used as collateral and the fluctuations in market price of the securities are of no concern.

The major participants in repos are securities dealers, corporations, and financial institutions. Unfortunately due to the large size of the transactions ($1 million or more), many individual investors do not invest directly in this type of money market security.

Money market securities discussed above offer investors the opportunity of having their short-term, liquid funds earn a return rather than allowing their money to sit in a non-interest-bearing or lower-interest-bearing bank account. The caveat with short-term money market securities is that over the long term, they do not provide a sufficient hedge against inflation.

MONEY MARKET MUTUAL FUNDS OR INDIVIDUAL SECURITIES?

Should you invest in money market mutual funds or in individual money market securities such as T-bills, CDs, bankers' acceptances, and commercial paper? Table 7-6 outlines the advantages of money mutual funds versus the individual money market securities.

Money market mutual funds have fixed share prices, which account for many of their advantages over the individual securities, in that they can be bought and sold without any tax consequences. Income from money market funds, however, is taxable. Buying and selling individual securities are not as simple as with money market mutual funds. T-bills are both liquid and marketable, but it would take at least three days to receive the proceeds from the sale of their T-bills in the secondary markets.

The other major advantage of money market mutual funds over individual securities is that if money is needed earlier than planned, there is no loss in principal. With T-bills, which are the most liquid and marketable of the individual investments, there might be a loss or gain in principal due to fluctuations in market rates of interest. Other than T-bills, individual money market investments may be more difficulties to liquidate. With CDs there are early withdrawal penalties.

The only disadvantage of money market mutual funds is that at times individual money market investments earn higher rates of return. Bear in mind, however, that the purpose of these money

TABLE 7-6

Money Market Mutual Funds or the Individual Securities?

	Mutual Fund	Individual Securities
Ease of Opening an Account	Yes	No, except for CDs, and Treasury bills
Liquidity and Marketability	Yes	Treasury bills
Loss of principal with early Redemption	No	Yes
Higher rate of return	No	Yes

market securities is to provide a parking place for emergency funds and short-term cash, and not be the cornerstone of the bulk of your investments.

Table 7-7 summarizes the advantages and disadvantages of individual money market securities.

TABLE 7-7

Individual Money Market Securities?

Security Type	Advantages	Disadvantages
Money market funds	Easy to invest and withdraw. Access to funds within 3 days or less. Higher rates of return than savings accounts. Overnight transfer of funds.	Interest income is taxed at federal, state (and local) levels. Earn lower rates of return than individual money market securities.
Treasury bills	No credit or default risk. Flexible range of maturities. Commission free if bought directly. Interest income is exempt from state (and local) taxes. Active secondary market.	Yields might be less than those on CDs and other short-term individual securities.
Certificates of deposit	Rates of return slightly higher than money market mutual funds. Bank CDs carry FDIC insurance.	Penalties for early withdrawal of funds. Secondary market only for negotiable CDs.
Commercial paper	Higher yields than T-bills with similar maturities	Difficult for individual investors to buy. Issued in large denominations. Interest is taxed at all levels. No secondary market.
Bankers' acceptances	Higher yields than T-bills with similar maturities. Secondary market	Difficult for individual investors to buy. Issued in large denominations ($25,000 to $1,000,000)
Repurchase agreements	Flexible terms and maturities for investors	Large denominations ($1 million or more) preclude individual investors.

REFERENCES

Saha-Bubna, Aparajita, "Commercial Paper Shows Some Stress," *Wall Street Journal,* August 8, 2007, page C2.

Schultze, Ellen E., "Parking Places for Cash Can Be Costly," *Wall Street Journal,* July 10, 1998, page C1.

Stigum, Marcia, and Frank Fabozzi, *Dow Jones Guide to Bond and Money Market Investments,* Homewood, IL: Dow Jones-Irwin, 1987.

CHAPTER 8

Treasury Securities

KEY CONCEPTS

- Treasury notes,
- Treasury bonds
- Treasury inflation protection securities
- Savings bonds
- Treasury bond mutual funds
- Treasury exchange-traded funds

Although all bonds have similar features, such as a coupon rate, a face value, and a maturity date, the types of bonds in the market have many differences between them. Treasury notes and bonds, for example, are free of credit and default risk. Some Treasury notes and bonds offer protection from inflation and are called Treasury inflation protection securities (TIPS). Municipal bonds provide interest income that is exempt from federal taxes, while some mortgage bonds provide monthly payments of interest and principal, and junk bonds have the capability of returning double-digit positive and negative returns likes stocks. Not only do these types of bonds differ, but you should understand the different characteristics of each type of bond before investing.

In deciding which types of bonds to buy, you must be aware of your reasons for investing in them. Bonds are generally safer than stocks and provide regular payments of income. Bonds, however, do not double their value overnight like some Internet and biotechnology stocks did in the late 1990s. Bonds provide protection for your portfolio if the stock market declines. You buy bonds, therefore, to provide insurance against large losses in the value of your portfolio and to provide a fixed stream of income.

The U.S government issues a wide variety of debt to fund operations and budget deficits. A budget deficit results when government spends more than the revenues it collects from taxes. The government raises money to fund its expenditures by issuing securities in the money and capital markets. The reason that Treasury securities are considered to be free of credit and default risk is that the government has few restrictions on its ability to raise money. The government has three major sources of money creation: it can print money, raise taxes, and issue more securities to sell to the public.

The U.S. government is the largest single borrower in the U.S. long-term bond market, and these securities attract a wide range of investors, individual U.S. residents, institutional investors (banks, mutual funds, hedge funds, insurance companies, pension funds), corporations (domestic and foreign), and foreign individual investors and foreign governments.

Treasury offerings consist of U.S. Treasury bills, U.S. Treasury notes, U.S. Treasury bonds, and TIPS. U.S. savings bonds are also issued by the government to fund the deficit. Treasury bills (discussed in Chapter 7) are non-interest-bearing, discount securities with an original maturity of one year or less. Treasury notes are intermediate securities with maturities ranging from 2 to 10 years, and Treasury bonds are long-term bonds that have maturities of over 10 years. Both Treasury notes and bonds are marketable securities that pay interest every six months until maturity. U.S. savings bonds are nonmarketable government debt. U.S. savings bonds are small denomination securities with various maturities designed to encourage savings by small investors. Savings bonds will be discussed after Treasury notes and bonds in this chapter.

TREASURY SECURITIES

The U.S. government issues Treasury bills, notes, bonds, TIPS, and savings bonds.

Treasury Notes and Bonds

Treasury notes and bonds are coupon securities issued by the Department of Treasury and backed by the U.S. government. *Treasury notes* are intermediate-term (1 to 10 years) coupon debt and *Treasury bonds* are long-term (more than 10 years) coupon debt issued by the U.S. Treasury. Because Treasury notes and bonds are coupon securities, they differ from Treasury bills. Coupon securities pay interest every six months, whereas Treasury bills are discount securities on which periodic interest payments are not made.

U.S. Treasury notes are issued with original maturities of 2, 5, and 10 years, and U.S. Treasury bonds have maturities of 30 years or more. Treasury notes and bonds are issued in denominations of $100 to $1,000,000. These issues are the safest intermediate and long-term bonds available. Consequently, yields on these issues are lower than those of comparable maturity U.S. government agency and corporate bonds. Treasury notes and bonds are not only more liquid than comparable maturity corporate, agency, and municipal bonds, because of the active secondary market for Treasury securities, but also have greater transparency in the pricing when buying and selling.

Interest payments from Treasury securities are exempt from state income taxes.

Buying and Selling Treasury Notes, Bonds, and TIPS

You can purchase new issues at auction or existing Treasury securities trading in the secondary market.

New Issues

You can purchase new issues of Treasury notes, bonds, and TIPS at auction or through brokerage firms and commercial banks. Buying through banks and brokerage firms involves paying commissions, which vary depending on the face value of the securities purchased and the markup charged for the purchase. To avoid having to pay commissions, you can purchase new issues auctioned directly through the Federal Reserve Bank.

Auctions of new issues take place on a regular schedule. Table 8-1 lists some of the auction schedule criteria for Treasury notes and bonds. Individual investors must first open an account online with the Treasury through the Treasury Direct program (same procedure as discussed in the Treasury bill section in Chapter 7), before being able to purchase Treasury notes, bonds, and TIPS directly from the Treasury. You can find information, updates on auctions, and news on all Treasury securities on this Web site: www.treasurydirect.gov.

By completing a New Account Request Form (see Figure 7-1), you can establish a Treasury Direct account where your Treasury securities are held in book form. Treasury certificates are no longer issued. After submitting this form to the Treasury, you will receive confirmation of your account and your own account number pertaining to the information in your account. This account number is used for all your purchases of Treasury securities (bills, notes, bonds, and TIPS) and is maintained free of charge up to $100,000. For security amounts over $100,000, there is a $25 fee per year.

Table 8-1

Treasury Note, Bond and TIPS Auction Information

Term	Minimum	Multiples	Announcement	Auction Date	Issue Date
2-year Note	$100	$100	3rd or 4th Mon of each month	Two days later	Last day of the month
5-year Note	$100	$100	3rd or 4th Mon of each month	Three days later	Last day of the month
10-year Note	$100	$100	First Wed. in Feb., May, Aug., and Nov.	2nd week of month	2/15, 5/15, 8/15, 11/15
30-year Bond	$100	$100	First Wed. in Feb., May, Aug., and Nov.	2nd week of month	2/15, 5/15, 8/15, 11/15
5-year TIPS	$100	$100	3rd week of April and October	Last week of month	Last day of month
10-year TIPS	$100	$100	Beginning of Jan, April July and Oct.	2nd week of month	Last day of month
20-year TIPS	$100	$100	3rd week of Jan. and July	Last week of month	Last day of month

You are now ready to fill out a tender form to buy Treasury notes, bonds, or TIPS at auction (see Figure 7-2 for a copy of the Treasury note, 30-year bond, and TIPS tender form). This is the same general form that is used for Treasury bills.

Besides filling in your personal information, you need to supply information about your bank account so that payments by the Treasury can be made by direct deposit to your account. The routing number is a nine digit number that identifies the financial institution where you bank. It can be found on the bottom corner of your check before your account number.

Investors have a choice of buying Treasuries using competitive or noncompetitive bids. However, in the Treasury Direct program you can only bid noncompetitively. Competitive bids are only allowed through brokers or dealers and through financial companies that participate in the commercial book-entry system. The commercial book-entry system records Treasuries bought through financial institutions and government securities dealers, whereas the Treasury Direct book-entry system records Treasuries bought directly at auctions. For competitive bids, investors submit a yield bid for the issue to two decimal places (e.g., 4.06 percent). If the yield is too high, investors run the risk of not having their bids accepted.

With noncompetitive bids, investors receive the full amount of the securities bid at the yield determined at the close of the auction. Noncompetitive bids are limited to $5 million per auction.

The pricing method used for 30-year Treasury bonds works in the following way. Investors submit their bids, and the Treasury accepts the bids with the lowest yields until the supply is sold. Thus, within the range of accepted bids, the accepted bidders who bid lowest are penalized with a lesser return than the accepted higher bidders. This phenomenon is known as the "winner's curse." However, investors who bid too aggressively run the risk of losing out in that auction by not having their bids accepted. Figure 8-1 illustrates results of a 30-year Treasury auction. The median yield was 5 percent, but competitive bidders who bid below 5 percent had their bids accepted from 4.9 percent to 5.059 percent. The highest yield accepted was 5.059 percent, which was the accepted yield for all the noncompetitive bids. The accepted price for noncompetitive bidders was $990.81933 per bond.

Treasury bills, notes, and TIPS are sold at single price auctions:

- Investors submit their bids.
- The Treasury starts accepting bids from the lowest yield on up to the yield until the supply of notes is used up.
- The difference in auction method is that all the winning bidders receive the highest accepted bids for the auction.

For example, if the Treasury announces the results of a $9 billion two-year note sale, and the range of accepted bids is between 4.72 percent and 4.74 percent, all the bidders receive 4.74 percent. This method eliminates the "winner's curse." All accepted bidders pay the same price for the issue.

When an issue date falls on a Saturday, Sunday, or holiday, investors in the issue are required to pay *accrued interest*. For example an issue dated on a Saturday is delayed until the following Monday, and investors holding that issue will receive the first interest payment for six months even though they held the issue for two days short of six months. Consequently, investors pay in the two days of interest to equalize the holding period to the exact length of time. For example, accrued interest for the Treasury bond auction, illustrated in Figure 8-1, is $12.50 per bond, which covers three months of interest in which investors did not own the bonds (May 15 through August 14, 2007). The bond was issued on August 15, 2007 (three months later), and the interest received by the holder of each bond on November 15, 2007, is $25, which is the interest amount for the first six months.

You have a choice on the form to buy Treasuries by using either a competitive or noncompetitive bid. More sophisticated investors use a competitive bid, where a yield bid to two decimal places (e.g., 4.06 percent) is submitted for the issue. You can get a clue about the probable range of the yield to submit by watching the pre-auction trading of that issue. Dealers begin trading these securities a few days before the auction on a "when issued" basis, and the when issued yield is often reported in the financial section of the *Wall Street Journal* and *New York Times*.

Investors submit sealed, written bids, and the Treasury accepts bids with lower yields than the stop-out yield until the supply is sold. All the winning bidders receive a single price.

FIGURE 8-1

Results of a 30-year Treasury Bond Auction

PUBLIC DEBT NEWS

Department of the Treasury • Bureau of the Public Debt • Washington, DC 20239

TREASURY SECURITY AUCTION RESULTS
BUREAU OF THE PUBLIC DEBT - WASHINGTON DC

FOR IMMEDIATE RELEASE   CONTACT: Office of Financing
August 09, 2007   202-504-3550

RESULTS OF TREASURY'S AUCTION OF 29-YR 9-MONTH BONDS

Interest Rate: 5%   Issue Date: August 15, 2007
Series: Dated Date: May 15, 2007
CUSIP No: 912810PU6   Maturity Date: May 15, 2037

High Yield: 5.059%   Price: 99.081933

All noncompetitive and successful competitive bidders were awarded
securities at the high yield. Tenders at the high yield were
allotted 76.79%. All tenders at lower yields were accepted in full.

Accrued interest of $ 12.50000 per $1,000 must be paid for the period
from May 15, 2007 to August 15, 2007.

AMOUNTS TENDERED AND ACCEPTED (in thousands)

Tender Type	Tendered	Accepted
Competitive	$ 14,109,500	$ 8,994,858
Noncompetitive	5,142	5,142
FIMA (noncompetitive)	0	0
SUBTOTAL	14,114,642	9,000,000 1/
Federal Reserve	4,846,153	4,846,153
TOTAL	$ 18,960,795	$ 13,846,153

Median yield   5.000%: 50% of the amount of accepted competitive tenders
was tendered at or below that rate. Low yield   4.900%: 5% of the amount
of accepted competitive tenders was tendered at or below that rate.

Bid-to-Cover Ratio - 14,114,642 / 9,000,000 - 1.57

1/ Awards to TREASURY DIRECT - $1,576,000

If you bid too aggressively, you run the risk of not having your bid accepted in that auction. If you do not want to run the risk of having your bid rejected, or if you do not know what to bid, you can submit a noncompetitive bid. You can then buy Treasury notes and bonds at the stop-out yield for as much as $5 million.

You can submit bids on tender forms by mail, electronically, or in person before the close of an auction. Competitive bids must be received by the time designated in the offering circular. Noncompetitive bids that are mailed must be postmarked by no later than midnight the day before the auction and received on or before the issue date of the securities.

Investors can sell their Treasury securities as soon as 45 days after issue through the SellDirect program, where requests to sell are transmitted to the Federal Reserve Bank of Chicago. The securities are sold to the highest bidding government securities broker and a charge of $45 is levied for this service.

Information, updates on auctions, and news on all Treasury securities can be obtained on the Web site www.publicdebt. treas.gov/.

Existing Issues

Investors buy (and sell) existing Treasury securities on the secondary market through banks or brokerage firms. Many issues are available with a wide range of maturities, trading at discounts or premiums depending on their coupon rates and length of time to maturity. Like corporate bonds, Treasury notes and bonds are quoted in the financial sections of newspapers under the Treasury Issues heading. Treasury note and bond prices are quoted as a percentage of par basis and the fractions of the percentage are 1/32 of a point. For example, a quoted price of $101:16 is $101 16/32, or $1,015.00.

The secondary market for Treasuries is an over-the-counter market, where dealers quote bid and ask prices. The spreads on Treasuries are the smallest (rarely more than a few cents) of all the fixed-income securities because of the liquidity of many of the issues. The market is active with large quantities of Treasuries traded.

Treasury Inflation Protection Securities

Treasury inflation protection securities (TIPS) are securities issued by the Treasury, whose interest and principal payments are adjusted for changes in inflation.

TIPS offer protection against rising inflation. Because inflation was historically low in the early years of the 2000s, these bonds did not generate much enthusiasm. TIPS are issued with a fixed coupon rate plus an amount that is indexed for inflation. The coupon rate is set at auction and remains fixed throughout the term of the security. The principal amount of the security is adjusted for inflation, but this inflation-adjusted premium is paid only at maturity. For example, if you purchase a bond with a $3\frac{1}{2}$ percent coupon rate at $1,000 and inflation averages 2 percent for the year, the price of the bond is adjusted for this inflation to $1,020. The $3\frac{1}{2}$ percent coupon rate is paid on the adjusted value of the bond ($3\frac{1}{2}$ percent × $1,020). The opposite is true if inflation falls. The price of the bond is adjusted downwards and the interest payments are calculated against the lower bond price. Semiannual interest payments are based on the inflation-adjusted principal amount at the time the interest is paid.

Yields on TIPS are generally lower than regular bonds during periods of low inflation, and you should compare yields and your expectations for inflation before investing. For example, if a 10-year Treasury bond is yielding 4.875 percent and a 10-year inflation-indexed bond is yielding 4.25 percent, in order to exceed the regular Treasury bond, inflation would have to increase by more than 0.625 percent (4.875 percent – 4.25 percent) over the next 10 years.

The auction process uses the single-priced, or Dutch auction method for these securities.

At maturity, TIPS are redeemed at the greater of their inflation-adjusted principal or par value. Table 8-2 summarizes the characteristics of TIPS.

The downside to an inflation-indexed Treasury is that its holders must pay federal income taxes on the interest plus the inflation adjustment, even though the inflation adjustment is paid out only when the bond matures. In other words, negative cash flow takes place on this "phantom" adjustment income, which makes this type of investment more suitable for a tax-deferred account. Like all other types of Treasury securities, interest income is exempt from state and local taxes. You purchase these issues in the same way as you purchase regular Treasury notes and bonds. Because of the relative newness of this type of security, you do not have many issues to choose from on the secondary markets.

This type of security, like all other fixed-income securities, is subject to interest rate risk. Yields on these securities are much lower than with regular Treasury issues, and if inflation remains low, any changes in interest rates will make the prices of these securities

Table 8-2

Treasury Inflation-Indexed Securities

- The interest rate, which is set at auction, remains fixed throughout the term of the security.
- The principal amount of the security is adjusted for inflation but the inflation adjusted principal is paid only at maturity.
- Semi-annual interest payments are based on the inflation-adjusted principal at the time that the interest is paid.
- Auction process uses the single priced or Dutch auction method for these securities.
- The securities are eligible for stripping into principal and interest components in the Treasury's Separate Trading of Registered Interest and Principal of Securities (STRIPS) Program. See the chapter on zero-coupon bonds for a more complete discussion on stripped securities.
- At maturity the securities are redeemed at the greater of their inflation-adjusted principal or par amount at original issue.

Source: www.publicdebt.treas.gov

more volatile, especially for 20-year issues that have longer periods until maturity.

However, this type of security protects against the ravages of inflation. But the opposite is also true: if inflation remains low, holders of TIPS receive lower returns than they would receive with regular Treasury notes and bonds that have the same maturities.

The Risks of Treasury Securities

Because Treasuries are direct obligations of the federal government, they have no credit risk and no default risk. Treasuries issued after 1985 are free from event risk and call risk, but they are subject to interest rate risk and inflation risk.

Avoid longer-term maturities unless you are confident that both inflation and market rates of interest are headed downward. As with all fixed-income securities, Treasuries are subject to *interest rate risk*. Bond prices react inversely to changes in market rates of interest, but prices are also tied to the length of time to maturity. Thus, long-term (30-year) Treasury bond prices experience the greatest volatility as a result of changes in market rates of interest.

The shorter the maturities, the lower the price volatility in relation to changes in interest rates.

Advantages of Treasury Securities

- They have virtually no credit or default risk.
- A wide range of maturities are available.
- Interest is exempt from state and local taxes.
- Treasuries can be purchased in the minimum denomination size of $100.
- They are extremely liquid and marketable due to the active secondary market.
- Transaction costs/fees can be avoided by buying directly from the Federal Reserve Bank/branches.
- Markups on trading Treasuries are the lowest of all the fixed-income securities.
- TIPS protect against inflation.

Disadvantages of Treasury Securities

- Yields on Treasuries are lower than agency and corporate bonds for comparable maturities.
- Treasury notes and bonds do not protect against rising inflation. Losses in purchasing power and investment capital would occur if the rate of inflation exceeds the coupon rate.
- For longer maturity Treasury bonds, there is interest rate risk. If interest rates go up after long-term bonds are bought, the market price of these bonds will go down. Investors could lose a significant part of their investment if they are forced to sell during these conditions before maturity.
- If inflation remains low during the life of a Treasury inflation indexed security, returns will be lower than regular Treasury notes and bonds of like maturities.
- Paying federal taxes on the inflation adjustment, which is only received at maturity, creates a negative cash flow.

Caveats

- Avoid longer maturities of Treasury notes and bonds unless you are confident that both inflation and market rates of interest are headed downwards in the future. If you anticipate inflation in the future, invest in Treasury inflation-indexed securities (TIPS).

Summary

Treasury notes and bonds are the safest of all the plain vanilla type bonds, but their yields are lower than other types of bonds. There is a wide range of maturities to choose from. Although yields offered by agency and corporate bonds are greater, they do not match the safety offered by Treasuries. If the yield differential between Treasuries and these other types of fixed-income securities is not very wide, Treasuries may be the better investment. However, when the yield differential is significant, you ought to consider their purchase over Treasuries.

Ownership of Treasuries can be staggered due to the wide range of maturities offered. For example, instead of buying 10-year or 30-year Treasuries, investors could apportion amounts to 2-, 3-, 5-, 10-, and 30-year issues. This approach provides a steady stream of income and frees up principal on a *piecemeal* basis as the shorter term issues mature. The advantages are that the effects of interest rate risk are avoided and yields are averaged over the time period.

Investors who are concerned about future inflation should invest in TIPS.

U.S. SAVINGS BONDS

U.S. savings bonds are nonmarketable securities issued and backed in full by the U.S. government. Rates of return on savings bonds are low and do not equal the returns of other comparable investments. Savings bonds are safe investments that can be purchased and sold directly from and to the government through the Treasury Direct program. Investors need to open a Treasury Direct account (see Figure 7-1) first before being able to buy savings bonds through the Internet. However, investors can also purchase paper savings bonds through banks and savings and loan institutions. The Treasury offers two series of savings bonds: EE Bonds and I bonds.

EE Savings Bonds

Series EE Bonds purchased on or after May 1, 2005, earn a fixed rate of return (3.4 percent in October 2007), whereas EE Bonds purchased between May 1997 and April 2005 earn a variable rate of return based on 90 percent of the six-month averages of five-year Treasury yields.

Electronic (purchased through the Treasury Direct program) EE Bonds are purchased at face value in amounts of $25 or more to the penny, whereas paper EE Bonds are purchased at half their face value ($25 for a $50 face value bond) in denominations of $50, $75, $100, $200, $500, $1,000, $5,000 and $10,000. Paper bonds are guaranteed to reach face value in 20 years. The maximum purchase in one calendar year is $30,000 for paper and electronic EE Bonds.

EE Bonds can be redeemed after 12 months, but there is a 3-month interest penalty for redeeming bonds in the first five years. For example, if after holding EE bonds for 18 months the holder cashes them in, interest paid will only be for 15 months. After a five-year holding period there is no penalty for redeeming savings bonds.

Interest compounds semiannually for 30 years. Interest is exempt from state and local taxes, but is subject to federal income tax. When EE Bonds are used to finance educational expenses, interest income may be excluded from federal taxes. Some restrictions do apply. See www.treasurydirect.gov for more information about EE bonds.

Inflation-Indexed Savings Bonds

Inflation-indexed savings bonds (I-Bonds), also known as series I savings bonds, are issued by the Treasury in paper form and electronically through the Treasury Direct program. I-Bonds are sold at face value with a minimum investment amount of $25 electronically and $50 for paper bonds, and a maximum of $30,000 per year.

Holders of these savings bonds receive a fixed rate of interest for the life of the bond plus an amount indexed for inflation, which is tied to the consumer price inflation index for urban workers (CPI-U). The Bureau of Public Debt announces the rates for the bonds in May and November. The semiannual inflation rate announced in May is the change between the CPI-U figures from the preceding six months of September through March. The inflation rate announced in November is the change between the CPI-U figures for the preceding March through September. Even if there is severe deflation in the economy, the inflation rate is never negative, so investors will never lose money with I-Bonds.

Interest payments are received at maturity or when the bond is cashed in. Holders of bonds do not have to pay taxes on their gains until they cash in their bonds. In other words, both the interest payments and the taxes on the gains are deferred until holders cash them in.

I-Bonds are similar to TIPS but there are some significant differences. Table 8-3 compares the characteristics of TIPS with those of I-Bonds.

Like the EE savings bond, I-Bonds offer investors with small amounts to invest the safety and stability of bank savings accounts plus inflation protection, should inflation increase.

Advantages of U.S. Savings Bonds

- U.S. savings bonds are safe investments because interest and principal are guaranteed by the U.S. government.
- There are no fees, handling charges, or commissions to buy and sell.
- Savings bonds provide a build-up of capital.
- Interest earned on U.S. savings bonds is exempt from state and local taxes.
- U.S. savings bonds are not subject to interest rate risk.
- Investors are assured a minimum rate of return on their EE bonds held for five years, even if market rates of interest fall to lower levels.
- For bondholders who qualify, interest received on the redemption of savings bonds may be excluded from

Table 8-3

TIPS versus I-Bonds

	TIPS	I-Bonds
Type of Investment	Marketable: can be sold in the secondary market	Non-marketable
How to Buy	At auction or through brokers	Electronically or through banks
Minimum Purchase Amount	$100 or increments of $100	$25 electronically or $50 in paper
Inflation Indexing	Inflation adjustments based on monthly published CPI-U	Semiannual inflation rate announced in May and November
Taxes	Interest and inflation adjustments are taxable in the year that they occur at the federal level; exempt from state and local taxes	Interest payments are deferred from federal taxes until bonds are redeemed or mature; exempt from state and local taxes
Maturity	5, 10 and 20-year bonds	Earns interest up to 30 years
How to Sell	Can be sold before maturity in the secondary market	Redeemable after 12 months with a 3-month penalty. No penalty after 5 years.
Interest payments	Interest paid semi-annually at the coupon rate	Interest accrues over the life of the bond and is paid on redemption.

federal taxes when applied to qualified higher education expenses for a spouse or dependents.
- I-Bonds can be purchased in amounts as little as $50.
- Returns on I-Bonds are pegged to inflation, which gives holders protection against rising inflation.

What Are the Disadvantages of U.S. Savings Bonds?

- Savings bonds must be held for five years in order to get the full interest rate. If held for less than five years, holders receive lower rates of interest due to the three-month penalty.

- EE bonds do not protect against rising rates of inflation.
- Investors are limited to $30,000 face amount per person per calendar year.
- Other securities pay higher rates of interest.
- Inflation-indexed savings bonds do not provide a good parking place for cash, or for funds, that are needed in less than five years. This is because of the penalty (three months of interest) if the bonds are sold within five years, and the fact that the bonds will only be redeemed six months after they are sold.

Caveats

- Compare the returns of other "safe" investments such as Treasury bills and Treasury notes: you may be able to increase your rate of return.

Summary

Savings bonds provide a safe, easy way to save money. There are no fees, handling charges, or commissions when you buy or sell I-Bonds.

TREASURY BOND MUTUAL FUNDS

Investors can invest indirectly in Treasury securities through Treasury mutual funds. The mutual fund investment company pools investors' funds and invests in different Treasury securities. Investors receive a number of shares proportionate to the amounts invested in the fund. Shareholders of the fund receive monthly dividends, whereas owning individual Treasury securities, investors receive interest semiannually.

How to Choose a Treasury Mutual Fund

Although the name Treasury bond mutual fund implies that the investment holdings should consist entirely of Treasury securities, this may or may not be the case. Many of these funds hold other types of securities besides Treasury issues, such as U.S. Agency bonds, corporate bonds, foreign bonds, zero coupon bonds, collateralized mortgage obligations (CMOs), and derivative issues tied to Treasury securities to boost the funds' returns. Looking at the name of the fund alone does not tell you very much about the fund's holdings.

Many mutual fund families, for example, the Vanguard Group, American Century, and Fidelity, offer Treasury mutual funds. Besides regular Treasuries, there are mutual funds that invest in TIPS. Examples are *American Century Inflation-Adjusted Treasury Fund* and *Vanguard Inflation-Adjusted Fund*.

In this category of funds, in order to determine what you are investing in, you should examine the prospectus of each fund that interests you.

The *objectives* of the fund specify the types of securities, the quality, and the maturity range of the issues. Generally, if a fund uses the name "Treasury" in its title, it must hold at least 65 percent of its investments in Treasury securities. However, from a risk standpoint, what the fund holds in the other 35 percent is, or should be, just as important to the investor. Zero coupon bonds, for example, can provide a wild roller-coaster ride when market rates of interest fluctuate. This result is not what an investor wants to see when the title of the fund implies conservative holdings.

Compare the characteristics of the funds you are interested in before investing:

- Examine the holdings of the fund. A telephone call to the mutual fund investment company might be required to ask specific questions about the holdings. For example, it is often difficult to distinguish whether a bond is a regular bond or a CMO from its name.

- Ask about the risks of the fund. Treasuries have no credit risks, but other types of securities held in the fund are subject to credit and default risks.

- Look at the average maturities of the holdings. In general, the longer the maturities, the greater the price fluctuations when interest rates change.

- Examine the fees charged by the funds, which can vary significantly. For bond funds of all types, it is always a good idea to go with the low-cost fund families.
- Don't choose a fund of this type based on the highest yield alone without looking at the other factors mentioned. In order to boost the returns over those yielded by Treasury securities, the fund could do any or all of the following:
  - Invest in other types of securities, which increases the credit risk and the risk of default.
  - Actively trade their holdings, which provides greater capital gains and/or losses.
  - Increase the maturities of their holdings.
  - Hedge its positions, which can be costly if circumstances change in an unanticipated direction.
  - Use derivative securities to boost returns, but which also increases risk.
  - Temporarily reduce their fees.

What Are the Risks of Treasury Mutual Funds

Individual Treasury securities have no *credit risks or default risk,* but there are no guarantees for the mutual fund, especially if the fund holds riskier non-Treasury securities as part of its other 35 percent holdings. Even so, the default risk generally is not large for Treasury mutual funds due to the diversification achieved by mutual funds. The risk of loss to an individual fund shareholder, due to the default of an issue in the fund's holdings, does not have as great an impact as it would had that investor held that issue in an individual portfolio (unless the investor has an abnormally large diversified holding of bond issues).

Interest rate risk impacts the share price of Treasury security mutual funds. The fluctuations will depend on the composition of the holdings and the maturity. In the early 1990s, some government mutual funds that held large mixes of derivative securities suffered much greater losses in share price when interest rates increased than those government funds with greater percentage holdings of Treasury securities. Longer duration maturity funds are more volatile than shorter-term maturity funds when interest rates change.

How to Buy Treasury Mutual Funds

Treasury mutual funds may be purchased directly through the mutual fund families or indirectly through brokers, financial planners, or banks. For the latter, a commission or fee is charged for the service (in the form of loads, which can be quite large).

Avoid load funds (funds that charge a commission to buy or sell shares) because the charge is a percentage of every dollar invested. To make up the charges, these funds have to work much harder to equal the results of a no-load fund. Treasury bond yields for each auction do not vary much, which means that, ideally, all Treasury bond mutual funds should earn similar returns. This phenomenon makes it more difficult for the load fund to equal the results of the no-load fund. Consequently, this explains why many funds also invest in riskier securities. A second factor is the fee that is charged for operating and administering the fund. Examine the prospectus of each of the funds that you are interested in for the different fees charged. For bond funds, it is a good idea to choose low-cost funds over high-cost funds. For equity funds, there is always the argument that the manager's stock-picking abilities are worth the additional charges. However, this has not been shown to bear out for bond funds.

Many mutual fund families have Web sites where you can download the prospectus and registration forms. Alternatively, mutual funds have toll-free telephone numbers where you can obtain this information to open an account.

What Are the Advantages of Treasury Bond Mutual Funds

- Treasury mutual funds offer investors the convenience of being able to invest funds at their discretion instead of having to wait for a particular auction date for individual Treasury securities.
- Shares in Treasury mutual funds are easier to sell than individual Treasury securities bought at auction before maturity.

What Are the Disadvantages of Treasury Bond Mutual Funds

- With Treasury bond mutual funds there is always the risk of capital loss from having to sell shares at a lower price than the purchase price, even with a long time horizon. This is because Treasury bond mutual funds never mature. When individual Treasury securities issues mature in the fund, they are replaced with new issues.

- Returns from holding individual Treasury securities may be higher than those of mutual funds that hold a large percentage of Treasury securities (as opposed to hybrid funds). This is mainly due to the annual fees and expenses charged by mutual funds.

- To boost the returns of Treasury bond mutual funds, many Treasury funds buy other types of bonds with greater risk.

- Mutual fund shareholders have no control over the distribution of the capital gains of a fund. This is particularly so for mutual funds, which actively trade their holdings to boost their overall returns.

- Holders do not know the composition of the investment holdings when they invest. Holdings are disclosed at the end of the quarter.

Caveats

- The risks of Treasury mutual funds may be higher than the risks of owning individual Treasury securities.

- Treasury mutual funds that hold other types of individual bond securities are subject to some state and local taxes on the interest earned.

Summary

Treasury mutual funds are convenient investments that are easy to buy, sell, and administer.

TREASURY EXCHANGE-TRADED FUNDS

A second method of investing indirectly in Treasury securities is through exchange-traded funds (ETFs). An ETF invests in a portfolio of securities that track an index, or in the case of some bond ETFs, track a specific duration. The following example illustrates the difference: Ameristock/Ryan's 5-Year Treasury ETF, ticker symbol GKC, tracks the most recently auctioned five-year Treasury note, whereas the iShares Lehman 1–3 Year Treasury Bond ETF, ticker symbol SHY, tracks an index with a range of bond durations between one and three years.

Buying Treasury ETFs that track a specific duration allows investors to tailor their bond holdings to a specific duration (e.g., investing funds needed in 2 years time in a 2-year duration ETF). Investors in Treasury ETFs that track an index should be aware that the indexes change with each new Treasury auction allowing the Treasury ETF (which holds a mixture of Treasuries) to more easily beat the performance of the index. The reason for this is that newly traded Treasury securities trade at a slight premium price to the market, causing the index to lag slightly after the auction.

As of May 1, 2008, Profunds Group launched two Treasury ETF funds that provide short exposure to intermediate- and long-term Treasury bonds. These two funds, Ultra Short Lehman 7–10 Year Treasury, ticker symbol PST, and Ultra Short Lehman 20+ Year Treasury, ticker symbol TBT, allow investors to benefit when Treasury prices fall. These funds provide twice the inverse of the daily Lehman Brothers 7–10 Year U.S Treasury Index and 20+ Year U.S. Treasury Index. For example, if the 7–10 Year Lehman Brothers U.S. Treasury Index declined by one percent, the Profunds ETF should increase by 2 percent before fees and expenses. The opposite is also true. These funds decline in price when the Lehman Brothers U.S. Treasury Index increases. The advantages of these two funds are that they allow investors to be able to short the bond market without having to open a margin account with a brokerage firm, and these funds can be owned in accounts that do not allow margin trading. Buying shares in these ETFs are as easy as buying common stock on the stock exchanges, but you need to be aware of the risk of loss of principal if the Lehman Bond Index increases instead of decreasing. This is especially so with the two-times inverse weighting of the daily performance of the Bond Index.

Because Treasury ETFs trade as stocks on the stock exchanges, investors can easily trade their shares throughout the business day. The following list provides you with some of the factors you should be mindful of when considering an investment in ETFs:

- With each trade, a commission (fee) is incurred because ETFs are bought and sold through brokers.

- Compare the bid-ask spreads of the different ETFs you are interested in before investing. The smaller the bid-ask spread, the lower the cost. Generally, the size of the spread indicates the trading activity. The more actively traded ETFs have lower spreads, and the inactively traded ETFs have wider spreads.

- Compare the expenses charged by the different ETFs by examining their prospectuses (can be done online). Choose the lowest cost Treasury ETF. The Vanguard Group has the lowest cost ETFs (0.11 percent expense ratio plus a bid-ask ratio of 0.07 percent, which is a combined total cost of 0.18 percent). A total expense ratio of 0.18 compared with 0.50 translates to a charge of $0.18 versus $0.50 per $100. These expense ratios are deducted from the dividends paid to shareholders when distributed. With Treasury yields at relatively low rates (3.5 to 4.5 percent depending on the maturity), these charges eat into dividends and over time make a considerable difference.

Risks of Treasury ETFs

There is no credit or default risk with Treasury securities, but investors in ETFs can lose part of their principal if the selling price of the ETF declines below the purchase price. Interest rate risk impacts the share price of the ETF. The longer the duration of the Treasury securities held in the ETF, the greater is the impact of changes in interest rates.

Advantages of Treasury ETFs

- Real time pricing and trading flexibility of ETF shares throughout the trading day.
- Investors do not need large amounts of money to invest in shares of Treasury ETFs.

Disadvantages of Treasury ETFs

- Returns of holding Treasury ETFs might be lower than those of comparable duration individual Treasury securities due to commissions charged to buy and sell ETF shares and expense ratios charged by ETFs.

Caveats

- The risk of loss in principal from Treasury ETFs might be higher than owning individual Treasury securities. By buying Treasury securities directly at auction through the Treasury Direct program and holding them through maturity, no fees are incurred, insuring that holders recover their principal. Treasury ETF share prices fluctuate, and investors might end up selling their shares at lower prices than their purchase prices.

SHOULD YOU CHOOSE INDIVIDUAL TREASURY SECURITIES, TREASURY MUTUAL FUNDS, OR TREASURY ETFS?

Buying individual Treasury securities directly at auction is not only easy but also free of fees. Investors who plan to hold their individual securities through maturity not only recover their principal investments in their entirety but also receive semiannual interest payments, which are not decreased by any fees or charges. Shares of Treasury mutual funds and ETFs fluctuate, which could result in holders losing part of their principal investments when they sell. Annual fees decrease dividends declared by mutual funds and ETFs. ETFs have added fees in the form of commissions charged to buy and sell shares over no-load mutual funds.

Prices of individual Treasury securities are the most transparent of all the categories of bond securities. The only disadvantage of owning individual Treasury securities purchased at auction is when the investor needs to sell the securities before maturity. Investors can only sell their Treasury securities (bought through the Treasury Direct program) 45 days after issue. Treasury securities bought through Treasury Direct can be sold through the SellDirect program where requests are sent to the Federal Reserve Bank of Chicago. Orders are sold at market price to the highest bidding government securities broker. A $45 fee is charged for this service.

Individual existing Treasury securities can also be bought and sold on an active secondary market. Not only is this market liquid, but because of the large quantities of securities traded, the bid-ask spreads are the smallest of all the different categories of bonds.

Individual Treasury securities have no credit and default risk, but because of the hybrid nature of some of the holdings of Treasury mutual funds, they don't have the same guarantees. The usual advantage of diversification achieved by mutual funds and ETFs does not apply for Treasury securities because of their safety from credit and default risk.

Investors in an individual Treasury note or bond receive a fixed yield (same amount of interest each semiannual period) through maturity whether interest rates rise, fall, or stay the same, but income from Treasury mutual funds and ETFs varies from period to period due to changes in their holdings. Treasury mutual funds pay dividends on a monthly basis, whereas some Treasury ETFs pay interest once a year. Check the prospectus for the payment policy.

Investors do not need large amounts of money to invest in individual Treasury securities as opposed to other types of bonds where round lots would need to be purchased. This makes it easy for small investors to invest in individual Treasury securities.

Summing up, for investors who are willing to purchase Treasury securities directly through the Federal Reserve banks and hold them through maturity, they would be better off with individual Treasuries. Their returns would be higher than those of Treasury mutual funds with 100 percent Treasury holdings and Treasury ETFs. There is a compelling case for choosing individual Treasury securities over Treasury mutual funds. However, for investors who have no desire to buy individual Treasury securities at auction, they would be better off with Treasury mutual funds or ETFs.

Table 8-4 summarizes some of the key differences between individual Treasuries, Treasury mutual funds, and Treasury ETFs.

Table 8-4

Characteristics of Individual Treasury Securities versus Treasury Mutual Funds and Treasury ETFs

	Individual Securities	Treasury Mutual Funds	Treasury ETFs
Ease of buying and selling	Easy to buy new Treasury securities at auction. Slightly more difficult to sell before maturity. Existing Treasuries trade actively during the day on the secondary market.	Easy to buy and sell shares. Trades occur only at the closing price at the end of the day	Easy to buy and sell shares at real time prices during the trading day.
Costs to trade	None when purchased at auction through the Treasury Direct program. Commission costs when buying and selling existing Treasury securities on the secondary market.	None when investing in no-load mutual funds.	Commissions incurred for each trade.
Income stream	Income stream remains fixed over the life of the security (interest paid semi-annually).	Income stream varies from month to month.	Income stream varies. Interest may be paid yearly or more frequently.
Management fees	None	Vary depending on the fund.	Vary depending on the ETF
Returns	Fixed return which is not diminished by fees.	Variable return reduced by the total fees charged by the fund.	Variable return reduced by the total fees charged by the ETF.
Tax planning	Easy to predict income and plan capital gains and losses.	Unpredictable distributions of income and capital gains can upset careful tax planning.	More tax efficient than a mutual fund.
Investment amounts	Requires a minimum of $100.	Required minimum investment amounts vary by fund.	Minimum purchase is a single share of stock.
Safety of principal	If Treasuries are held through maturity, principal is recovered.	A chance that principal may not be fully recovered if share price is below the purchase price when shares are sold.	Fluctuating share price could result in a loss of principal.
Holdings	Known	Not disclosed until the end of the quarter.	Known

CONCLUSION

Treasury securities are the safest and also the lowest yielding fixed-income securities. Regular Treasury notes and bonds provide higher returns than TIPS, if inflation remains at its low current levels. However, if inflation rises, TIPS will provide higher returns that would be pegged to the increase in inflation.

Regular and inflation-indexed savings bonds are for the most conservative investors. Inflation-indexed savings bonds provide for additional returns if inflation rises. Yields on savings bonds are less than those provided by regular Treasury notes and bonds, which means that they do not provide growth to a portfolio of investments. Instead, savings bonds are viewed as good alternatives to bank accounts.

Investors should consider the yield differential between Treasuries and other types of bonds before investing. If the yield differential is not significant, Treasuries may be a better investment. However, when the yield differential is significant, you ought to consider their purchase over Treasuries.

CHAPTER 9

Government Agency and Pass-Through Securities

KEY CONCEPTS

- Government agency securities
- Mortgage pass-through securities
- Types of mortgage pass-through securities
- Government National Mortgage Association (GNMA) securities
- Federal National Mortgage Association (FNMA) securities
- Federal Home Loan Mortgage Corporation (FHLMC) securities
- Collateralized mortgage obligations
- Collateralized debt obligations
- Government agency and pass-through security mutual funds
- Government agency and pass-through exchange-traded funds

Government agency bonds are debt securities issued by either agencies of the government or government-sponsored entities (GSEs). GSEs are privately owned entities that have a public charter and were created by Congress. Agency bonds are issued by the major federally sponsored agencies such as the Federal Home Loan Mortgage Corporation (FHLMC), Federal National Mortgage

Association (FNMA), Federal Home Loan Bank (FHLB) System, Farm Credit Banks, the Student Loan Marketing Association (SLMA), and many others. The first three of these agencies (FHLMC, FNMA, and FHLB) provide funds to the mortgage and housing sectors of the economy. The Farm Credit Banks provide funds for the agricultural sector, and SLMA (Sallie Mae) provides funds for loans for higher education. Government agencies issue traditional debt securities (agency debt), as well as mortgage pass-through securities. Mortgage pass-through securities are debt issues whose interest and principal payments made by borrowers are passed through to investors after a fee is deducted. Government agency bonds and pass-through securities appeal to investors who are interested in high-quality bonds with higher yields than Treasury securities.

GOVERNMENT AGENCY SECURITIES

Many different government agencies issue debt securities, and the characteristics of the securities vary. However, they do have many common features:

- New issues of agency securities are sold through a syndicate of dealers. These dealers also buy and sell these securities in the secondary markets.
- Large agency issues are marketable and fairly liquid.
- Agency securities are exempt from registration with the Securities and Exchange Commission (SEC).
- Some agency issues have tax advantages in that interest income is exempt from state and local taxes.
- Agency securities have either de facto or de jure (actual or by right) backing from the federal government, making them safer than corporate bonds.

Agency securities tend to offer greater yields than Treasuries with comparable maturities, but lower than the yields of most Aa- or Aaa-rated corporate bonds. The different agency securities with their wide range of offerings and maturities appeal to investors who like the slightly higher yields than those offered by Treasuries, without sacrificing much credit risk. The Federal government does not guarantee agency bonds, but it is not likely to allow any of its agencies to default on their interest and principal obligations. The Tennessee Valley Authority and the World Bank are two examples of agency debt.

Agencies issue debt with maturities ranging from a few days to 30 years, at fixed or floating rates, which also can have call provisions. Before investing, you should check the characteristics of the agency bond issue.

MORTGAGE-BACKED OR PASS-THROUGH SECURITIES

Mortgage-backed or pass-through securities are debt securities issued by government agencies or GSEs that pass through the payments received from mortgage borrowers to investors. Mortgage pass-through securities are much more complex than regular fixed-income securities. Mortgage pass-through securities are created from mortgage transactions. Most home purchases are financed with borrowed funds from financial institutions such as mortgage companies and banks that issue mortgages. Borrowers promise to repay, in monthly payments throughout the life of the mortgage loans, the amounts that are loaned. However, most banks and mortgage companies do not hold these mortgages to maturity. Instead, they sell the mortgages to other (government and private) institutions that package the mortgages into pass-through securities and then sell them to investors. Homeowners continue to make their same monthly payments to the newly assigned financial institutions. Figure 9-1 illustrates how mortgage-backed pass-through securities work.

These financial institutions pool their mortgages and sell shares in those pools to investors. Mortgage pools are collections of similar mortgages. Mortgage pass-through securities are shares in pools, which are collections of similar mortgages. The investor then receives monthly interest and principal repayments (minus a modest fee, normally about one half of 1 percent), hence, the term *pass-through securities*. The size of mortgage pools varies, with some consisting of several thousand mortgages and others having just a few mortgages. These pools normally are issued with a minimum of at least $1 million.

FIGURE 9-1

How Mortgage-Backed Securities Work

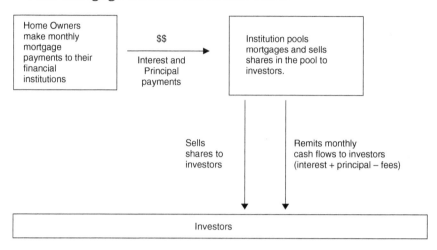

TABLE 9-1

Amortization Schedule of $1 million (30-years, 9 percent) Mortgage

Month/Year	Payment	Int. (9.00%)	Principal	Loan Balance $1,000,000.00
1/2008	8046.23	7500.00	546.23	999,453.77
2/2008	8046.23	7495.90	550.32	998,903.45
3/2008	8046.23	7491.78	554.45	998,349.00
4/2008	8046.23	7487.62	558.61	997,790.39
5/2008	8046.23	7483.43	562.80	997,227.59
6/2008	8046.23	7479.21	567.02	996,660.57
7/2008	8046.23	7474.95	571.27	996,089.30
8/2008	8046.23	7470.67	575.56	995,513.75
9/2008	8046.23	7466.35	579.87	994,933.87
10/2008	8046.23	7462.00	584.22	994,349.65
11/2008	8046.23	7457.62	588.60	993,761.05
12/2008	8046.23	7453.21	593.02	993,168.03

You can better understand pass-through securities by examining how mortgages work. Suppose that a $1 million mortgage pool consists of a single conventional 30-year mortgage of $1 million at 9 percent. The monthly payment the homeowner makes to the mortgage lender is $8,046.23. This payment consists of interest and a portion that goes toward the reduction of the principal balance. Table 9-1 shows the amortization schedule for the first 12 months of this mortgage. In the first payment, the amount of interest is $7,500 ($1 million × 9 percent/12) and $546.23 ($8,046.23 – $7,500) is applied to the principal balance, reducing it from $1 million to $999,453.77. The interest rate is 9 percent per year and the interest rate per month is 9 percent/12 or 0.0075. You calculate the interest expense by multiplying the monthly rate by the mortgage balance. The interest for the first payment is $7,500 (0.0075 multiplied by $1 million).

The monthly payments are designed to reduce the mortgage balance to zero at the end of the mortgage term (30 years or 360 payments). As you can see from the first 12 payments, the amount of interest expense declines each month, which means that more of the monthly payment is applied to reducing the outstanding loan (mortgage) balance. In other words, the fixed amount of the payment is the same, but the proportionate amount of interest received declines and the proportionate amount of the principal repayment increases.

In this case, an investor in this pass-through security receives his or her share of the pass-through interest and principal minus the servicing fees and any other charges by the servicing institution. Investors cannot always count on the monthly amount being the same because mortgage borrowers have the option to prepay their mortgages. The payment might be the entire amount of the mortgage or only a part of it. For example, if the mortgage borrower in this example prepays an additional $1,000 per month, the mortgage pass-through security investor receives a proportionate share of this additional payment, which is, in essence, a return of the pass-through investor's principal or investment capital.

For many reasons, mortgage borrowers prepay the entire amount of their mortgages before the maturity dates. Homeowners sell their homes or refinance their mortgages when interest rates decline; or in the case of fire and other casualties in which the property is destroyed, insurance proceeds are used to pay off the mortgage.

Consequently, in a mortgage pool, if numerous mortgages are prepaid, the amounts of the cash flows to investors are not regular (they may fluctuate from month to month), and neither is there certainty about the length of time to maturity of the pool. Investors also cannot be certain about the timing of monthly cash flows. Suppose that mortgage payments are due on the first day of the month. If borrowers are late in sending in their payments and the processing of those payments is delayed, payments to investors also are delayed. The length of the delay also varies according to the type of pass-through security. In addition to the level-payment, conventional mortgage described (see Table 9-1), which is the most common type for pass-through securities, other types of mortgages (adjustable rate mortgages, graduated payment mortgages, and interest-only mortgages) are available to be used as pass-through securities.

An *adjustable rate* mortgage (ARM) has a floating rate of interest, which varies according to a particular index. For example, if the adjustable rate mortgage is tied to the rate of short-term Treasury notes, the rate is reset up or down with the movement of the rate on Treasury notes every six months, one year, or whatever period the lender chooses at the outset of the mortgage.

Most ARMs have periodic caps on interest rates. They can only increase or decrease by a certain number of percentage points within a period of time, and there usually are also lifetime caps on interest rates. They can only increase or decrease by a certain number of percentage points over the life of the mortgage.

Cash flows of ARMs are even more difficult to predict, which means that monthly amounts received by investors fluctuate more than those received on conventional mortgage pools. There is also prepayment risk with ARMs.

Although ARMs have been blamed for the credit crunch and subprime home loan fiasco in 2007, because of a few disreputable lenders extending credit beyond their borrowers' abilities to repay their mortgages, and resetting the floating interest rates at excessively high levels, ARMs still offer homeowners a flexible method for purchasing homes.

Graduated payment mortgages (GPMs) have also been used for pools or pass-through securities. With a GPM, the level monthly payments in the early years of a mortgage, for example, the first 5 years, are less than the level payments in the later years of the mortgage. The interest rate is fixed, like a conventional mortgage, but in some instances the monthly payments in the initial years might not be enough to cover the interest expense each month, resulting in negative amortization. As a result, the shortfall in interest expense is added back to the mortgage balance. Instead of decreasing, the mortgage balance increases, and so do the monthly payments when it resets. Consequently, at the end of the mortgage term, the home borrower will have repaid a greater amount of principal than was originally borrowed at the inception of the mortgage.

Interest-only mortgages schedule monthly payments that consist only of interest for a specified period (5 to 10 years). The monthly payments do not include amounts for the repayment of principal; consequently, the loan (mortgage) balance remains unchanged at the end of the specified period. In general, interest rates tend to be higher on interest-only mortgages than ARMs or fixed-rate mortgages. Often ARMs are packaged with interest-only options and the interest rate charged is lower than a fixed-rate mortgage purely because it is combined with an adjustable rate.

All types of mortgages are subject to prepayment risk, which affects the amount of the cash flows for investors in pass-through securities. However, there is a level of comfort for those investors in that historically, during times when mortgage rates have fallen to 5 percent, there are still some homeowners who hang on to their 7 percent mortgages.

Besides prepayment risk, mortgage pass-through securities present a challenge for investors in terms of valuation. Since mortgages are self-amortizing (the principal gets paid back in monthly amounts throughout the mortgage term) they cannot be valued like other fixed-income securities, such as Treasury bonds, where the entire principal is returned at maturity.

THE TYPES OF MORTGAGE-PASS-THROUGH SECURITIES

Various types of mortgage pass-through securities are available, each with its own nuances. Despite these differences, investors in all mortgage pass-through securities are concerned with the following criteria:

- The safety of the issue
- The liquidity and marketability of the issue
- The overall rate of return of the issue
- The expected maturity of the issue

The majority of pass-through securities have been issued by three government agencies, namely GNMA, FNMA, and FHLMC. There has also been a marked growth in the number of mortgage pass-through securities issued by private issuers since the mid–1980s.

Government National Mortgage Association

The Government National Mortgage Association, also known as *Ginnie Mae,* is a wholly owned agency of the Housing and Urban Development Department (HUD). Hence, the timely interest and principal payments of Ginnie Mae pass-through securities are guaranteed by the full faith and credit of the U.S. government. They have zero credit risk, which is appealing to investors.

The agency does not issue pass-through securities but rather insures them. These securities are issued by mortgage bankers and thrift institutions. Many of these institutions bundle their mortgages into pools of at least $1 million. These mortgage bankers apply to GNMA for backing and, if accepted, get a pool number. Shares of these pools are sold to investors, consisting mainly of banks, pension funds, and insurance companies. The minimum purchase amount is $25,000, which explains why the majority of investors in these pools are institutions. After all the shares of the GNMA pool are sold, the GNMA securities are traded on the security markets.

GNMA accepts only Veterans Administration (VA) and Federal Housing Administration (FHA) mortgages, which are assumable mortgages. This feature makes prepayment less variable than on mortgages that are not assumable.

A number of Ginnie Mae pools exist. The major pools are GNMA I and GNMA II. GNMA I has fixed-rate 20- to 30-year mortgages totaling a minimum face value of $1 million, all with the same interest rates. GNMA II pools are larger than GNMA I pools and have mortgages with a variety of interest rates and maturities.

There are a number of different GNMA pools, such as midgets (mortgages with a 15-year term), GNMA GPMs, GNMA ARMs, GNMA mobile home pools, GNMA buydowns, and GNMA FHA projects. The different types of mortgages, maturities, interest rates, and pool sizes make the analysis more difficult for each type of pool. Generally, larger pool sizes have more liquid payments and are less affected by prepayments. The shorter the term of the mortgages, the shorter is the average life and half-life of the pool of pass-through securities.

Average life, defined as the weighted-average time that each dollar of principal is outstanding, is a measure of the investment life of mortgage-backed securities in the pool. The pool's average life depends on the prepayment rate. The greater the number of prepayments in the pool, the shorter is the average life, and the weighted-average life, and the lower the volatility in price of the GNMA security. GNMA and other types of mortgage securities are traded on their assumed average life as opposed to their maturity dates, as with other bonds.

Half-life is the time it takes to return half the principal in a pool. The average life and half-life are useful measures for comparison purposes because you would use these concepts, not the length of time to maturity, to compare GNMAs with other fixed-income investments. For example, if you want to compare the yield on a GNMA with a 5-year half-life and a maturity of 12 years with a Treasury note, you would compare it to Treasury notes with 5-year maturities.

GNMA investments are much more complex than other fixed-income investments because of the uncertainties about not only the length of time to maturity for that investment, but also the amount and timing of the cash flows. GNMA provides statistics about prepayment histories for each GNMA pool, but these statistics are not cast in stone and can vary. The estimated payments, therefore, are revised continually.

Yields on GNMA securities are also difficult to determine accurately, as you might expect. If you are not sure about the size, frequency, or regularity of the cash flow, you cannot determine the investment's precise yield. However, various calculation methods have been developed based on different assumptions of prepayment speed (fast, average, and slow). On an offering sheet, a number of yields are quoted depending on the FHA estimated experience of prepayment speed. The slowest speed offers the highest yield. From a safety point of view, therefore, whenever you buy GNMA securities, assume that you will earn the lowest of the predicted yields.

When you are comparing the estimated yields on GNMA securities with yields on other fixed-income securities you need to keep these issues in mind:

- Reinvestment risk is greater for GNMA securities than for other fixed-income securities because interest and the return of principal payments are made monthly for pass-through securities, as opposed to semiannually or annually for regular bonds. For example, if a significant downturn occurs in market rates of interest, the returned interest and principal are reinvested at lower rates, and the total return is lower for the GNMA investment than the quoted yield to maturity assuming reinvestment at the quoted yield.
- Exact rates of return cannot be determined because of the uncertainty of reinvestment risk.
- If the monthly interest and principal payments are spent rather than reinvested, the total rate of return is even lower.
- Principal repayments should not be included in the cash flow yield because they are a return of the investor's initial investment.

GNMA securities and all pass-through securities, like all other fixed-income securities, are sensitive to changes in market rates of interest. When market rates of interest rise, bond prices decline. When market rates of interest decline, many homeowners prepay their mortgages and then refinance them with mortgages at lower rates. This process acts as a ceiling on GNMA prices, so they do not increase as much, generally speaking, as regular bond prices when market rates decline. You not only receive your principal earlier, but you are also faced with reinvesting the proceeds in investments with lower yields.

How to Buy

You can purchase GNMA securities directly from the issuer through dealers or brokers. Minimum purchase amounts are $25,000. However, you can buy GNMA mutual funds or unit investment trusts by investing as little as $1,000 to $2,500 (the minimum amount specified by the GNMA mutual fund or investment trust). Government agency and GNMA exchange-traded funds (ETFs) can also be purchased for amounts that are less than the minimum purchase amount for individual GNMA securities. You can also buy and sell existing GNMA securities that are traded on the secondary market. GNMA securities are both marketable and liquid because of the large volume of issues traded. When you are buying from a broker or bank you should be aware of these guidelines:

- Prices quoted in the newspapers or offering sheets are for large buyers (institutions); small investors are quoted larger spreads (difference between bid and ask prices).
- The yields that are quoted are based on prepayment assumptions. If only one yield is quoted, ask your broker for the different prepayment assumptions and their corresponding yields. Use the most conservative yield because even it may not be realized.
- The remaining term of the mortgage pool or length of time until maturity is not as important as the weighted-average life because the former assumes no prepayments. The assumption in the secondary market is that a 30-year GNMA will be repaid, on average, in 12 years.
- Price is important. If a GNMA security is trading at a premium, you might be more inclined to suffer a capital loss. If interest rates decline, homeowners might prepay their mortgages in the pool faster than estimated. Then you might not recover the premium that you paid over the face value for the security, and you also have to reinvest the cash flow received at lower interest rates. Buying at a discount offers the opportunity of capital gains, but the coupon yield for the GNMA is lower than coupons offered at that time.

What Are the Advantages of GNMA Securities?

- Large sophisticated investors can use the futures market to hedge their portfolios against adverse swings in interest rates.
- GNMA securities offer investors cash flows on a monthly basis as opposed to semiannually or annually for other fixed-income investments.
- GNMA securities have no credit risk because interest and principal payments are guaranteed by the U.S. government.

- GNMA securities are marketable due to the large size of the GNMA market. They are also liquid in that the bid and ask spreads tend to be similar to those for Treasury securities (about 1/8 of a point), and less than most corporate bonds.
- Thirty-year GNMA securities are not as volatile as 30-year Treasuries, because part of the principal on the GNMA is repaid on a monthly basis.
- Yields on GNMA securities tend to be higher, than those on Treasuries but lower than those offered by corporate bonds.

What Are the Disadvantages of GNMA Securities?

- It is difficult to determine the amount of monthly cash flows due to prepayments of mortgages in the pools.
- It is difficult to determine the exact yield for GNMA securities due to the uncertainties of the cash flows.
- Reinvestment risk is greater for GNMA securities than for Treasuries and corporate bonds, particularly when market rates of interest decline.
- Interest is fully taxable at the federal, state, and local levels, whereas Treasuries and certain agency issues are exempt from state and local taxes.
- GNMA securities are subject to interest rate risk. Prices of GNMA securities move in the opposite direction to changes in interest rates.

Caveats

- To reduce prepayment risk, investors should avoid buying GNMA securities from small mortgage pools. By buying into large mortgage pools, investors spread out their prepayment risk. For this reason, small investors might consider GNMA mutual funds where diversification is achieved through the size of the mutual fund's investments in these securities. By investing in one or a few pools, investors with relatively small amounts cannot achieve the diversification that mutual funds can.
- With GNMA securities, investors receive a return of principal and interest monthly. Investors should not spend

their entire monthly checks, but rather should invest a portion of their proceeds to keep their investment capital intact.

- When GNMA securities are trading at a premium price, their coupon yields are greater than current coupon rates for new GNMA securities. Investors should be cautious in buying at a premium because prepayment volatility is greatest for GNMA securities whose coupons exceed current mortgage rates by 3 percent (Hayre and Mohebbi, 1989). A faster rate of prepayments can lead to a capital loss.

Federal Home Loan Mortgage Corporation

The Federal Home Loan Mortgage Corporation, or "Freddie Mac," is the second largest issuer of pass-through securities. Shares of Freddie Mac, a government-sponsored enterprise, are traded on the New York Stock Exchange under the ticker symbol FRE.

The participation certificates offered by Freddie Mac are similar in many ways to GNMA securities. The major differences are as follows:

- Participation certificate pools contain conventional mortgages (most are single-family loans with 30-year terms) that are underwritten and purchased by Freddie Mac. These pools tend to be larger than those of GNMA pools.
- Freddie Mac guarantees the timely payment of interest and, ultimately, the repayment of principal (within a year). Because Freddie Mac is an agency, its guarantee is weaker than the federal government's "full faith and credit" provision for GNMA securities. Some participation certificates guarantee only the timely payment of interest.
- Participation certificates are not as marketable as GNMA securities because fewer participation certificates are traded in the secondary market. To improve the marketability of its participation certificates, Freddie Mac buys them back directly from holders.
- Yields on participation certificates are slightly higher than the yields on GNMA securities because of the slight discrepancy in safety and the slightly lesser degree of marketability. This statement does not mean that

participation certificates are not safe or marketable. Compared with GNMA securities, their level of credit risk is slight (far less than a corporate issue) and they are marketable (and liquid), but because GNMA securities have a greater presence in the marketplace, they are not as marketable or liquid.

The Federal Home Loan Mortgage Corporation has, in addition to participation certificates, a mortgage pass-through security called a *guaranteed mortgage certificate* (GMC). The GMC was designed for institutional investors with minimum amounts of $100,000 (as opposed to $25,000 for GNMA securities and participation certificates) and it pays out interest and principal semiannually. Freddie Mac guarantees its interest payments and the full payment of principal.

Federal National Mortgage Association Securities

The Federal National Mortgage Association, also known as "Fannie Mae" or FNMA is a quasi-private organization whose common stock is traded on the New York Stock Exchange. Fannie Mae was established by Congress in 1938, but was then rechartered by Congress to become a private corporation in 1968 with a mandate to assist in the development of a secondary market for conventional mortgages.

Some of the features of Fannie Mae pass-through securities are:

- FNMA guarantees timely interest and principal payments—a weaker guarantee than the one given for GNMA pass-through securities.
- FNMA pools tend to be larger than GNMA pools.
- FNMA securities are not as marketable as GNMA securities, and yields on FNMA securities tend to be higher than those offered on GNMA securities.

Table 9-2 discusses current events that have affected the safety image of mortgage-backed agency securities.

To offset the prepayment and cash flow uncertainties of agency pass-through securities, collateralized mortgage obligations were developed in the private sector.

TABLE 9-2

Are Government-Sponsored Mortgage Companies Safe and Sound?

Has the accounting scandal virus that affected so many companies such as Enron, WorldCom, and Global Crossing reached the government-sponsored agencies? The Office of Federal Housing Enterprise Oversight (Ofheo) does not think so. According to Ofheo, Freddie Mac and Fannie Mae have adequate capital on hand to protect themselves against certain risks. However, their definition of core capital excludes losses that have built up over the years, thereby overstating their true capital (Weil, 2003). In its core capital definition, Ofheo has ignored losses on cash flow hedges, which have been greater at Fannie Mae than at most banks (Weil, 2003). Cash flow hedges are side bets used to protect cash flows from interest rate volatility and are commonly used by Freddie Mac and Fannie Mae. If these cash flow hedges are perfectly offset against changes in interest rates, then there are no fluctuations in income, which is a big "if."

Freddie Mac also used swap-type maneuvers, which had the effect of moving $400 million of operating earnings from 2001 into future years. Swaps are paired contracts between two parties that allow them to trade cash flows. For example, Freddie Mac might pay fixed-rate income immediately in return for receiving fixed-rate income in the future. Freddie Mac was concerned that a combination of new federal accounting standards and falling interest rates would increase earnings in the short-term, but then lead to earnings disappointments in the future. This action amounts to a manipulation of earnings using complex financial maneuvers and accounting schemes.

Freddie Mac went even further in 1998 by removing bonds that were in default off its balance sheet. It set up an offshore special purpose entity (SPE), á la Enron, in the Channel Islands, which sold high-yield bonds to institutional investors, enabling Freddie Mac to shift bonds in default off its balance sheet. Due to a restatement of its financial statements, this debt is back on Freddie Mac's balance sheet.

Attention to these corporate shenanigans has put downward pressure on these agencies' bond prices. A rumor surfaced on July 28, 2003, that the European Central Bank was selling all the bonds it owned of Freddie Mac and Fannie Mae, and recommended that its national central banks do the same. If there was any truth to this rumor, it would have affected the bond markets in general and the mortgage- and housing-related sectors in particular. Foreign investors hold a large percentage of agency debt, and if they stopped investing, Fannie Mae and Freddie Mac's borrowing costs would increase, driving up mortgage rates and squeezing profits.

Freddie Mac and Fannie Mae are backed by the federal government and are at the center of the U.S. housing market. Should they be allowed to violate accounting procedures to manipulate earnings? The answer is no, and federal regulators and the U.S. Congress should step up to the plate to make sure that there is not a repetition of the Enron debacle in the agency-sponsored market.

Visit GNMA, FNMA, and FHLMC Web sites to determine information about the issuers, their new issues, and mortgage rates at:

www.ginniemae.gov
www.fanniemae.com
www.freddiemac.com

Source: Weil, Jonathan, "Regulator's Core Capital Gauge for Fannie, Freddie May be Off," *Wall Street Journal Online*, July 22, 2003.

Collateralized Mortgage Obligations

Collateralized mortgage obligations (CMOs) are mortgage pass-through securities that provide more predictable interest and principal payments than GNMA, FNMA, and Freddie Mac pass-through mortgage securities. CMO pools are split into tranches (or slices), which are classified according to expected maturities of the securities and specific payment rules. The first CMO was issued in 1983. The main innovation of the CMO is that it provides investors with a steady stream of income for predictable terms. A CMO is a debt security based on a pool of mortgages (like GNMA securities) in which the property owners make their interest and principal payments on a monthly basis. However, the return of principal payments is segmented and paid sequentially to a number of different portions of the pool's investors.

CMOs are created when pools are divided into tranches ranging in number from 3 to 17. Investors buy bonds with varying maturities in these tranches. For example, the classic CMO has four tranches; the first three (class A, class B, and class C) pay interest at the stated coupon rate to bondholders of each tranche. The fourth tranche (often referred to as a class Z or a Z bond class) resembles a zero coupon bond where interest is accrued. The last tranche is always the Z tranche.

The cash flows received are used first to pay the interest on the first three classes of bonds and then to retire the bonds in the first tranche at maturity. All prepayments are applied to the first tranche, class A; then, when all the bonds are retired, the prepayments continue to the next tranche, class B. This process continues until class B bonds are paid off, and then C bonds follow. Z bonds receive no payments (interest and principal) until all the other tranches are paid off. Subsequent cash flows are used to pay off the accrued interest, and then the return of principal to retire the Z bonds.

Z bonds are much more complex than the A, B, or C bonds in CMOs for a number of reasons. First, the length of time to maturity cannot be accurately predicted (for Z bonds), whereas regular A, B, and C tranches have stated maturities. Second, Z bonds are long-term bonds—people investing in them face greater risks than with shorter-term securities. For this reason, Z bonds can be quite volatile, and you should understand the risks before buying Z tranche bonds in a CMO. Your credit risk varies depending on the backing of the CMO pool. If GNMA or FNMA backs CMO pools, then the credit risk is minimal. The risks rise for private issuers who are not as creditworthy.

Advantages of CMOs

- Greater certainty exists for cash flows (quarterly or semiannually) of earlier tranches, than for tranches with longer terms to maturity.
- Earlier tranches have shorter and more predictable maturities, and, consequently, less exposure to interest rate risk.
- Later tranches have greater prepayment risk than earlier tranches (because investors cannot receive any principal payments until the earlier tranches have been paid off).
- CMO pools are much larger than GNMA pools.
- Depending on the backing of the mortgages, CMOs can have very little to no credit risk. Some pools are backed by GNMA, FNMA, or FHLMC, which have no credit risk. Privately backed pools have pool insurance, but they also may have greater credit risks.
- Depending on the brokerage firms selling CMOs, minimum investment amounts can be as low as $10,000.
- Yields on Z tranche bonds are higher than those of GNMAs, but risk is also much greater for Z tranche bonds.

Disadvantages of CMOs

- CMOs are less liquid and may be less marketable than GNMA, FNMA, and Freddie Mac securities.
- Z tranche bonds can be quite volatile when market rates of interest change.
- Yields on the earlier tranches tend to be lower than those on GNMAs.
- Z tranche bonds have more complicated tax aspects in that interest is taxed as accrued even though the investor does not receive the actual interest payments in the early years (only when the Z tranche pays out).

Caveats

Before investing in CMOs, investors should:

- Understand the characteristics of each tranche, the relationships between the tranches, and the prepayment structure.
- Understand who has guaranteed or insured the mortgages in the pools.
- Ascertain from the brokerage firm selling the CMOs whether they make a market in the securities. If not, the CMOs may be difficult to sell. Table 9-3 outlines some of the difficulties in pricing some of these privately packaged collateralized loans.

Many different classes of CMOs have evolved. These have different features, and the complexities of each specific class have increased with the evolution of CMOs. CMOs offset some of the problems of the traditional pass-through securities by providing a stream of cash flows for a relatively predictable maturity (particularly for early tranches).

GOVERNMENT AGENCY AND PASS-THROUGH MUTUAL FUNDS

Government agency mutual funds often contain a mixture of different bond securities issued by the federal government and corporations. If a fund has "government agency" in its title it must hold 65 percent of the fund's security holdings in government agency securities. The other 35 percent could consist of any other securities such as Treasuries, foreign government bonds, corporate bonds, zero coupon bonds, or convertible bonds.

Since not all agency bonds are guaranteed or backed by the U.S. government, and these other types of bonds, besides Treasuries, vary in credit risk, investors should examine the holdings of these types of mutual funds before investing. Credit risk and the risk of default can vary considerably, depending on the holdings of the mutual fund.

The same may be said of the holdings of GNMA and other pass-through mutual funds, which hold a variety of mortgage pass-through securities of varying degrees of credit quality. In a GNMA fund, the majority of the holdings would be GNMA securities, but the other 35 percent might consist of riskier securities

---

TABLE 9-3

Are Collateralized Mortgage Obligations and Collateralized Debt Obligations Too Risky for Investors?

Collateralized debt obligations (CDOs) are pools of subprime mortgages, home equity loans, conventional mortgages, other debt securities, and preferred trust securities that are packaged into tranches (or slices) and then securities are sold to investors based on these underlying assets based on their risk. The senior tranches contain good quality securities with ratings of AAA, mezzanine tranches contain securities with AA-BB ratings, and equity tranches have risky securities with higher default and credit risks along with higher yields. CDOs bear some similarities and differences to collateralized mortgage obligations (CMOs), which is illustrated in Figure 9-2. The main difference between CDOs and CMOs is that with CDOs, risk and yield are defined. CDO equity tranches have the highest risk of default and pay the highest yields. The equity tranche, also known as toxic waste or first loss tranche, is the most vulnerable to default risk. Thus, when default occurs, it is borne by the equity holders' tranche, and then moves up sequentially to the next tranche when losses exceed the size of the equity tranche.

Administrative expenses are deducted from cash flows (paid monthly by mortgage and debt holders). The senior tranche investors are paid first from the cash flows, followed by the mezzanine tranche investors. Only after all investors in the other tranches have been paid do equity tranche investors get paid. Uncertainty exists for investors with regard to the amount and timing of cash flows after senior tranche investors have been paid.

CDO administrators frequently buy and sell their collateral assets to increase returns for their investors. The intent is to seek capital gains rather than focusing on income by investing in higher-yielding investments. With the housing meltdown and increasing defaults in subprime mortgages in 2007, many CDOs that held large percentages of subprime mortgages were downgraded by the ratings services and pricing the underlying securities became a problem. CDOs could not sell their risky mortgages because there were no buyers. This lack of pricing explains why Bear Stearns' two hedge funds failed in July 2007: there was no value in the subprime mortgages that they held in their portfolios.

CDOs and CMOs are complex in their structures, and investors need to understand not only how they work but also need to be aware of the risk of the underlying securities held in their tranches. For CDOs, investors should choose the tranche with the risk/return characteristics that they feel comfortable with.

---

such as CMOs, collateralized debt obligations (CDOs), and derivative securities.

There are also ARM mutual funds, which purchase mortgage securities with adjustable rates. Although many of these mortgages may be guaranteed by federal agencies, the credit risk can also vary on these funds for the same reasons as cited above. These funds may hold risky CMOs, CDOs, and derivative securities in addition to their holdings of ARM securities.

FIGURE 9-2

Similarities and Differences Between Collateralized Mortgage
Obligations (CMOs) and Collateralized Debt Obligations (CDOs)

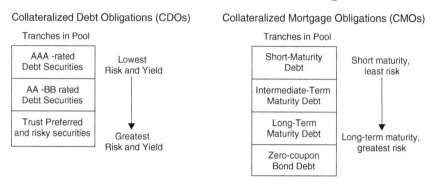

What Are the Risks of Government Agency and Pass-Through Mutual Funds?

Government agency and pass-through mortgage securities provide higher yields than Treasuries because they are subject to greater risk. The same holds true of mutual funds with these holdings. Besides *credit risk* and the *risk of default*, which both rise as mutual funds increase their holdings of CMOs, derivative securities, corporate bonds, zero coupon bonds, and bonds of the less creditworthy agencies, there are other risks.

Government agency and pass-through mortgage mutual funds are subject to *interest rate risk*. Generally, when market rates of interest fall, prices of existing fixed-income securities rise. However, as mentioned earlier in this chapter there is a ceiling on the rise in price of pass-through securities. The reason for this is many homeowners are likely to refinance their older higher interest mortgages for lower interest mortgages. Thus, with falling rates of interest, prices of pass-through securities do not rise as much as other fixed-income securities. The flip side of the coin is that when interest rates rise, homeowners do not refinance their mortgages. The result is that holders of pass-through securities receive lower yields than other securities, because pass-through pools have longer lives and holders do not receive their principal back to reinvest at the higher prevailing interest rates. With rapid swings in interest rates, pass-through securities do not perform as well as other fixed-income securities. In other words, pass-through security mutual funds do not perform well during times when interest rates fluctuate rapidly. ARM funds theoretically should perform better when there are rapid swings in interest rates, but this was not the case historically when ARM funds returned lower yields than money market funds.

Pass-through mortgage securities are complex; payments are unpredictable and yields are only estimates at best. This makes it more difficult to analyze the risks of pass-through mortgage securities, and in particular, pass-through security mutual funds. For these reasons, with pass-through security mutual funds there is always the *risk of loss of principal* due to the volatility of mutual fund share prices.

How to Buy Government Agency and Pass-Through Security Mutual Funds

Government agency and pass-through security mutual funds may be bought directly through the mutual fund families or indirectly through brokers, financial planners, and banks. To save on sales commissions, you are better off investing directly with the mutual fund family in no-load funds, especially in light of the share price volatility of pass-through security mutual funds. In addition, look for low expense ratio funds. Lower expenses can make quite a difference to overall returns over long periods of time. High expense ratio funds have to earn greater returns than low expense ratio funds just to equal the same total returns.

Many financial magazines and newspapers publish quarterly, yearly, and longer-term operating results of the different agency and pass-through mortgage mutual funds. From such a list, investors can narrow the list of potential funds by examining the following in the prospectus:

- The objectives of the fund, which determines the latitude the fund manager has to purchase riskier securities for the fund
- The types of securities held in the fund
- Whether the fund charges a load (front-end and/or back-end)
- The expense ratios of the fund

A prospectus and application form may be obtained off the Internet from the mutual fund company's Web site or by calling the fund's toll free number.

What Are the Advantages of Government Agency and Pass-Through Mutual Funds?

- Although mortgage pass-through and government agency mutual funds may hold riskier securities in their portfolios to boost their yields, they still offer mutual fund shareholders a more diversified portfolio than if they were to invest in individual agency or pass-through securities. The greater diversification achieved by mutual funds can lessen the impact of credit and default risk.
- The minimum purchase amount for individual pass-through securities such as GNMA and FNMA is $25,000, which makes pass-through security mutual funds, with lower minimums of around $1,000, more accessible for investors who have less money to invest.
- When interest rates move within a narrow range, government agency and pass-through security mutual funds offer the potential for greater returns than Treasury mutual funds.

What Are the Disadvantages of Government Agency and Pass-Through Mutual Funds?

- Wide swings in market rates of interest can make the prices of pass-through security mutual funds quite volatile, causing potential losses in principal should mutual fund shareholders have to sell when their shares are at lower prices than their purchase prices.
- Due to the unpredictability and unevenness of the cash flows of mortgage pass-through securities, yields on pass-through security mutual funds are not comparable with those of government agency, Treasury, and corporate bond mutual funds.

Caveats

- Not all agency securities are exempt from state and local taxes, which may mean that a portion of the dividends received from these mutual funds may be subject to state and local taxes.

GOVERNMENT AGENCY AND PASS-THROUGH SECURITY EXCHANGE-TRADED FUNDS

As of September 2007, there were 17 government bond ETFs (www.ici.org). All of these funds have a blend of bond holdings that include government agency and mortgage pass-through debt. For example, Barclay's ishare Lehman Intermediate/Credit Bond fund (ticker symbol GVI) had 22 percent of its holdings in government agency and pass-through securities and the Lehman Government/ Credit bond fund had 18 percent of its holdings in government agency and pass-through securities in November 2007. As of this date there are no pure play government agency and mortgage pass-through security ETFs. The holdings of these ETFs also change over time, and so if investors are looking to invest primarily in an ETF with the largest holdings of government agency and government pass-through securities, they will need to research each of the funds to determine which hold the greatest percentage of this category of bonds.

ETFs generally have the advantage of having lower expense ratios than mutual funds. Consequently, it is possible to buy and sell ETFs, which include commission costs, and still come out ahead against a higher expense ratio mutual fund. Expense ratios of ETFs and mutual funds can be compared by going to the sponsors' Web sites.

Risks of Government Agency and Pass-Through Security ETFs

There is always the risk of loss of principal when investing in bond ETFs (having to sell at a lower price than the purchase price). Prices of bonds rise and fall conversely to changes in interest rates. When interest rates decline, maturities of government agency and pass-through security bonds decline, and when interest rates increase, holders of these securities find that maturities of these securities increase. The result is that investors in pass-through securities generally do not benefit as much from declines in market rates of interest, as with other types of bonds (Treasury and corporate). However, as a practical matter, government ETFs contain a combination of different types of bonds (Treasuries, government agency, and pass-through bonds, in addition to corporate bonds), making it difficult to predict the swings in prices as a result of changes in market rates of interest.

GNMA bonds generally deliver higher yields than Treasury notes and bonds, but it is hard to predict how an ETF will perform because its holdings of GNMA securities are a small percentage of the fund.

Credit and default risk depend on the quality of the holdings of the ETF.

Advantages of Government Agency and Pass-Through ETFs

- It is easy to buy and sell shares at real time prices at any time during the trading day.
- Investors do not need large amounts of money to invest in government agency and pass-through security ETFs.
- Investors can sell short shares of ETFs.
- ETF shareholders own a diversified portfolio of bonds.
- ETF shareholders are not liable for capital gains on their holdings until they sell their shares.

Disadvantages of Government Agency and Pass-Through ETFs

- There are currently no ETFs that invest in only government agency and pass-through securities. The holdings of government ETFs include other types of bonds.

SHOULD YOU CHOOSE INDIVIDUAL GOVERNMENT AGENCY AND PASS-THROUGH SECURITIES, GOVERNMENT MUTUAL FUNDS, OR GOVERNMENT ETFS?

Buying individual government agency and pass-through securities is a complex undertaking for lay investors, but government mutual funds and ETFs make it easier for investors to participate in this group of debt securities. Similarly, government agency and pass-through mutual funds and ETFs offer investors professional management, diversification, smaller investment minimums, and the ease of owning a share in these otherwise complex securities.

Should investors want to invest in riskier CMOs, mutual funds offer the advantage of a diversified portfolio of holdings, which can lessen the risk of loss due to defaults of individual securities. Currently there are not that many ETFs in this category of bonds to choose from, whereas mutual funds offer investors greater choices, such as, for example, GNMA, ARM securities, and government agency bonds.

Annual fees and expense ratios decrease dividends declared by mutual funds and ETFs. The disadvantage of ETFs is that there are additional fees in the form of commissions charged to buy and sell shares over no-load funds. However, with ETFs, holders can pick the price at which they choose to sell their shares, because of the transparency of prices of shares traded on the stock exchanges. Mutual fund holders can only buy and sell shares at the closing price of the mutual fund at the end of the day, which is unknown to the holder.

There is always the risk of loss of principal with mutual funds and ETFs, but buying individual government agency bonds and pass-through bonds and holding them to maturity ensures that holders will not lose any principal.

Investing in individual pass-through securities and government agency bonds over mutual funds and ETFs allows investors the freedom to choose their portfolios of securities and their risks, along with being able to eliminate the fees that they would pay for mutual funds and ETFs. Consequently, overall returns may be higher by investing in individual bonds. Table 9-4 summarizes some of the differences between individual government bonds, government mutual funds, and government ETFs.

TABLE 9-4

Characteristics of Individual Government Securities versus Mutual Funds and ETFs

	Individual Securities	Mutual Funds	ETFs
Ease of buying and selling	Difficult to buy and sell individual bonds.	Easy to buy and sell shares. Trades occur only at the closing price at the end of the day	Easy to buy and sell shares at real time prices during the trading day.
Costs to trade	Commission costs when buying and selling existing government agency bonds on the secondary market. Lack of transparent pricing of bonds.	None when investing in no-load mutual funds.	Commissions incurred for each trade. Transparent prices of shares.
Income stream	Income stream remains fixed for some agency bonds and varies for pass-through securities.	Income stream varies from month to month.	Income stream varies.
Management fees	None	Vary depending on the fund.	Vary depending on the ETF
Returns	Return is not diminished by fees.	Variable return reduced by the total fees charged by the fund.	Variable return reduced by the total fees charged by the ETF.
Tax planning	Easy to predict income and plan capital gains and losses.	Unpredictable distributions of income and capital gains can upset careful tax planning.	More tax efficient than a mutual fund.
Investment amounts	Requires a minimum of $25,000- $50,000.	Required minimum investment amounts vary by fund.	Minimum purchase is a single share of stock.
Safety of principal	If agency and pass-through bonds are held through maturity, principal is recovered.	A chance that principal may not be fully recovered if share price is below the purchase price when shares are sold.	Fluctuating share price could result in a loss of principal.
Holdings	Known	Not disclosed until the end of the quarter.	Known, although they can change over time.
Diversification	Need large amount of money to build a diversified portfolio	Small investment buys a holding in a diversified portfolio.	Small investment buys a holding in a diversified bond portfolio.

REFERENCE

Hayre, Lakhbir S., and Cyrus Mohebbi, "Mortgage Pass-Through Securities," in Frank J. Fabozzi (ed.) *Advances and Innovations in the Bond and Mortgage Markets*, New York: McGraw-Hill, 1989.

CHAPTER 10

Corporate Bonds

KEY CONCEPTS

- The features of corporate bonds
- The types of corporate bonds
- The risks of corporate bonds
- Junk bonds
- Corporate inflation-linked notes
- How to buy and sell corporate bonds
- The advantages and disadvantages of corporate bonds
- Caveats
- Quasi-corporate debt preferred stock securities
- Corporate bond mutual funds
- How to choose corporate bond mutual funds
- The risks of corporate bond mutual funds
- How to buy corporate bond mutual funds
- The advantages and disadvantages of corporate bond mutual funds
- Caveats
- Corporate exchange-traded funds (ETFs)
- Corporate bonds, corporate bond mutual funds, or corporate bond ETFs

Corporations, like governments and government agencies, issue bonds as a primary source of capital. Corporations can issue debt privately (to large, sophisticated companies such as insurance companies and pension funds) or to the general public. Many more individual investors are investing directly in bonds due to the move to make the pricing of bonds more transparent, and bypassing corporate bond mutual funds. However, corporate bonds have become more volatile in recent years partly as a result of the largely publicized bankruptcies of supposedly safe corporations such as Enron and WorldCom. Another development has been a growing category of corporate junk bonds, which has led many individual investors to question the safety of corporate bonds. Despite the apprehension about credit risk and the risk of default, investors still find corporate bonds to be attractive investments, because they offer higher yields than Treasury securities, government agency bonds, certificates of deposit, and money market funds. To protect the safety of their principal, investors need to become more aware of the bond's features and risks.

WHAT ARE THE FEATURES OF CORPORATE BONDS?

Bonds are debt instruments, and all bonds have similar features. A corporate bond is a loan made by a corporation in return for a specified amount of interest and the repayment of the face value of the bond at a specified maturity date. The interest (coupon) rate is generally fixed for the life of the bond (exceptions are variable rate bonds), and the face (par) value of the bond is usually $1,000. The maturity date is when the par value of the bond is returned to the bondholder. Thus, a corporate bond with a coupon of 7 percent and a maturity date of July 1, 2015, pays interest of $70 per bond every year up to July 1, 2015, when the corporation returns the face value of the bond ($1,000) to the bondholder.

If a bond has 20 years to maturity at the date of issuance, it is said to have an *original* maturity of 20 years. After a year, that same bond will have a *current* maturity or term to maturity of 19 years.

TYPES OF CORPORATE BONDS

Corporate bonds can be classified in many different ways: their seniority, whether they have collateral backing, the industry category of the issuer, the bond's coupon structure, or the types of provisions embedded in the bond's indenture.

Seniority

The expectations of bondholders are that they will receive regular interest payments and their principal from corporations when their bonds mature. However, if a corporation with many different bond issues outstanding has difficulties in making these payments, there is a hierarchy of claims as to which bondholders get paid first, and who is last in line. Senior bonds have a higher claim on the company's assets than other bonds. The bond issues' indenture generally specifies whether that bond issue has seniority. Mortgage bonds, for example, are secured by property, which gives holders the legal right to foreclose on the property in order to satisfy unpaid debt obligations. Consequently, mortgage bondholders' claims are considered to be senior to the claims of debenture bondholders, whose claims on the company's assets are satisfied only after senior bondholders' claims are satisfied. Debenture bonds are unsecured and their claims are satisfied after all senior claims, if there are any assets left. Consequently, it is important to invest in senior bonds of less creditworthy corporations than to speculate on their debenture issues.

Industry Category

Bonds can also be classified by industry category:

- The utilities, which consist of bonds issued by the telephone and electric companies. These securities tend to be viewed as safe, conservative investments.
- The transportation group, which consists of bonds issued by the railroads and the airlines.
- The industrials, which consist of bonds issued by industrial companies.

- The finance companies, such as insurance companies and banks.

Within these groups, there are many types of bonds, such as mortgage bonds, debenture bonds, variable interest bonds, convertible bonds, and zero coupon bonds. These bonds are either secured or unsecured. For *secured bonds*, the issuer pledges an asset as collateral, and in the event of a default, the creditor can seize the asset (after proceeding to court). An example of a secured bond is a mortgage bond, which is frequently issued by utility companies. Investors should sleep well at night knowing that their bonds are backed by a power plant. But do investors have the expertise to operate the power plant in the event of default by the utility company? Although pledging assets increases the safety of the principal of the bonds, in this case investors should hope that the utility company does not default on its interest and principal payments.

The transportation group issues bonds known as equipment trust certificates, which are secured by equipment such as airplanes and railroad cars. This equipment may be more marketable than power plants, but investors could still lose some of their principal in the event of a default.

Unsecured bonds or *debenture* bonds are backed only by the issuer's creditworthiness (ability to pay annual interest and principal at maturity). Some companies issue *subordinated debenture* bonds, which are riskier in the event of insolvency, since subordinated debenture holders are last in the line of lenders to be repaid. Seniority becomes important during bankruptcy because secured bonds and senior debt are first in line to be repaid. Riskier issues tend to offer higher coupon rates to entice investors.

Generally, investors should be concerned with the issuer's ability to service their debt (or creditworthiness) rather than with the security alone. In the event of bankruptcy, pledged property may not be marketable, and it may involve litigation, which can be time consuming.

Bond Coupon Structure

Most bond issues have fixed coupon rates, but there are variable coupon rate bonds and zero coupon bonds. With a fixed coupon rate, a bond issue pays the same amount of interest every period (at the stated coupon rate) over the life of the bond. A variable or floating coupon rate bond has its rate pegged to the movement of a specified interest rate index, such as London Interbank Offered Rate (LIBOR) or the U.S. prime rate, and changes when the index is adjusted. *Zero coupon* bonds are issued at deep discounts with coupon interest paid at maturity.

Bond Provisions

The most common provision included in corporate bonds is a call provision, which gives the issuer the right to call in the bonds before maturity. A put provision allows holders of the bond issue to sell their bonds back to the issuer at a predetermined price at a particular date. A bond issue with a sinking fund provision enables the issuer to retire a predetermined amount of the bond issue according to a posted schedule in the indenture. A bond with a provision that links inflation to coupon rates has recently been offered by some corporations. A convertible bond issue allows bondholders to convert their bonds into a specified number of shares of the company's common stock.

FORMS OF BONDS

Bonds are issued in registered or book-entry form. *Registered* form is similar to owning stock certificates. Bonds are registered in the owner's name, and the interest payments are mailed to the owner. When the bond is sold, the transfer agent registers the bond in the name of the new owner.

With *book-entry* form bonds, bondholders receive a confirmation with a computer number, which signifies ownership, instead of receiving a bond certificate. Interest payments are deposited directly into bank accounts designated by their holders.

WHO SHOULD KEEP YOUR BOND CERTIFICATES?

Investors often debate whether to take possession of their bond certificates or whether they should leave them with their brokerage firms.

The advantages of leaving them in the custody of the broker-age firm are:

- They are protected against physical loss if that brokerage firm is covered by the Securities Insurance Protection Corporation (SIPC).
- In the event that your bonds are called, the brokerage firm is more likely to become aware of the call and redeem the bonds immediately.

The disadvantages of keeping them in the custody of the brokerage firm are:

- Should you decide to sell your bonds through another broker, you must have your existing brokerage firm trans-fer them to the new broker's firm. You have three days after the date of sale to deliver the securities before the brokerage assesses a late charge.
- Some brokerage firms are slow in remitting interest payments.
- When bonds with a sinking fund provision are left in the brokerage firm's name, the brokerage firm chooses which customer's bonds are to be redeemed early. A sinking fund is used by companies to redeem a certain number of bonds each year before maturity. The corporation notifies bond-holders through the mail and in the newspapers of redemptions. This is particularly relevant for the small investor. With a sinking fund provision, investors are bet-ter off holding their own bonds, which can be called directly, but it is not left to the brokerage firm to choose which client's bonds to redeem.

WHAT ARE THE RISKS OF CORPORATE BONDS?

The *risk of default* is more of a concern for investors in corporate bonds than for investors in other types of bonds such as U.S. Treasuries and government agency bonds, where the risk of default is much less. U.S. Treasuries are considered to be free of default risk. This is why corporate bonds offer higher yields than Treasuries and government agency bonds. The greater the risk of default, the higher is the coupon rate for that issue.

To evaluate the risk of default on individual corporate bond issues, most investors rely on the ratings of the issues given by the commercial rating companies, such as Standard & Poor's, Moody's, and Fitch. However, as pointed out in an earlier chapter, these ratings are not foolproof and they are also subject to change. A company's financial position can deteriorate after being rated. For example, Enron bonds were only downgraded by the commercial ratings services to speculative shortly before they declared bankruptcy.

In addition to commercial ratings, an investor can evaluate a bond issue on her or his own by looking at the bond's prospectus or the corporation's financial statements for:

- The amount of debt that the company has
- Where the bond issue stands in the claim's line as to claims in the event of bankruptcy

There is another risk that affects prices of existing bond issues called *event risk*. Event risk occurs in a leveraged buyout where a corporation raises capital by issuing substantial amounts of debt to purchase the shares of another corporation. The additional debt issues of the combined company could result in the existing bond issues of the combined company being downgraded and hence plummeting in price. As a result, investors are careful as to which corporate bond offerings to invest in. To entice investors to buy new corporate issues, corporate issuers introduced provisions that make takeovers more expensive. This provision in a bond's indenture is referred to as a "poison put," which allows bondholders to sell their bonds back to the issuer at par in the event of a takeover. This provision protects bondholders from deterioration in credit quality. Before buying a new corporate issue, check with your broker whether there is a "poison put" protection clause. The advantages of a put feature in the bond's indenture are often paid for through lower yields on the bonds.

All bonds, except for floating rate bonds, are subject to *interest rate risk*. Citicorp was the first corporation to introduce floating rate bonds in the 1970s. These were unique at the time in that the coupon rate fluctuated with the rate of Treasury bills, and after a two-year period (after issuance) the bondholders could redeem the bonds at par value. Therefore, unlike prices of regular fixed-income bonds, floating rate bonds do not fluctuate very much in price when interest rates change. As pointed out in previous chapters, bond prices fluctuate inversely with market rates of interest. The longer the maturity of the bond, the greater is the price fluctuation in relation to changes in interest rates.

The impact of interest rate risk can be lessened by:

- Spreading out the maturities of the different bond issues in your portfolio to even out the impact of changing market rates of interest. For example, instead of investing only in bonds with 20-year maturities, ladder the maturities between 2, 5, 10, 15, and 20 years.
- Diversifying your bond portfolio by buying different types of bonds.
- Purchasing good quality bonds.
- Lessening the length of the maturities.
- Buying bonds with a put feature, which allows bondholders to sell their bonds back to the issuer at face value when interest rates rise.

The downside is that bonds with these features have lower coupon rates and shorter maturities. However, in theory, the optimum strategy is to invest in short maturities when market rates of interest are increasing and then when they peak, to buy long maturity bonds to lock into the high coupon rates. The obvious question is how do you know when market rates of interest are going to peak? Locking in at the peak of market interest rates is not as important as at least trying to follow the strategy.

Many corporate bonds have call features, which involves *call risk*. The call feature allows the issuer to retire the bonds prior to maturity. When a bond is called, interest no longer accrues, which forces bondholders to retire their bonds. The call feature benefits the issuer rather than the bondholder, primarily because issuers tend to call their bonds after a period of high interest rates. For example, if a corporation issued 11 percent coupon bonds when interest rates were high, and then rates dropped to 7 percent, it would be advantageous for the issuer to refund the old bonds with new bonds at a lower coupon rate.

Early repayment is always disadvantageous for investors, as issuers rarely refund bonds early when market rates of interest are rising. This is especially disadvantageous for investors who had bought the bonds when interest rates were at a peak.

Investors should pay particular attention to a bond issue's call and refunding provisions. There are three types of call provisions:

1. Noncallable bonds offer investors the most protection, but there are many loopholes. *Noncallable* implies that the bonds cannot be called before maturity. However, there are cases where noncallable bonds have been called, such as in the case of a fire or act of God; or when a healthy company stops making its interest payments on the bonds, and the trustees call them in and the debt is paid off early. Noncallable for life bonds are listed in the dealer's quote sheets as NCL.

2. Freely callable bonds offer investors no protection as issuers can call them anytime.

3. Deferred callable bonds offer some protection since the bonds cannot be called until after a period of time (for example, 5, 10, or 15 years after issue). A bond that is noncallable until 2009 would be listed as NC09 on the dealer's quote sheet.

The call provision of the bond specifies the price above the face value that the issuer is willing to pay. This is referred to as the *call premium,* which frequently equals the coupon rate of the bond. It is important to check the call provision of a bond issue before buying. For new issues you may want to go one step further and insist on a final copy of the prospectus from the broker. Often the preliminary prospectus is skimpy on early call details (Antilla, 1992). Even when buying noncallable or deferred callable bonds, seek written assurances from your broker as to their call status.

Besides the call provision, the refunding provision in the bond indenture is important. There are nonrefundable bonds that can indeed be called and refunded. However, the refunding must be with "clean money," which is raised either from internal sources of funds or the selling of stocks or assets. Nonrefundable bonds cannot be repaid from the proceeds of selling lower coupon rate debt. May Department Stores was named in a lawsuit for redeeming more than $160 million of high-interest bonds with a simultaneous offering of new bonds at a lower coupon rate. May Department Stores used a technique known as a STAC, which is the simultaneous tender offer and cash call.

A STAC works in the following way: the company with outstanding bonds announces to its bondholders that they can voluntarily turn in their bonds at a premium price. A heavy hand is applied to those bondholders who do not voluntarily turn in their bonds. They are told that their bonds will be called for cash later at a lower price. In other words, the gist of a STAC is: turn in your bonds for a higher price because if you don't, the company has enough cash to call them in.

Call and refunding provisions are important to investors, particularly if the bonds are purchased at a premium price and/or market rates of interest are at or near their trough.

WHAT ARE JUNK BONDS?

Junk bonds are not a special type of bond; they are regular high-risk, low-rated bonds. These corporate bonds have ratings of BBB (Standard & Poor's) and Baa (Moody's Investor Services) or less, which includes a range of poor quality debt close to default. Some of these bonds have no ratings.

In order to entice investors, coupon rates of junk bonds are higher than the coupon rates of investment-grade bonds. There are two major reasons for these higher coupon yields:

1. The issuers of junk bonds are generally young growth companies with weak balance sheets or financially troubled companies for whom junk bonds are one of the few alternatives left to raise capital. However, large, established companies that are financially troubled also issue junk bonds.

2. Many corporations have used junk bonds to finance the takeovers of other corporations.

The junk bond market has grown since the 1980s, when Michael Milken and Drexel Burnham and Lambert opened up the junk bond market and sold these bonds directly to the public. By establishing a network of potential investors, companies had a lower-cost alternative to raising funds versus the traditional sources of borrowing from banks prior to the growth of the junk bond market. The junk bond market is now an important part of the corporate bond market.

Junk bond prices are more volatile than better quality debt, but over the years default rates have not been significantly higher than better quality issues. Junk bonds do not perform well for investors when the economy moves into recession. In 1990, for example, junk bond prices plummeted and many junk bondholders found that they held illiquid investments (no buyers for their bonds). Then, with the steep declines in bond prices, the junk bond market proved to be an attractive speculation and the junk bond market rallied for about 18 months into 1992, providing holders with capital appreciation akin to stockholders.

For investors who buy and sell junk bonds at the right time, the rewards are large. The risks are high, though, and that is why yields of junk bonds are so attractive. Investors are giving up a degree of safety because junk bonds have greater price swings and have the overhanging specter of default.

Various studies quote different rates of default, and there are studies done by brokerage firms that tout the relative safety of high-yield junk bonds. In general, junk bonds do well in a strong economy because there is less risk of default. In a weak economy, the risk of default rises. Broad diversification of junk bond issues can lessen the risks of default.

Regardless of which study you choose to believe, you should carefully weigh the following risks against the "promised" higher returns:

- If interest rates decline, there is the risk that issuers of the high-yielding junk bonds will call them and refinance with lower-yielding securities.
- There is the risk that junk bond prices could plummet and investors could lose part of their initial investments.
- There is the risk that during sell-offs in the junk bond market; investors could find that there are no buyers for their bonds.

Investing in junk bonds is not for unsophisticated investors, but for those who are able to analyze the financial statements of companies in order to differentiate the "quality" high-yield bonds from those that are descending along the path to bankruptcy. Some advice for those who are not deterred by the risk of junk bonds:

- Buy only publicly listed bonds so you can follow the price quotes in the newspapers when you buy and sell. The junk bond market has gained a reputation that has not enhanced its credibility. As trading is unregulated and investors do not have access to accurate price information, prices quoted by dealers can vary significantly. For example, Equitable Bag Company was quoted by one dealer at a bid and asked price of 80 and 90, respectively, while a second dealer quoted an 85 bid and a 90 asked price on the same bonds (Mitchell, 1992). By 2004, excessive markups and markdowns of junk bond pricing had not been solved. Several large brokerage firms were fined by the National Association of Securities Dealers (NASD) for excessive markups and markdowns that ranged from 9 to 30 percent. A normal spread between the bid and ask should be no higher than 3 percent for junk bonds. Individual investors are therefore at a disadvantage if they need to buy or sell quickly.
- Diversify your purchases to spread your risk. If you cannot afford to buy many different corporate junk bonds, invest in junk bond mutual funds or ETFs to achieve diversification.
- Avoid buying bonds that are part of small issues (less than $75 million). They can be illiquid.
- Limit the amount that you invest in junk bonds to a small percentage of your portfolio. That percentage should vary according to your investment objectives, risk, level of income, stage of the life, and other personal characteristics.

CORPORATE INFLATION-LINKED NOTES

Rising inflation adversely affects the value of a fixed-income bond by eroding its purchasing power. *Corporate inflation-linked notes* pay monthly interest that exceeds inflation (as measured by the consumer price index) by a specified amount. Consequently, large corporations, including banks and brokerage companies, have issued corporate inflation-linked notes with varying maturities, most typically ranging from 5 to 12 years. Corporate inflation-linked notes differ from Treasury inflation protection securities (TIPS) in the following ways:

- Corporate inflation-linked notes pay interest monthly, whereas TIPS pay semiannually.
- Interest payments on corporate inflation-linked notes are adjusted for inflation monthly, whereas TIPS pay principal adjustments for inflation only at maturity or when the bond is sold.
- Interest payments on corporate inflation-linked notes are taxable at the federal, state, and local levels. Interest on TIPS is not taxable at the state and local levels.
- TIPS investors are required to pay taxes on the inflation-adjusted principal even though this adjustment is not received until maturity or when the bond is sold, whereas corporate inflation-linked note holders receive their yearly inflation adjustments (and pay taxes on the received amounts).
- Corporate inflation-linked notes usually pay higher coupon yields than TIPS to compensate investors for the additional credit and default risk of corporate inflation-linked notes.
- There is a secondary market for both TIPS and corporate inflation-linked notes, but spreads to buy and sell corporate inflation-linked notes are much greater than for TIPS.

Corporate inflation-linked notes provide protection against rising inflation in that monthly payments increase with the increases in inflation. However, if inflation decreases, monthly interest payments also decrease, depending on the decline in the 12-month consumer price index. Like corporate bonds, corporate inflation-linked notes are subject to interest rate risk and credit risk. Before buying, check the credit quality of the issuer of the notes.

HOW TO BUY CORPORATE BONDS

Corporate bonds are bought and sold in the same manner as common stocks. Bonds are bought through brokerage firms with cash or on margin. Purchasing bonds on margin means the investor uses borrowed funds from the brokerage firm to purchase the bonds (stocks). The amount that can be borrowed depends on the margin requirement (set by the Federal Reserve), which is the percentage requirement that must be put up by the investor in cash. The rest may be borrowed. As of June 2008, the margin requirement was 50 percent.

Using borrowed funds to buy bonds could lead to problems if the bonds do not return more than the interest cost on the borrowed funds. On the other hand, if the investment does well, the rate of return is greater for the investor since the investor has invested less of his or her own money.

When you buy a new issue of bonds, you pay no commission. It is absorbed by the issuing corporation. Before investing in a new issue, you should examine the company's prospectus to assess the overall risk.

From the balance sheet, you can determine the level of debt and the number of debt issues that are senior to this one. In the event of bankruptcy, the greater the number of senior issues to this one, the lower the priority of this bond investor's claims.

From the income statement, you can determine whether the level of earnings provides adequate coverage of the interest payments on all the debt issues outstanding, including the issue to be financed. If there is a downturn in sales, you would want to see how much of an interest cover the company has before the earnings become insufficient to service its debt.

If the company is currently selling off assets to generate funds and the debt-to-total assets ratio is high, warning flags should go up about this issue. This process of analyzing the financial statements is particularly important when considering the purchase of new, lower quality, corporate issues. The financial statements of listed companies can be obtained from the Internet on the government Web site www.edgar-online.com.

Existing corporate bond issues trade on the over-the-counter market and a number of corporate issues are listed on the New York Stock Exchange (NYSE). Trading of listed bonds does not take place in the same location as common stocks. In April 2007 the NYSE replaced its older automated bond system with a new online system, based on its electronic equity market Arca, to trade corporate bonds. The goal of the new system is to improve pricing transparency and increase its trading volume. Individual investors are able to obtain bond prices and trading details on the NYSE's Web site www.nysedata.com. Another Web site to obtain bond prices is www.bondsonline.com.

The advantage of buying listed bonds is that their prices also appear in the daily newspapers, which gives investors the opportunity to check up on closing prices of bonds. Bonds that trade over the counter are unlisted, and bond price quotes vary considerably from dealer to dealer. This is especially true for lower quality, inactively traded bonds where the size of the spread between the bid and ask prices can be quite large. The junk bond market is noted for unruly trading. Only when a system is in place where dealers report their prices will inefficiencies disappear. Thus, when buying unlisted bonds, it is almost imperative that investors shop around for the best quotes from different brokers.

It is always a good idea to ask for both the bid and ask price of the bond that you are interested in buying, because the size of the spread tells you much about that bond issue.

- A large spread (4 percent or more) indicates that the bond is more than likely illiquid (cannot resell quickly), inactively traded, and possibly linked to some other bad news such as a potential downgrading in ratings (Thau, 1992).
- A small spread indicates the opposite: active trading with little risk of resale.
- Higher transaction costs are charged if investors buy or sell a small number of bonds (less than 10 bonds).

For existing bond issues, you will not see a prospectus, but before investing, you should request the latest company information from your broker or research the company's financial statements on the company's Web site.

When buying bonds, investors might pay more than the ask price due to *accrued interest* on that bond. Bonds earn interest daily, but corporations only pay out the interest once or twice a year. Therefore, if a bond is purchased between the dates that interest is paid, the buyer then owes the seller for the accrued interest for the number of days that the seller owned the bond. The amount of accrued interest is added to the purchase price of the bond. The accrued interest is stated separately on the confirmation statement sent from the brokerage firm when the bonds are bought or sold. Table 10-1 illustrates how accrued interest is computed.

TABLE 10-1

Accrued Interest

When you purchase a bond between coupon interest dates, you need to pay the amount of interest that is owed up to the date of purchase, called accrued interest. For example, suppose you purchase a bond on October 1, with a coupon of 6 percent, paid semiannually on June 1 and December 1 that matures in 4 years. You owe the seller for 4 months of interest, because on December 1 you will receive 6 months of interest (even though you only owned the bond for 2 months). The coupon interest paid on June 1 and December 1 is $30. Consequently, accrued interest of $20 (4/6 × $30) is added to the purchase price of the bond. So if the bond is selling for $870.73 on October 1, this price includes $20 of accrued interest. When the price includes accrued interest, it is referred to as the *dirty price*. The *clean price* is the price minus accrued interest.

Bonds that are in default do not pay interest and are said to trade *flat*. These bonds do not trade with accrued interest. In the bond quotes in the financial pages of the newspapers, an F next to the bonds signifies that it is trading flat.

Bondholders can sell their bonds in the secondary market before maturity or call. For listed bonds, investors can get an idea of the price from the newspapers. Bear in mind that newspapers only list one price for bonds, whereas bonds have a bid and ask price. Investors buy at the higher price (ask) and sell at the lower price (bid). The difference or spread is how dealers and brokers make their money from the trade. Unlisted bonds that are traded in the over-the-counter market are likely to trade with higher spreads than listed bonds.

Online bond trading has been slow to take off with individual investors and hasn't met with the same success as online stock trading. There are several reasons for this:

- Bond dealers make their money from buying and selling bonds, and if the spreads narrow, their profits are reduced. Hence there is resistance to providing greater transparency in bond pricing. Consequently, bond market pricing is fragmented.
- A greater number of bonds than stocks trade over the counter, which means that individual investors are not aware of the different issues available.
- Investors cannot check the prices of these bonds unless they call up their individual brokerage firms.

- Placing trades online does not ensure that investors are getting the best prices because of the fragmented nature of pricing bonds.

Electronic bond trading may take off in the future, but even with electronic trading, investors should pay attention to finding the lowest costs for their transactions (Zuckerman, 1998).

As mentioned earlier, bonds may be retired before their maturity dates. Many corporate bonds have *sinking fund* provisions in their indentures, which are used to help with the retirement of the bond issues. Instead of the entire bond issue being retired at maturity, a sinking fund allows the corporation to make periodic payments to retire parts of the bond issue before maturity.

With one type of sinking fund, the company randomly selects the bonds to be retired, and then calls them for redemption. Once these bonds are called, they no longer earn interest. For bonds with this kind of sinking fund provision, you would not want to leave your bonds in street name (in the custody of the brokerage firm), unless you are a large investor with tremendous clout in that brokerage firm, and therefore know that they will turn in other investors' bonds first.

In another type of sinking fund, a corporation makes payments to a trustee who invests the money, and then the entire amount accumulated is applied to retiring the bonds at maturity.

Corporations may also repurchase their bonds in the bond market and retire them. This practice occurs more frequently when the bonds are trading at a discount. Investors who sell their corporate bonds do not know if it is the issuing corporation who is buying them back.

Corporations might announce their intentions to repurchase their bonds and offer a set price to buy them back. In such a situation, bondholders are not required to sell their bonds back to the corporation if they don't want to.

WHAT ARE THE ADVANTAGES OF CORPORATE BONDS?

- Corporate bonds pay higher coupon yields than Treasuries and agency bonds of similar quality. Generally, good quality corporate bonds can pay coupon rates of 1 to $1\frac{1}{2}$ percent more than those of Treasuries. Junk bond coupons are much greater in order to compensate investors for greater credit and default risk.

- Corporate bonds pay higher total returns relative to other fixed-income securities. Investors can increase their current rates of return by purchasing lower quality bonds, but they face increased risk of default on interest and principal.

- Income and principal are relatively safe on high-quality corporate bonds.

- Investors can receive capital gains from purchasing bonds when market interest rates are falling (bond prices and interest rates move in opposite directions). However, capital losses may be incurred if bonds are sold when market interest rates are rising. For investors willing to take higher risks, the junk bond market provides investors with opportunities for larger capital gains and higher returns.

- Corporate inflation-linked notes protect against the erosion of purchasing power from rising inflation.

WHAT ARE THE DISADVANTAGES OF CORPORATE BONDS?

- Corporate bond prices are adversely affected by rising inflation and rising interest rates. This affects all fixed-income securities and is a basic disadvantage of all bond investments.

- Interest from corporate bonds is taxable at all levels (federal, state, and local) whereas interest from Treasuries and certain agency bonds are exempt from state and local taxes.

- Corporate bonds are exposed to greater credit risk (than Treasuries and government agency bonds) as well as to event risk. The latter risk is nonexistent for both Treasuries and government agency bonds. The lower the quality of a corporate bond, the greater is the credit risk.

- Investors selling corporate bonds may face illiquidity for several reasons:
  - If the ratings of the issuer decline or there is bad news concerning the issuer's financial position, holders may have difficulty selling their bonds without sacrificing

large price concessions. This is especially true in the junk bond market where nervousness can send junk bond prices on a downward spiral.

- If investors only have a small number of bonds to sell, there might be large price concessions when selling.
- When market interest rates are rising, existing bond prices are driven down further.
- When spreads widen between bid and ask prices, it may be more difficult to buy or sell specific amounts of bonds.

- Corporate bonds with call provisions can be called when investors least want their principal returned to them (after market rates have fallen).
- Spreads between bid and ask prices on corporate bonds are greater than those on Treasuries and government agency bonds.
- Spreads on unlisted junk bonds can be quite large.
- The junk bond market has been plagued by some abusive practices as well as large market moves in prices before important corporate news announcements, implying insider trading on advance knowledge.

CAVEATS

Before buying corporate bonds, check the following:

- The credit ratings of the issue.
- The seniority of the issue.
- The call and refunding provisions. Investors can avoid losses of principal by not buying higher premium priced bonds with higher coupon rates than market rates that could be called at lower premium prices. In other words, check whether the premium price exceeds the call price.
- The sinking fund provision.
- Whether there is "poison put" protection against event risk.
- Whether the bonds are part of a small issue, less than $75 million—avoid buying bonds of small issues.
- Whether the bonds are listed or whether they trade over the counter.

- The maturity of the bond. The longer the maturity, the greater is the risk. Every now and again, corporations issue bonds with 50-year and 100-year maturities. With this time period, a lot can happen to affect the company's ability to repay the issue. The Disney Corporation issued a 100-year bond that will mature for the next generation's children, grandchildren, or great-grandchildren. With this time span, stocks are a better investment.
- Risk-averse investors should buy good-quality corporate bond issues.
- Investing in corporate bonds requires large sums of money to achieve a diversified portfolio to lessen the risks of default.
- Investors in junk bonds should not invest a large portion of their investment funds in this category.

Be sure to first compare the coupon yield of the corporate issue to the yields offered on similar maturity Treasuries and government agency bonds to see if the spread warrants the additional risks that corporate bonds are exposed to. For investors who cannot tolerate higher risks, avoid junk bonds, which only guarantee sleepless nights. For risk-averse investors, choose high-quality corporate issues.

QUASI-CORPORATE DEBT PREFERRED STOCKS

Quasi-corporate debt preferred securities are hybrid securities with features of both debt and preferred equity. Each sponsor or investment bank has its own acronym for these securities: MIPS (monthly income preferred securities), TOPrS (trust originated preferred stock), QUIDS (quarterly income debt securities), QUIPS (quarterly income preferred securities, or Corts (corporate-backed trust securities).

The common features of these securities are:

- A par value of $25 instead of the traditional $1,000 par for a bond.
- Listed on the stock exchanges as opposed to the bond exchanges.

- Pay regular interest at more frequent intervals than bonds.
- Most have a maturity date. There are some issues that are perpetual like common stock.
- Many of these issues have call provisions.
- If the issuer has financial difficulties, it can delay interest payments without any comeback from holders of the securities.
- In bankruptcy, bondholders are paid first before holders of these securities.

Generally, these securities are easier to buy than regular bonds, because they are listed on the stock exchanges where prices are available, and they do not require as large a capital outlay with the lower par value. Table 10-2 lists some of these securities.

The first of the issues listed is JC Penney's corporate-backed trust securities (Corts) with a coupon of 7.625% with a maturity on March 1, 2097. The closing price of this issue as of July 2006 was $25.58, which is a slight premium to its par value. The rating of this trust preferred issue is the same as the JC Penney 7 5/8 percent bonds in the trust. There is a call provision for this issue that inserts a ceiling on the appreciation of the issue when interest rates decline. If this issue is bought at $25.58 per share and held to maturity in the year 2097, the yield to maturity will be 7.5 percent (Faerber, 2008).

JC Penney's corporate asset-backed corporate (Cabco) securities were also issued with a 7.625 percent yield and trade under the ticker symbol PFH, pay a dividend of $1.91, and were trading at $25.26 per share in July 2006. In the early 2000s, JC Penney was not

Table 10-2

Quasi-Corporate Debt Preferred Securities Issues

Company	Symbol	Div	Price (close)*	Yield	Net Change
Cort JC Penney	KTP	1.91	$25 .58	7.5%	I0.18
Cabco JC Penney	PFH	1.91	25.26	7.6%	0.06

* July 2006
Source: Esme Faerber. *All about Stocks* 3rd Ed. McGraw-Hill Publishing Co. 2008, p. 41

as financially sound as it is in 2007, and its Cabco securities were listed as junk bonds.

There are some caveats that investors should be aware of:

- Be cautious when paying a premium for an issue with a call provision. If the issue is called, you receive the par value, $25, or the call price, which means that you can lose some of your capital.
- These companies can suspend their interest (dividends) during times of financial hardship.
- Companies with balance sheets that may be over-leveraged might use this type of security to raise funds. Consequently, you should look for issues with strong credit ratings.

CORPORATE BOND MUTUAL FUNDS

Instead of investing directly in individual corporate bond issues, investors can invest indirectly in these issues through corporate bond mutual funds. A mutual fund pools the money from investors and invests in different corporate bond issues. Investors receive shares in the fund that are proportionate to the amount of their investments.

HOW TO CHOOSE A CORPORATE BOND MUTUAL FUND

The types of corporate bonds chosen by the fund are determined by the fund's objectives. Corporate bonds may be categorized in terms of:

- *Quality.* The higher the credit quality of the fund, the lower the risk and the yields. The lower the credit quality of the fund, the higher the risk and potential returns.
- *Maturity.* This is the average length of time of the maturity of the corporate bonds in the fund. These are generally classified as short-term, intermediate-term and long-term. The longer the maturity, the greater the risks and the greater the potential returns (assuming a normal yield curve).

Table 10-3 shows the types of bond funds issued by mutual fund families using these two dimensions. Not every fund family will offer all nine permutations of these corporate bond funds, but this is a good planning tool to use to determine which type of corporate bond fund (funds) to invest in.

High-quality bonds have a low risk of default. Low-quality bonds (junk bonds) have a high risk of default.

Shot-term bond funds have an average maturity of 1 to 3 years for their bonds. Intermediate-term bond funds have an average of 7 to 10 years for their bonds. Long-term bond funds have an average maturity of 15 to 25 years for their bonds.

The lower your risk tolerance, the more you would move to the left side of the table, and depending on your time horizon, to the top, middle, or bottom of the table. If you have a long time horizon, you would choose the middle or bottom rows (intermediate-term and long-term funds), which are also most sensitive to changes in market rates of interest.

This grid is a good tool to identify the corporate bond mutual fund or funds that best conform to both your time horizon and level of risk tolerance. If you cannot determine which types of funds are suitable, it is not advisable to invest in all nine different

Table 10-3

Types of Corporate Bond Mutual Funds

M a t u r i t y		High-quality	Medium-quality	Low-quality
	Short- term	High-quality Short-term fund	Medium-quality Short-term fund	Low-quality Short-term fund
	Medium term	High-quality Intermediate-term fund	Medium-quality Intermediate- term fund	Low-quality Intermediate-term fund
	Long term	High-quality Long-term fund	Medium-quality Long-term fund	Low-quality Long-term fund
		High	Medium	Low

Quality

Source: Morningstar Funds

corporate bond funds by default. This would be overkill. Nor is it advisable to have all your eggs in one basket so to speak. You do want some diversification in your bond portfolio.

What Are the Risks of Corporate Bond Mutual Funds

In addition to the risks that pertain to mutual funds, corporate bond funds are exposed to many of the same risks as the corporate bonds that are their underlying assets.

The *risk of default* is a greater risk for corporate bonds than for other types of bonds. However, with corporate bond mutual funds, the risk of loss from the default of an individual corporate bond issue is lessened. The diversification achieved by bond mutual funds lessens the impact of the loss from unexpected defaults, because the percentage share of each individual bond issue is a small part of the total value of the bond fund.

There is always the *risk of loss of principal* when investing in bond mutual funds. Unlike money market funds, in which the net asset values (the share prices) are held constant, the share prices of bond mutual funds fluctuate. This is because bonds held by the funds fluctuate in value daily, responding to changes in interest rates, credit quality, and the length of time to maturity. If the share price of the bond mutual fund falls below the purchase price of the shares at the time of sale, the investor experiences a loss of principal invested.

Interest rate risk impacts the share price of bond funds differently depending on the composition of the bonds in the funds. For example, the share prices of two different long-term bond funds might react differently to the same increase in market rates of interest. If the one bond mutual fund has an average maturity of 15 years and the other 25 years, the latter fund is exposed to a greater fall in share price when market rates of interest rise. Similarly the quality of the bonds also affects the volatility of the share price. A high ratio of low-quality bonds (i.e., junk bonds or below investment grade) are much more volatile than a fund composed of higher-quality bonds. For this reason it is important to read the prospectus of each mutual fund before investing. The stated objectives of the fund determine the latitude the mutual fund manager has in choosing investments. For example, if the stated objective of the mutual fund is to invest 65 percent in investment-grade corporate bonds, the investor then knows that the other 35 percent should be examined for credit quality. The mutual fund manager can then increase the overall yield of the fund by investing that 35 percent of the fund in higher yielding lower quality bonds.

How to Buy Corporate Bond Mutual Funds

Corporate bond mutual funds can be purchased directly through mutual fund families or indirectly through brokers, financial planners, and banks. The key difference between buying mutual funds directly and indirectly is that in the latter case you are paying a load or commission. When you buy indirectly through a broker and financial planner, you pay a commission to the broker for the advice. Load funds (which charge a commission to buy or sell shares) have to work harder to recoup the charges to equal the results of no-load funds where all the invested funds are put to work.

Why then do investors buy load funds? The first reason seems to be that many investors feel insecure about choosing a fund on their own. Buying through a broker seems to give them peace of mind that someone else has made the appropriate choice of mutual funds for them. Yet when you compare the mutual funds offered by the brokerage houses such as Merrill Lynch with those offered by the Vanguard family of funds, the over-riding difference boils down to cost. The brokerage house mutual funds charge loads and the operating costs of these funds are much higher than the no-load Vanguard funds, which have the lowest operating costs in the mutual fund industry. These operating costs are paid for by none other than you the investor!

Second, many brokers advocate that load funds outperform no-load funds. This is a stretch for bond mutual funds. After loads are deducted, it is very hard for a load corporate bond fund to catch up to the no-load fund let alone outperform the no-load fund. The reason is because bonds are not like stocks where skill in picking stocks is a factor. If investment grade bonds return 6 percent, the only way a mutual fund manager can boost returns of his investment-grade corporate bond fund is to invest in higher risk, lower quality bonds. As pointed out in the previous section, buying a corporate bond fund for higher yields can also result in a greater loss of capital should interest rates increase.

No-load corporate bond mutual funds can be purchased directly through the mutual fund family. Financial magazines and newspapers, and fund family Web sites publish quarterly results of the different bond funds. By analyzing the long-run performances of these funds, you can narrow your list of prospective funds to choose from. Call the toll free numbers of these funds to obtain the prospectuses of each of the funds. You can also download a fund's prospectus from the fund family's Web site. Examine the fund's objectives, expense ratio, quality of holdings, and total returns before you invest.

When you decide on a bond mutual fund, you need to fill out an application form that can be sent through the mail, or you can sign up with the fund over the Internet.

Investors should also determine whether a fund has a *back-end load.* This is a charge deducted from your proceeds when you sell your shares in a fund. Many funds include this back-end fee and advertise that there is no front-end load when shares are bought. Look for this fee in the prospectus of the fund. A no-load fund could have this back-end fee, which is as insidious as a front-end load. If a fund has this back-end fee, look for another fund to invest in.

By doing your own research, you can increase your overall return by making your own choice of corporate bond mutual funds to invest in.

What Are the Advantages of Corporate Bond Mutual Funds?

- Corporate bond mutual funds offer individual investors the opportunity to own a fraction of a diversified corporate bond portfolio. By investing the minimum amounts allowed by corporate bond mutual funds, investors own a proportionate share of an excellent cross section of corporate bonds, whereas buying individual corporate bond issues would require an investment of at least $100,000 for a diversified portfolio.
- Corporate bond mutual funds are professionally managed. This is particularly advantageous for investors who do not

have the time or inclination to research and evaluate individual corporate bond issues.

- Mutual funds offer a range of different corporate bond funds with different characteristics. Investors can choose those corporate bond funds that are consistent with their time horizons and level of risk tolerance.
- The shares of corporate bond mutual funds are easier to sell than individual bond issues.
- Corporate bond mutual fund yields are generally higher than those of other types of bond funds. This is especially so for high-yield junk bond funds, which if purchased when interest rates are declining offer an opportunity for greater capital gains than other lower yielding funds.
- When there are small increases in market rates of interest, the share prices of high-yielding corporate bond mutual funds may not fall by as much as the share prices of lower yielding corporate bond funds. However, the higher yielding funds also may have greater risk of default, which could cause the share prices of these junk bond funds to fall more than better quality funds.

What Are the Disadvantages of Corporate Bond Mutual Funds?

- With corporate bond mutual funds there is always the risk of capital loss from having to sell shares at a lower price than the purchase price, even with a long time horizon. The reason is because corporate bond mutual funds never mature. When individual bonds in the fund mature, they are replaced with new issues.
- Corporate bond mutual funds pay dividends that are taxed at all levels of government, whereas municipal bond and Treasury bond mutual funds offer some tax breaks.

Caveats

- Load bond funds rarely outperform no-load bond funds. To increase total returns over long periods, stick with no-load corporate bond funds.

- In periods of rising inflation and rising interest rates, share prices of corporate bond mutual funds decline, resulting in capital losses for shareholders. High-yielding corporate junk bond funds may not give shareholders immunity from sliding share prices due to the increased default risk from the lower quality bond issues in those funds.
- Choose corporate bond funds from mutual fund families that have a wide range of different funds, allowing you greater flexibility to transfer from one fund type to another.

CORPORATE BOND EXCHANGE-TRADED FUNDS

Barclays iShares and the Vanguard Group offer investors choices in their selection of corporate bond ETFs. In April 2007, Barclays launched a high-yield (junk bond) ETF and the Vanguard Group has expanded their offerings by including four funds that are tied to existing bond index funds. There are fundamental differences between the ETFs offered by these two sponsors. The Vanguard Group's ETFs track bond indexes and generally hold many more bonds in their funds, providing broader coverage of the indexes. Barclays uses representative sampling to choose the bonds for its funds, which is a small subset of the index. Consequently, the number of bonds held in the Barclays ETFs (about 140 bond issues in the AGG bond ETF) is quite small by comparison with the Vanguard Group's Total Bond Fund (greater than 2,500 bond issues). The second difference is the expense ratios charged by the two groups of ETFs. Vanguard's bond ETFs have, as of December 2007, lower expense ratios than the Barclays iShares Bond ETFs (11 basis points charged for Vanguard's BND fund versus 20 basis points for Barclay's AGG fund). In a low interest rate environment, it is more difficult for funds that charge more to outperform funds with lower expense ratios.

Barclay's iShares high yield (junk bond) ETF, ticker symbol HYG, gives investors more flexibility to be able to own a share of a diversified portfolio of junk bond securities for a relatively small investment. The default rate of junk bonds is low (1 to 1.8 percent) as of December 2007. The default rate is one of the main variables that determine the spread between Treasury security yields and junk bond yields. As of December 2007, the spread is quite low (2.9 percent; 290 basis points). Spreads range from less than 3 percent to 10 percent, with an average around 4.7 percent.

Junk bonds are volatile and have the potential to deliver double-digit returns, as well as double-digit losses.

Risks of Corporate Bond ETFs

Corporate bond ETFs are affected by changes in interest rates and inflation in the economy. Corporate bonds have higher coupon yields than Treasury and agency securities, and when market interest rates decline, corporate bonds appreciate more than lower yielding coupon bonds. However, when market rates of interest increase, it raises a fear of default by weaker corporate issuers and prices of such bonds decline by significant amounts.

A historically wide spread between Treasuries and corporate bonds indicates that there is higher credit and default risk from issuers. Credit and default risk depend on the quality of the holdings of the ETF. Both the quality and the length of time to maturity of the issues of the bond holdings have a bearing on the volatility of the share price of the ETF. An ETF with higher quality issues is less volatile in price than an ETF that holds lower quality debt issues. Similarly, an ETF with longer average maturities than the holdings of another ETF is also more volatile in price.

Advantages of Corporate Bond ETFs

- It is easy to buy and sell shares at real time prices at any time during the trading day.
- Corporate bond ETFs allow investors to own a portfolio of corporate bonds and by-pass the lack of pricing transparency of corporate bonds.
- Investors do not need large amounts of money to invest in corporate bond ETFs in order to own a part of a diversified bond portfolio.
- Investors can sell short their shares of ETFs.

- Expense ratios of some ETFs are lower than some mutual funds.
- ETF holders are not liable for capital gains on their holdings until they sell their shares.

Disadvantages of Corporate Bond ETFs

- Commissions charged to buy and sell shares and the expense ratios charged diminish returns.

SHOULD YOU CHOOSE INDIVIDUAL CORPORATE BONDS, CORPORATE BOND MUTUAL FUNDS, OR CORPORATE BOND ETFS?

The lack of pricing transparency and the fragmentation of the corporate bond market make it difficult for individual investors to know whether the prices that they receive to buy and sell bonds are reasonable. Corporate bond mutual funds and corporate bond ETFs alleviate this disadvantage. Mutual funds and ETFs also offer the advantages of diversification, smaller investment minimums, and the ease of owning a corporate bond portfolio. Corporate bond mutual funds offer professional management, whereas some corporate bond ETFs track an index.

Mutual funds and ETFs offer investors an easy way to participate in the junk bond market. It is more risky to invest in individual corporate junk bond issues than corporate junk bond funds. The diversification achieved by mutual funds minimizes the impact from any unexpected defaults.

Annual fees and expense ratios decrease dividends paid by mutual funds and ETFs. In addition, there are commission costs when buying and selling shares of ETFs. There are no commission costs when buying and selling no-load funds that have no redemption (exit) fees. The advantage of ETFs over mutual funds is that shares of ETFs can be traded at real time prices throughout the trading day, whereas mutual fund shares of mutual funds are transacted at the closing price (which is not known) at the end of the day. Investors in individual corporate bonds avoid the fees charged by mutual funds and ETFs, which reduce the returns of mutual funds and ETFs. If you invest in funds or ETFs, look for those funds that have low operating fees and expense ratios. Investors in individual corporate issues have the potential to earn higher total returns than mutual funds depending on the composition of the bond investments.

Investing in individual corporate bonds allows investors to hold their bonds to maturity to ensure that principal invested is not lost, assuming the bond issuers do not default on their interest and principal payments. With ETFs and mutual funds there is always the risk of loss of principal, because when bonds mature the funds replace them with new bonds.

Table 10-4 summarizes some of the major differences between individual corporate bonds, corporate bond mutual funds, and corporate bond ETFs. Corporate bond mutual funds have an advantage over ETFs in that shareholders of mutual funds can elect to receive their dividends and capital gains distributions in the form of new shares, without paying any commissions or fees. Before purchasing mutual funds or ETFs, choose the funds with the lowest expense ratios. An ETF with the lowest bid-ask spread indicates that the fund is more actively traded.

Table 10-4

Characteristics of Individual Corporate Bonds versus Mutual Funds and ETFs

	Individual Corporate Bonds	Mutual Funds	ETFs
Ease of buying and selling	Difficult to buy and sell individual bonds.	Easy to buy and sell shares. Trades occur only at the closing price at the end of the day	Easy to buy and sell shares at real time prices during the trading day.
Costs to trade	Commission costs when buying and selling existing corporate bonds on the secondary market. Lack of transparent pricing of bonds.	None when investing in no-load mutual funds.	Commissions incurred for each trade. Transparent prices of shares.
Income stream	Income stream remains fixed.	Income stream varies from month to month.	Income stream varies.
Management fees	None	Vary depending on the fund.	Vary depending on the ETF

	Individual Securities	Mutual Funds	ETFs
Returns	Return is not diminished by fees.	Variable return reduced by the total fees charged by the fund.	Variable return reduced by the total fees charged by the ETF.
Tax planning	Easy to predict income and plan capital gains and losses.	Unpredictable distributions of income and capital gains can upset careful tax planning.	More tax efficient than a mutual fund.
Investment amounts	Requires a minimum of $25,000- $50,000.	Required minimum investment amounts vary by fund.	Minimum purchase is a single share of stock.
Safety of principal	If high quality bonds are held through maturity, principal is recovered.	A chance that principal may not be fully recovered if share price is below the purchase price when shares are sold.	Fluctuating share price could result in a loss of principal.
Holdings	Known	Not disclosed until the end of the quarter.	Known, although it can change over time.
Diversification	Need large amount of money to build a diversified portfolio.	Small investment buys a holding in a diversified portfolio.	Small investment buys a holding in a diversified bond portfolio.

REFERENCES

Antilla, Susan, "Nonrefundable Bonds Can Indeed be Refunded." *New York Times*, November 21, 1992.

Mitchell, Constance, "Hourly Price Quotes on Some Junk Bonds Planned in Bid to Curb Unruly Trading." *Wall Street Journal*, November 11, 1992, p. C1.

Faerber, Esmé, *All About Stocks*, Chicago: McGraw-Hill, 2008.

Thau, Annette, *The Bond Book*, Chicago: McGraw-Hill, 1992.

Zuckerman, Gregory, "Online Push Barely Budges Bond Trading," *Wall Street Journal*, December 28, 1998, pp. C1, C15.

CHAPTER 11

Municipal Bonds

KEY CONCEPTS

- What is different about municipal bonds?
- Are municipal bonds suitable for you?
- The types of municipal bonds
- The risks of municipal bonds
- How to buy and sell municipal bonds
- The advantages and disadvantages of municipal bonds
- Caveats
- Municipal bond mutual funds
- Municipal bond exchange-traded funds

Municipal bonds are bonds issued by state, county, city, or other political entities. Ownership of municipal securities is diverse: individual households hold municipal bonds directly and/or indirectly through mutual funds, unit trusts, and exchange-traded funds (ETFs).

WHAT IS DIFFERENT ABOUT MUNICIPAL BONDS?

Interest paid by most municipal bond issuers is exempt from federal income taxes and from state and local taxes if the bonds are issued in the state and local tax area. In such a case, the issue would be triple tax exempt. For example, if you live in a high tax state, you may want to buy bonds issued by your state or local government, which can improve your yield by a percentage point or so. This federal tax exemption benefits not only individuals who buy municipal bonds, but also the states and localities issuing them, since they can pay lower coupon yields than regular taxable bonds.

Most municipal bonds issued are tax exempt at the federal level, but there are some that are not tax exempt at the federal level. With the Tax Reform Act of 1986, Congress deemed municipal issues with nonessential purposes to be taxable at the federal level. However, these bonds are exempt from state and local taxes. Nonessential purposes include those issued to raise funds for sports stadiums, parking facilities, conventions, industrial parks, and pollution control facilities.

Another tax wrinkle from the Tax Reform Act of 1986 involves industrial development bonds issued after 1986. Industrial development bonds are those where 10 percent or more of the proceeds raised by the sale of the bonds are used by private firms. For example, a state may issue industrial development bonds to finance a building, which it leases to a private corporation.

Interest income received from industrial development bonds is treated as a preference item and may be subject to the alternative minimum tax (AMT) that some individuals pay. The AMT is an additional tax that individuals in high income tax brackets with large deductions may pay. The AMT is designed to ensure that individuals in high income tax brackets who may not be subject to regular federal income taxes (due to large deductions) are required to pay some federal taxes.

Thus, interest income from industrial development bonds that is exempt from federal income taxes can trigger the AMT. This would not concern investors who are not subject to the AMT. In fact, industrial development bonds are attractive to investors as they tend to have slightly higher yields than tax-exempt bonds that are not subject to the AMT.

Investors in high tax brackets can circumvent the AMT by buying tax-exempt bonds issued before August 7, 1986, in the secondary market. This is the good news. The bad news is that the supply of these bonds is limited due to institutional investors such as mutual funds, which have already purchased them. Thus, industrial development bonds may not be that attractive to investors who are subject to the AMT.

There is always an exception to the rule. It is 501(c) bonds, which are not subject to the AMT. These are the bonds issued by private, nonprofit hospitals and universities.

Despite the fact that private activity bonds are not tax exempt (at the federal level), and industrial development bonds issued after August 7, 1986, can trigger the AMT, the vast majority of municipal bonds issued by state and local governments and their authorities are tax exempt at the federal level. It is this freedom from federal and possibly state and local taxes that makes municipal bonds so appealing to investors in the higher tax brackets.

ARE MUNICIPAL BONDS SUITABLE FOR YOU?

Most investors want to lower their tax bills, but municipal bonds may not be the right investment for everyone. Buying tax-exempt issues purely to lower tax liability may mean that some investors in some cases may earn more on an after-tax basis if they had bought taxable bonds. This may be true for investors in low tax brackets, who might earn more from taxable bonds even after paying the taxes.

In order to compare municipal bonds with taxable bonds, you need to convert the tax-exempt yield of a municipal to the equivalent yield of a taxable bond. See Table 11-1 for some examples of what taxable bonds would have to yield in order to equal the yields of municipal bonds.

A municipal bond with a tax-free yield of 4.5 percent has an equivalent taxable yield of 5.29 percent for an investor in the 15 percent marginal tax bracket. The equivalent yield of a taxable bond at the investor's tax bracket is the yield an investor would have to earn (on a taxable bond) to equal the yield on a municipal bond. For example, an investor in the 15 percent tax bracket purchasing a taxable bond with a yield of 7.05 percent would earn the equivalent from a 6 percent tax-exempt municipal bond. Put another way, the investor in the 15 percent tax bracket would purchase a municipal bond yielding 6 percent only if taxable bonds of similar maturities were yielding less than 7.05 percent. If this investor could earn more

Table 11·1

Comparison of Taxable Bond Yields to Those of Municipals at Different Tax Brackets

A Municipal Bond with a Yield of:			
4%	4 1/2%	5%	6%
would be equivalent to a Taxable Bond Yield of:			
Federal Income			
Tax Bracket			
15%	4.71%	5.29%	5.88%	7.05%
28%	5.55	6.25	6.94	8.33
33%	5.99	6.72	7.46	8.96
35%	6.15	6.92	7.69	9.23

than 7.05 percent on taxable bonds, municipal bonds would not be considered. However, for investors in higher tax brackets, the taxable equivalent yield is much greater. In the 35 percent tax bracket, the taxable equivalent yield on a 6 percent municipal bond is 9.23 percent. As tax brackets (rates) increase, the taxable equivalent yields increase, and municipal bonds become more attractive.

The following formula shows how to compute the taxable equivalent yield of a municipal bond:

$$\text{Taxable equivalent yield} = \frac{\text{Tax-free yield}}{(1 - \text{Marginal tax rate})}$$

Municipal bonds present earnings opportunities for investors in the highest tax brackets when comparing their yields with 10-year Treasury bonds, which are currently yielding less than 5 percent. Before buying tax-free municipal bonds, you should decide whether the yield at your tax bracket is high enough to warrant the purchase.

A 6 percent coupon municipal bond bought by an investor in the 28 percent marginal tax bracket will have a before-tax return of 8.33 percent:

$$\text{Taxable equivalent yield} = \frac{6\%}{1 - 0.28}$$
$$= 8.33$$

Some states have higher rates of taxation than other states, and this brings the next question to mind: should you buy an in-state or out-of-state bond?

Most states give favorable tax treatment to in-state municipals by exempting the income from state taxes. This also applies at the local tax level if the issue is a local issue. This exemption from state and local taxes increases the taxable equivalent yield when comparing an in-state municipal bond with a taxable bond. To answer the question of whether to buy an in-state or out-of-state bond requires another simple calculation.

Suppose that you are considering an out-of-state municipal bond with a yield of $6\frac{1}{2}$ percent with an in-state bond with a yield of $5\frac{3}{4}$ percent, and the state and local taxes combined are 6 percent.

$$\text{The } after\text{-}tax\ out\text{-}of\text{-}state\ yield = (1 - \text{tax rate}) \text{ multiplied by the}$$
$$\text{out-of-state yield}$$
$$= (1\text{-}0.06) \times 0.065$$
$$= 6.11\%$$

The after-tax yield on the out-of-state bond is 6.11 percent, which is higher than the in-state bond yield, and so the out-of-state bond would be more attractive in this case. High tax states like New York and California have such a high demand for their in-state issues that their yields are often lower than out-of-state municipal bond issues. Bear in mind for comparison purposes that Treasury issues and certain government agency issues are also exempt from state and local taxes but they are not exempt from federal taxes.

Investors who are subject to the AMT should consult their tax advisors or accountants to determine their equivalent yields.

Tax laws change continually, and investors should keep abreast of these changes as to the effects on their investments. Municipal bonds are probably the last great tax shelter left in the code. However, they do not benefit all investors. Generally, investors in the higher tax brackets benefit the most from municipal bonds and those in the lower tax brackets may not find them particularly advantageous to own.

TYPES OF MUNICIPAL BONDS

State and local governments (and their agencies) issue a variety of debt instruments that are classified either by the length of time to maturity or by the way in which the debt is supported. In the case of the former, the debt is classified as short-term or long-term, depending on the time to maturity. In the latter type, the debt issue is secured either by the taxing power of the issuer, in which case it is a general obligation bond, or by the revenues generated by the project, called a revenue bond. There are three types of categories of municipal bonds: general obligation bonds, revenue bonds, and prerefunded bonds.

General Obligation Bonds

General obligation bonds are issued and backed by the full faith and credit of states, counties, cities, towns, schools, and special districts. The interest and principal payments are secured by the taxing power of the issuing authority. In other words, the interest paid to bondholders comes from unlimited taxing authority, but in reality, it might not be easy to enact their "unlimited" taxing powers. For example, New York City defaulted on its general obligation notes in 1975 and California's Orange County declared bankruptcy in 1994. These two highly publicized bankruptcies have tarnished the so-called ironclad security of general obligation bonds. It is apparent that not all general obligation bonds are equal. Their safety in terms of credit and default risks depends on the economic and financial strengths of the issuers. Just because the issue is a general obligation bond backed by the taxing power of the issuer does not mean that there are no credit risks.

Some obligation bonds are not secured by the unlimited taxing power of the issuer. There are limits on their taxing sources and these are known as *limited-tax general obligation bonds*. There are also certain obligation bonds, which, besides their own characteristics, have certain features of revenue bonds.

Revenue Bonds

Revenue bonds are municipal bonds whose interest and principal payments are made only if there is sufficient revenue generated by the issuing authority. Revenue bonds are issued by states, municipalities, and public agencies such as hospitals, universities, airports, toll roads, and public utilities to increase the revenues generated by the enterprises from their projects, which are used to pay the interest on the debt.

For example, airport revenue bonds might generate revenues based on traffic usage at the airport or from revenues generated by the use of the airport facilities such as leasing a terminal building. In the former case of revenue collection, bondholders should determine whether a growing demand exists for both passenger and airline traffic use of the airport; in the latter form of revenue collection, bondholders should determine whether the lease payments are sufficient to service the debt.

Proceeds from highway revenue bonds might be used to build toll roads or bridges or to make improvements to the highway infrastructure. Bondholders have a claim to tolls collected on the roads and bridges, but what about the improvements to the highways? Improving a highway does not generate revenue. Revenue bonds that are not self-supporting have revenues earmarked to secure the debt. Some examples are gasoline taxes, license fees, and automobile registration fees.

The security or safety of the revenue bonds depends on how essential the services are that the enterprise provides, the flow of revenues, whether these revenues are increasing or decreasing, and whether any other claims to the revenues are made before those of the bondholders. The relative strength of the issuer of the revenue bonds to generate revenues and the ease with which the issuer can cover the interest payments determine the rating of the revenue bonds.

Prerefunded Bonds

For risk-averse investors who want a safe investment with some tax advantages, there are *prerefunded municipal bonds*. These bonds are not backed by their issuers but instead are backed by U.S. Treasury bonds. Prerefunded bonds are created when an issuer of municipal bonds refinances an existing issue with new lower rate bonds. The proceeds are used to buy zero coupon Treasury securities, which are used to back the old bond issue. The bonds from the old issue become the prerefunded bonds. The Treasuries are used as security for the first issue of bonds (prerefunded), which will not mature at the stated maturity but instead will be called at the first call date. Figure 11-1 illustrates how prerefunded issues are created.

Prerefunded municipals have AAA ratings and generally pay slightly higher premium coupons. The disadvantages are that they generally sell at premium prices and they have relatively short maturities in that they are called within a few years after they become prerefunded bonds.

Besides general obligation, revenue bonds, and prerefunded bonds, state and local governments issue short-term municipal notes, which have maturities for periods up to three years. *Anticipation notes* are issued to even out the irregular cash flows of the treasuries of the state and local governments. Among anticipation notes are *tax anticipation notes* (TANs), which are issued in anticipation of taxes to be collected; *bond anticipation notes* (BANs) in anticipation of the proceeds from the sale of long-term bonds; *revenue anticipation notes* (RANs), which are issued in anticipation of revenues coming in; and *tax and revenue anticipation notes* (TRANs), which are a combination of taxes and revenues coming in.

FIGURE 11-1

How Prerefunded Issues Are Created

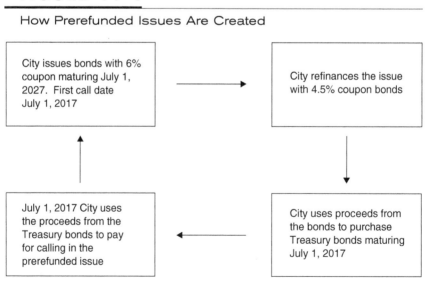

Municipal bond issues might also have special features. Most tax-exempt securities are issued with *call provisions*. In periods of falling interest rates, municipal bond issuers are apt to call in their bonds. Thus, municipal bonds tend to appreciate much less than Treasuries and corporate bonds during bond market rallies. This has a direct effect on the performance of municipal bond mutual funds.

Zero coupon municipal bonds are like regular zero coupon bonds in that they are sold at a deep discount to their face values. Interest is paid at maturity when the investor receives the face value of the bond. The zero coupon municipal bond offers tax advantages over regular zero coupon bonds. The interest that accrues is not subject to federal income taxes. For regular zero coupon bonds, interest accrues each year and is subject to federal income taxes, even though the interest is not received until the bond is sold or matures. These bonds are discussed in more detail in Chapter 13.

Put or option tender municipal bonds are those in which bond-holders have the option of returning the bond to the bond trustee before maturity at face value. Typically, this type of bond is either backed by the revenues of the issuer or by a letter of credit from a bank. The put feature is the opposite of a call feature in the bond provision.

WHAT ARE THE RISKS OF MUNICIPAL BONDS?

Although the number of defaults on municipal bond issues has been small historically, some highly publicized examples have made investors quite conscious of the *risk of default*. Table 11-2 outlines some steps you can take to reduce the risk of default.

Interest rate risk can be greater than the risk of default for quality tax-exempt issues. This situation is not unique to municipal bonds but applies to all fixed-income securities. The longer the term to maturity, the greater is the price volatility because of fluctuations in interest rates. Although you receive greater yields from long-term (30-year) than shorter-term municipals, you face increased volatility and must consider the fact that yield spreads between maturities tend to be wider for municipals than they are for bonds in the taxable bond market.

TABLE 1 1 - 2

Reducing the Risk of Default for Municipal Bonds

The following steps might reduce the risk of default for municipal bonds:

- *Ratings.* You should consider the ratings of a bond offering. Moody's and Standard & Poor's rate these offerings based on a substantial amount of financial information. Because municipal bonds do not have to be registered with the Securities and Exchange Commission, little information about the issuer's financial status is available for investors. States and municipalities might not publish their annual financial statements. To minimize your risk of default, limit purchases to AAA or AA ratings. Because ratings can change over time, do not base your decision on ratings alone.

- *Insurance.* Determine whether the issue is insured. Bond insurance can increase the ratings of an issue. When a bond is insured, it is given an AAA rating even if the bond had a lower rating before the insurance was issued. A bond issue that has a rating of AAA or AA without insurance is a stronger offering than an insured bond with AAA ratings. Insurance corporations, such as Municipal Bond Insurance Association (MBIA) and Financial Guaranty Insurance Co. (FGIC), sell insurance policies guaranteeing the interest payments and the return of principal. The quality of the insurance company will also affect the ratings of the issue.

- *Credit enhancements.* Some issuers have letters of credit from banks and insurance companies. A letter of credit does not guarantee interest payments by a bank or insurance company. Rather, it offers the issuer a line of credit. If the issuer does not have enough cash to cover the interest payments, the bank or insurance company lends the issuer the money. Because this method offers a lower degree of protection than insurance does, you should check the ratings of the bank or insurance company providing the line of credit.

- *Official statement.* Obtain a copy of the official statement or offering circular, which is like the prospectus for corporate securities. In the statement, review:
  - The legal opinion. If there is any doubt as to the tax exemption avoid the issue.
  - A statement of how the issue will be repaid. This ought to be fairly clear.
  - Qualifying phrases. If you read phrases that make you nervous such as "no assurance can be given," find another issue to invest in.

- *Diversification.* Purchase bonds of different issuers, which spreads the credit and default risks associated with any single issuer.

The *risk of a municipal bond being called* is a common risk. Most municipal bonds have call or refunding provisions that allow issuers to call in the bonds when interest rates decrease significantly. You should read the call provision before a purchase to see whether it has any unusual features. Because housing revenue bonds, for example, might not stipulate a call date, they could be called anytime after they are issued. Be careful if a premium is paid on these bonds, because if they are called, you may not recoup your premium price.

Because municipal securities are not as actively traded as government bonds, the spreads between the bid and ask prices tend to be relatively wide, even for the most actively traded issues. This wide spread makes municipal bonds less liquid than Treasury issues and agency bonds.

The larger issues of general obligation bonds and the well-known authorities tend to be marketable, but the smaller, thinly traded issues are less marketable. For some small issues, in fact, the only market that exists might be the issuing locality.

You run the *risk of paying excessive markups on the pricing of individual municipal bonds.* Under current pricing practices, you do not know whether you are being charged an excessive markup by your brokerage firm when you buy individual municipal bonds because these bonds are traded on the over-the-counter markets, where prices are not publicized. When you call your brokers and ask for a price quote, the broker can quote any price (because the prices are not quoted in the newspapers, as they are for stocks). Shopping around at other brokerage firms is difficult unless the investor has an account.

For example, a brokerage firm might buy a particular bond issue at $90 per bond and sell it to investors for $99 per bond. This is a $9 markup, or 9.89 percent. This price is in lieu of commissions because the brokerage firm owns the bonds, and it bears the risk of the bond prices falling. Another brokerage firm might have bought the same issue of bonds at $89 and is offering it to investors at $93 per bond. Lack of pricing information is a big disadvantage, because investors never know whether they are paying excessive markups on the individual municipal bonds that they purchase and sell. You should buy bonds and hold them to maturity, therefore, rather than use them as trading vehicles for capital gains, because this lack of pricing also affects the sale of the bonds.

HOW TO BUY AND SELL MUNICIPAL BONDS

Investors buy municipal bonds at issue or on the secondary market. Financial newspapers, *Barron's,* the *Wall Street Journal*, and the *New York Times* publish weekly the forthcoming sales of new municipals. *The Bond Buyer*, a trade publication about municipal bonds, also provides information about forthcoming sales, in addition to the results of the preceding week's sales of municipal bonds.

State and local governments market their issues in some cases by placing them privately in the market, usually directly to institutional buyers. Mostly, new municipal bonds are placed through investment bankers who offer them for sale to the investment community (the public). The investment banker then forms a syndicate of brokerage firms to sell the new issue. Investors place orders through their brokerage firms for these issues. If their brokerage firms are part of the syndicate, they earn no sales commission on the purchase. The other advantage of buying at issue is that the bonds are priced uniformly (at the syndicate offering price) until all the orders for the syndicate have been filled. Only then can the bonds trade at market prices.

Buying municipals on the secondary market is slightly more difficult because the financial newspapers only print the prices of some popular revenue bonds. Prices of government obligation bonds are not quoted in the newspapers. To learn which bonds are available in the secondary market, you can get a copy of the *Blue List*, published daily by Standard & Poor's. It lists the bonds that dealers currently own in their portfolios and want to sell. The listings of each bond generally include this information:

- The number of bonds for sale in each issue
- The name of the issuer
- The coupon rate and maturity date
- The price (not including the bid and ask spread)
- The name of the dealer selling the bonds

Because a subscription to the *Blue List*, which is the best source of information, is costly for most individual investors, ask your broker for a copy. You should not be surprised to find that by the time that you see the *Blue List,* some of the bond issues already might be sold. Because the bid and ask spreads are not quoted, expect some deviation from the price quoted in the *Blue List*.

Some Internet sites provide daily information about municipal bonds. The Web site www.bondmarkets.com has many municipal bond links. Other Web sites are www.investinginbonds.com and www.municipalbonds.com, which list municipal bonds traded on preceding days, yields, and credit ratings.

Many municipal bond dealers throughout the United States support the municipal bond secondary market. Brokers serve as intermediaries between dealers and institutional and individual investors in municipal bond issues. Many brokerage firms maintain markets in their local and regional issues.

The pricing of municipal bond issues can vary significantly from dealer to dealer, so when you are buying or selling, you should get several quotes from different brokerage firms. The bottom line: shop around, because paying high commissions and wide spreads lower overall returns.

Municipal bonds on the secondary market can trade at either a discount or a premium, depending on a number of factors such as quality, coupon yield, issuer, and length of time to maturity. When you buy municipal bonds at a discount or premium, be aware of the likelihood of incurring capital gains when the bonds are sold or called. For example, if you bought 50 municipal bonds with a face value of $50,000 at a discount of $45,000 in 2007, and in 2007 you bought another 50 municipal bonds with a face value of $50,000 at a premium of $55,000 with both issues maturing in 2007, $5,000 is subject to capital gains in 2007. Puzzled? Most people are.

According to the Internal Revenue Tax Code (Section 171), tax-exempt bonds offer no allowable deduction for amortization of the premium. In other words, you cannot offset your $5,000 gain against your $5,000 loss because the loss is not recognized (the loss cannot be deducted). The premium is amortized over the life of the bond to maturity or until it is called, which results in municipal bondholders being penalized twice:

1. You can buy coupon bonds at a premium, only to find that they could be called at a lower price (than the premium purchase price paid).
2. The loss is not deductible against other capital gains.

The nondeductibility of the amortization is unique to tax-exempt bonds, and you should be aware that you might be liable for taxes because of gains from buying bonds at a discount and through the process of amortization of a premium. To illustrate the latter process, suppose that you buy a tax-exempt bond at a premium of $1,200 and sell the bond five years later for $1,200. As a result of having to amortize or "write down" the premium over time, the adjusted basis of the tax-exempt bond is less than $1,200. A taxable gain occurs, therefore, between the adjusted basis and the selling price.

Municipalities often issue *serial bonds*, which are groups of bonds with different maturities within an issue. Bear in mind that with a serial issue, you can choose the maturity when the issue is originally sold in the market.

The Bush Jobs and Growth Tax Relief Reconciliation Act of 2003, signed into law on May 28, 2003, reduced the amount of taxes that shareholders pay on the receipt of corporate dividends. Shareholders are taxed on their dividend income from qualifying corporations at a rate of 5 or 15 percent, depending on their marginal tax bracket. The prospect of reduced taxes on corporate dividends has had a marked effect on the bond markets, especially municipal bonds.

Municipal bonds, whose interest is tax exempt, are most directly affected by the dividend tax reduction because the tax exempt advantage that municipal bonds offer is sharply reduced. Municipal bond investors usually are attracted to the contractual tax-free interest payments and the return of principal at maturity. In other words, municipal bond investors seek income and capital preservation. Stocks paying dividends offer yields that may be as attractive as the yields offered by municipal bonds along with the possibility of capital appreciation (or, on the downside, capital loss).

Some other advantages of common stocks over municipal bonds might not be as obvious. Transaction costs are higher for municipal bonds than for stocks, making bonds more conducive to buy and hold to maturity rather than as a trading investment. Spreads (the difference between bid and ask prices) on stocks have narrowed to pennies on the dollar, whereas the spreads on municipal bonds are considerably larger. Consider the following spreads on two municipal bonds sold in January and February of 2003, respectively (Foust, 2003):

    Calvert County Pollution   Bought $60 Sold $100
        Control 5.55% 2014

> Boston Water & Sewer   Bought $100 Sold $129
>   10.875% 2009

The Web site www.municipalbonds.com lists prices of bonds that have traded on preceding days, and even though the site does not quote bid and ask spreads, it will flag those issues where the spreads are excessive. The site also lists those municipal bonds that have traded with the largest spreads. In 2003, Bedford County, PA, Redevelopment Authority Revenue bonds with a coupon of 6.75 percent maturing on December 15, 2026, traded with a spread of 34 percent, where an investor sold at $659.88 per bond and another investor bought the bonds at a price of $1,000 per bond.

In addition to excessive markups in price, the municipal bond market is both less liquid and less marketable than the stock market. Many municipal bonds have call features that allow issuers to buy back bonds early, before maturity and often at the par price. Any municipal bonds bought at a premium price (above $1,000) with this type of call feature pose a risk for investors. If the bonds are called at par, investors do not receive the interest to cover the premium, leaving them short of their principal investments.

With these potential pitfalls in the municipal bond market, dividend-paying stocks with the reduction in federal taxes on dividends become much more attractive for investors seeking income with the potential for capital gains. Table 11-3 illustrates how you can compare the yields from municipal bonds with those of common stocks. Another factor to consider as to when to invest in municipal bonds is to look at how expensive municipal bonds are in relation to Treasury bonds. Municipal bonds usually trade at 80 to 90 percent of Treasury bond yields, but as of January 1, 2008, municipal bonds were yielding the same or more than Treasury bonds, making municipal bonds inexpensive to buy (Pollock, 2008).

WHAT ARE THE ADVANTAGES OF MUNICIPAL BONDS?

- Interest on most municipal bond issues is exempt from federal income tax, and it may be exempt from state and local taxes if issued in that state and locality. This benefits high-income investors in the higher tax brackets.

TABLE 11-3

Comparing Yields of Dividend-Paying Stocks and
Municipal Bonds

Qualified dividends from stocks (both common and preferred) are taxed at lower rates
than ordinary income. The maximum tax rate for qualified dividends is 15% for taxpayers in marginal tax brackets greater than 15%, and 5% for taxpayers in lower tax
brackets. The equation for converting dividend yields into after-tax yields is:

$$\text{After Tax Dividend Yield} = \frac{\text{Dividend}}{\text{Purchase price of stock}} \times (1 - \text{investor's dividend tax})$$

A stock purchased at $19 pays a dividend of $1.08 per year. The after-tax dividend
yield for a taxpayer in the 35% marginal tax bracket is 4.83%:

$$\frac{\$1.08}{19} \times (1 - 0.15)$$
$$= 4.83\%$$

If you are seeking investments yielding income, you can compare this after-tax dividend yield with municipal bond yields. A municipal bond with a yield to maturity of
4.5%, therefore, might not look as attractive as the yield from this stock, assuming
that the risk of the company issuing the stock and the authority issuing the municipal
bond is similar.

- They provide regular interest payments for income-depen-
  dent investors.

WHAT ARE THE DISADVANTAGES OF MUNICIPAL BONDS?

- Municipal bonds are less liquid and less marketable than
  government bonds. Investors may have difficulty in selling
  some of the smaller, less actively traded issues in the
  secondary market.
- Many high-coupon municipals have call provisions. Be
  aware of the call provision, especially when buying a tax-
  exempt bond trading at a premium. You could lose part of
  your investment if the issue is called at a lower price than
  the purchase price.

- When bonds are called, investors are exposed to the reinvestment risk of having to reinvest their money into lower-yielding securities.
- Default risk is of increasing concern owing to a number of defaults in the past.
- Municipal bond prices fluctuate with changes in interest rates. The longer the maturity of the issue, the greater is the price volatility.
- Dealer spreads can be quite wide and vary considerably among dealers, resulting in excessive markups for investors.

CAVEATS

- Before investing, taxpayers in lower marginal tax brackets should compare the yields of taxable bonds with those of municipal bonds.
- Municipal bonds are not entirely risk free. Buy municipals with the highest quality ratings and stay away from small, unrated issues and speculative revenue bonds.
- When buying a new issue, check the offering circular for the legal opinion, and the ratings for the issue.
- Be aware of the tax nuances—the possibility of incurring capital gains on the redemption of municipals bought at a discount or premium price.
- Interest on industrial development bonds (IDBs) issued after August 7, 1986, is treated as a preference item, which may trigger the AMT for high-income investors.
- Interest on private activity bonds for nonessential purposes is not tax exempt from federal income taxes.
- Investors should not buy municipal bonds for their IRAs, Keough, or tax-deferred pension accounts. They are already tax deferred.
- As an alternative to municipal bonds, investors in high tax brackets seeking income from their investments should compare the yields of blue chip stocks with the after-tax yields of municipal bonds.

MUNICIPAL BOND MUTUAL FUNDS

Instead of investing in individual municipal bonds, investors can choose municipal bond mutual funds. The two major types of municipal bond mutual funds are general tax-exempt funds and single-state tax-exempt funds. In addition, there are other choices pertaining to the length of maturities, and high yield versus high grade.

General municipal bond funds invest in the fixed-income securities issued by states and localities throughout the United States. *Single-state municipal bond funds* invest primarily in the obligations issued by a single state and the localities in that state, such as the Pennsylvania tax-exempt mutual fund, or the New York tax-exempt mutual fund. The primary advantage of single-state municipal bond mutual funds is that for residents of that state, the interest income generated by that fund is exempt not only from federal taxes, but also state and possibly local taxes. This is particularly advantageous if you live in a high tax state like New York, Massachusetts, or California. Investing in general municipal bond mutual funds means that investors are required to pay state and possibly local taxes on the interest income of the fund, generated by the obligations of the states outside of their state of residence. Keep in mind that capital gains generated by the fund are taxed at the federal and state levels. The decision of whether to invest in a general tax-exempt mutual fund or a single-state tax-exempt fund is determined by your after-tax returns. If you are in a low tax state, it might not be necessary to invest in a single-state fund.

A *well-diversified* fund is exposed to fewer risks of loss from default and credit than a concentrated fund. Although historically there have not been many defaults by states and municipalities, there is always the possibility of the specter of another Orange County. In 1995, Orange County declared bankruptcy and defaulted on some of its short-term taxable and tax-exempt obligations. In this case, the mutual fund families bailed out many of their affected funds so that the shareholders did not have to bear the losses.

Investors can follow the ratings of their tax-exempt mutual funds, which will expose the credit risks of the fund. Standard & Poor's rates municipal bond mutual funds.

Another feature that differentiates municipal bond funds is *insurance*. Some funds are insured. How this works is that the mutual fund pays an insurance company to insure the principal and interest payments of at least 65 percent of the bonds in the portfolio. The insurance gives the mutual fund portfolio manager more leeway to increase the proportion of riskier, high-yield bonds held in the fund. This then becomes a trade-off between the higher costs of the insurance premiums and the higher yields from the riskier bonds. Paying for insurance reduces the overall returns to shareholders.

The *quality* of the holdings of the mutual fund is another consideration. A municipal bond fund with investment-grade holdings typically has lower yields than one with lower than investment-grade bond holdings. However, the share prices of the lower quality funds may be more volatile than the higher quality funds when there are changes in market rates of interest. In general, the higher the credit quality of the fund, the lower the risks and the returns. The lower the credit quality, the higher the risk and the potential returns.

Municipal bond funds vary as to the average length of *maturity* of their bond holdings. They may be classified as short term, intermediate term, and long term. The longer the maturity of the fund, the greater the potential returns (assuming a normal yield curve) and risks. Not all funds in these classifications have exactly the same maturities.

WHAT ARE THE RISKS OF MUNICIPAL BOND MUTUAL FUNDS?

Municipal bond mutual funds are exposed to many of the same risks as their underlying assets, municipal bonds, in addition to those affecting mutual funds.

Interest rate risk impacts the share price of bond funds differently, depending on the composition and length of maturity of the bonds in the funds. Share prices of municipal bond funds with longer average maturities are more volatile when market interest rates change than share prices of shorter average maturities. A composition of low-quality municipal bonds is more volatile in price than a composition of high-quality bonds when interest rates fluctuate. Insured municipal bond mutual funds that hold a large portion of low-quality bonds are not immune to the volatility in share price because of the insurance.

Credit risk and the risk of default are always possible with municipal bonds. Municipal bonds in a mutual fund can be downgraded, which would result in a decline in the share price of the fund. Nor are insured mutual funds immune to credit risk. The municipal bond insurer could be downgraded, which would affect the share price of an insured fund. Diversification diminishes credit risk and the risk of unexpected defaults of single issues. This point illustrates the diversification benefits of general funds over single-state funds. California municipal bond funds that held the defaulted Orange County securities were much harder hit than general mutual funds, which likely held a smaller percentage of those obligations.

There is always the *risk of loss of principal* for mutual fund shareholders, since mutual funds do not have a maturity date on which the original principal is returned. To reduce the risk of loss of principal, investors should choose average maturities of funds that match or exceed their needs for the funds invested.

HOW TO INVEST IN MUNICIPAL BOND MUTUAL FUNDS

Municipal bond mutual funds may be bought directly through the mutual fund families or indirectly through brokers, financial planners, and banks. Buying indirectly results in investors paying sales commissions. By choosing the mutual fund family and the specific municipal bond fund, investors save on paying commissions, but in so doing, investors should make sure that they are selecting funds that do not have loads, either front end or back end. Second, investors should choose low expense ratio funds, which will increase the overall returns over time. The Vanguard family of funds offers several general and single-state municipal bond funds of varying qualities and maturities, which are all low expense ratio funds.

In order to compare the overall returns of the different municipal bond mutual funds, investors should review quarterly, yearly, and longer-term results, which are published in the financial newspapers and business magazines on a quarterly basis. The next step is to request a prospectus from each of the potential fund families.

This can be done by using the toll-free telephone numbers that are published in the quarterly results in the financial newspapers and magazines. The fund's prospectus also may be downloaded from the fund families' Web sites on the Internet. Vanguard's Web site, for example, is www.vanguard.com.

The prospectus should be examined for the following:

- The objectives of the fund, which determine the fund manager's latitude in purchasing riskier securities
- The types of bonds held in the fund
- The expenses charged by the fund
- Whether the fund charges a front-end load and/or back-end load
- The total returns of the fund

It is important to examine the objectives and the holdings of the fund because this will determine the risks of the fund. If the fund manager has the latitude to invest in less than investment-grade securities, investors should not be surprised to find that the share price of this fund is much more sensitive to changes in interest rates and credit scares than funds with higher quality bonds.

Before investing in a fund, an application form needs to be filled out and sent to the mutual fund company with a check for the initial investment amount. Investors can add to their fund's investments by sending checks with an investment stub showing the account number and the amount being invested. Similarly, withdrawals can be made as easily. Investors select the methods of withdrawal from the fund on their application form. They notify their fund either in writing or telephonically as to the amount they wish to withdraw and the money is either sent by check through the mail, transferred electronically to their accounts, or transferred to another type of fund in the family of funds.

WHAT ARE THE ADVANTAGES OF MUNICIPAL BOND MUTUAL FUNDS?

- Municipal bond mutual funds offer investors the opportunity to own a fraction of a diversified municipal bond portfolio. By investing the minimum amounts allowed by the mutual fund, investors can own a proportionate share of a cross-section of municipal bonds, whereas buying individual municipal bond issues would require an investment of over $100,000 for a diversified portfolio.

- With the interest income exemption from federal taxes, municipal bond mutual funds offer investors in higher tax brackets the opportunity for higher after-tax returns than other types of bonds.

- Investors can lower their taxes by investing in a single-state municipal bond fund (same state where they reside), which means that interest income is exempt from federal, state, and possibly local taxes.

- Shares in municipal bond mutual funds are easy to buy and sell.

WHAT ARE THE DISADVANTAGES OF MUNICIPAL BOND MUTUAL FUNDS?

- With municipal bond mutual funds, there is always the risk of capital loss if investors are forced to sell shares at a lower price than the purchase price. The reason is because mutual funds do not mature.

- Some municipal bond mutual funds may hold a percentage of other bond securities, which are not exempt from federal taxes, which means that shareholders may incur some federal taxes on the interest income from those bonds.

CAVEATS

- For high-income taxpayers, some municipal bond mutual funds could trigger the AMT due to their holdings of industrial development bonds that were issued after August 7, 1986. Before investing, check with the mutual fund whether it is subject to the AMT.

- All capital gains incurred by the fund are taxable at all levels of government.

- Do not consider municipal bond funds for your tax-deferred accounts, since they are already tax-deferred.
- Risk-averse investors should seek funds with high-quality bond holdings.

EXCHANGE-TRADED MUNICIPAL BOND FUNDS

As of January 1, 2008, there are at least nine ETFs that track municipal bond indices for investors to choose from. Among the choices are single-state (New York and California), AMT-free, and regular national municipal bond ETFs offered by State Street Corporation, Power Shares Capital Management, and Van Eck Global Group. The Van Eck Group offers the Market Vectors Lehman Brothers AMT-free long-term Municipal Index ETF with a maturity of 17 years or more (ticker symbol MLN), and an intermediate-term AMT-free municipal bond ETF (ticker symbol ITM). Power Shares offers an insured long-term municipal bond ETF.

Because municipal bond ETFs are relatively new to the market, their shares are not actively traded on the exchanges, which results in higher than average bid and ask spreads when investors buy and sell their shares (Anand, 2007). Expense ratios of these ETFs tend to be lower than those of the average municipal bond mutual funds.

RISKS OF MUNICIPAL BOND ETFS

Municipal bond ETFs are affected by changes in interest rates and inflation in the economy. Prices of municipal bonds react inversely to changes in interest rates: when interest rates increase, prices of municipal bonds decline, and when interest rates decline, prices of municipal bonds increase. ETFs that hold bonds with longer-term maturities fluctuate more in price when interest rates change than shorter-term maturity funds.

Credit and default risk depend on the quality of the holdings of the ETF. Both the quality and the length of time to maturity of the issues of the bond holdings have a bearing on the volatility of the share price of the ETF. An ETF with higher quality issues is less volatile in price than an ETF that holds lower quality debt issues. Similarly, an ETF with longer average maturities than the holdings of another ETF is also more volatile in price.

ADVANTAGES OF MUNICIPAL BOND ETFS

- It is easy to buy and sell shares at real time prices at any time during the trading day.
- Municipal bond ETFs allow investors to own a portfolio of municipal bonds and bypass the lack of pricing transparency of corporate bonds.
- Investors do not need large amounts of money to invest in municipal bond ETFs in order to own a part of a diversified bond portfolio.
- Investors can sell short their shares of ETFs.
- Expense ratios of some ETFs are lower than some mutual funds.
- ETF holders are not liable for capital gains on their holdings until they sell their shares.
- ETF fund managers do not have to sell bond issues to raise cash when investors redeem their shares, because investors trade their shares with other investors.

DISADVANTAGES OF MUNICIPAL BOND ETFS

- Commissions charged to buy and sell shares and the expense ratios charged diminish returns.
- Commissions are charged to reinvest the interest paid by the ETF into new shares.

SHOULD YOU INVEST IN INDIVIDUAL MUNICIPAL BONDS, MUNICIPAL BOND MUTUAL FUNDS, OR MUNICIPAL BOND ETFS?

The lack of pricing transparency of municipal bonds makes it difficult for individual investors to know whether the prices that they receive to buy and sell these bonds are reasonable. Municipal bond mutual funds and municipal bond ETFs alleviate this disadvantage.

Buying and selling shares in a mutual fund is far easier than the buying and selling of individual municipal bond issues, particularly with the lack of published pricing information.

Mutual funds and ETFs also offer the advantages of diversification, smaller investment minimums, and the ease of owning a municipal bond portfolio. Mutual funds offer professional management, whereas some municipal bond ETFs track an index.

Mutual funds and ETFs offer investors an easy way to participate in the lower-quality, higher-yield municipal bond market. The diversification achieved by mutual funds minimizes the impact from any unexpected defaults. Single-state municipal bond mutual funds and ETFs offer triple tax-free investing for investors living in those states.

Annual fees and expense ratios decrease dividends paid by mutual funds and ETFs. In addition, there are commission costs when buying and selling shares of ETFs. There are no commission costs when buying and selling no-load funds that have no redemption (exit) fees. The advantage of ETFs over mutual funds is that shares of ETFs can be traded at real time prices throughout the trading day, whereas shares of mutual funds are transacted at the closing price (which is not known) at the end of the day. Investors in individual municipal bonds avoid the fees charged by mutual funds and ETFs, which reduce the returns of mutual funds and ETFs. If you invest in funds or ETFs, look for those funds that have low operating fees and expense ratios. As of January 2008, average expense ratios of municipal bond ETFs are lower than the average charged by municipal bond mutual funds. Investors in individual municipal issues have the potential to earn higher total returns than mutual funds, depending on the composition of the bond investments.

Investing in individual municipal bonds allows investors to hold their bonds to maturity to ensure that principal invested is not lost, assuming the bond issuers do not default on their interest and principal payments. With ETFs and mutual funds there is always the risk of loss of principal, because when bonds mature the funds replace them with new bonds.

Table 11-4 summarizes some of the major differences between individual municipal bonds, municipal bond mutual funds, and municipal bond ETFs. Municipal bond mutual funds have an advantage over ETFs in that shareholders of mutual funds can elect to receive their dividends and capital gains distributions in the form of new shares, without paying any commissions or fees. An advantage of ETFs over mutual funds is that when mutual fund shareholders redeem their shares, the fund manager might have to sell some of their bond holdings to raise cash to pay shareholders for the shares sold. Investors buying and selling shares of ETFs trade their shares with other investors. Before purchasing mutual funds or ETFs, choose the funds with the lowest expense ratios. An ETF with the lowest bid-ask spread also indicates that the shares of that fund are more actively traded.

One method of protecting against interest rate risk with individual municipal bonds is to "ladder" your portfolio. Laddering is a technique of buying several different municipal bond issues with different maturities over a period of time. Investors receive their principal back on the shorter maturities, which can then be reinvested at current market rates of interest. If rates go up, investors reinvest at higher rates. Of course, if rates go down, the coupons of the reinvested securities are lower. In essence, with this technique investors can average market rates of interest over the time period.

Most of all, choose good-quality municipal bond issues. The yield gap between good-quality and lesser-quality municipal bonds is not large enough to justify the risks of buying lesser-quality issues.

Table 1 1 - 4

Characteristics of Individual Municipal Bonds versus Mutual Funds and ETFs

	Individual Securities	Mutual Funds	ETFs
Ease of buying and selling	Difficult to buy and sell individual bonds because of murky pricing.	Easy to buy and sell shares. Trades occur only at the closing price at the end of the day	Easy to buy and sell shares at real time prices during the trading day.
Costs to trade	Commission costs when buying and selling existing municipal bonds on the secondary market. Lack of transparent pricing of bonds.	None when investing in no-load mutual funds.	Commissions incurred for each trade. Transparent prices of shares.
Income stream	Income stream remains fixed.	Income stream varies from month to month.	Income stream varies.

	Individual Securities	Mutual Funds	ETFs
Management fees	None	Vary depending on the fund.	Vary depending on the ETF
Returns	Return is not diminished by fees.	Variable return reduced by the total fees charged by the fund.	Variable return reduced by the total fees charged by the ETF and commissions charged to buy and sell shares.
Tax planning	Easy to predict income and plan capital gains and losses.	Unpredictable distributions of income and capital gains can upset careful tax planning.	More tax efficient than a mutual fund.
Investment amounts	Requires a minimum of $25,000–$50,000.	Required minimum investment amounts vary by fund.	Minimum purchase is a single share of stock.
Safety of principal	If high quality bonds are held through maturity, principal is recovered.	A chance that principal may not be fully recovered if share price is below the purchase price when shares are sold.	Fluctuating share price could result in a loss of principal.
Holdings	Known	Not disclosed until the end of the quarter.	Known, although it can change over time.
Diversification	Need large amount of money to build a diversified portfolio.	Small investment buys a holding in a diversified portfolio.	Small investment buys a holding in a diversified bond portfolio.

REFERENCES

Ablan, Jennifer, "Bonds Bushwacked," Barron's, January 13, 2003, p. MW10

Anand, Shefali, "Municipal Bonds Are Awkward Fit in ETF World," *Wall Street Journal*, October 20–21, 2007, p. B1.

Foust, Dean, "Munis: What's a Fair Price?" Business Week, July 14, 2003, pp. 90- 91.

Mitchell, Constance, "Latest Muni Derivative Gets U.S. Scrutiny," *Wall Street Journal*, February 11, 1993, p. C1.

Pollock, Michael A., "Bonding Time," *Wall Street Journal*, January 3, 2008, p. R7.

CHAPTER 12

Convertible Bonds

KEY CONCEPTS

- Convertible securities
- Their features
- How they work
- The different types of convertibles
- Their risks
- How to buy and sell convertibles
- Their advantages and disadvantages
- Caveats
- Their suitability for investors
- Convertible mutual funds
- Their risks
- How to buy
- Their advantages and disadvantages
- Should you invest in individual convertible securities over mutual funds?

Convertible bonds are hybrid securities that in some years have outpaced all other investments, including stocks. In 1992, for example, convertible bonds as measured by Smith Barney's convertible index increased by 25 percent, which was more than six times the increase in the Dow Jones Industrial Average and the Standard & Poor's 500 Index (Bary, 1993). Convertible bonds also presented opportunities for companies issuing them. During the 1990s, convertible bonds were almost synonymous with free money, in that companies issued these bonds, which were then converted into the stock of these companies, resulting in an avoidance of ever having to repay the initial bond investors. However, if the stock price of a company never appreciates above the conversion price, companies that issued convertible bonds would have to come up with the cash to repay convertible bondholders when the debt matures.

WHAT ARE CONVERTIBLE SECURITIES?

Convertibles are hybrid securities that come in two primary forms: convertible bonds and convertible preferred stock. These convertibles are bonds or preferred stock that can be exchanged for a specified number of common shares of the issuing corporation, at the option of the convertible holder. In a few cases, convertible bonds have been exchanged for preferred stock or other bond issues. However, there are some other rare types of hybrid convertibles, which include payment in kind (PIK) hybrid convertibles, liquid yield option notes (LYONs), commodity-backed bonds, and stock-indexed bonds. Each of these different types of securities has conversion options or relationships to other types of securities or assets. PIKs, for example, pay their holders more of the same units of securities they hold. These are all discussed in more detail later in the chapter.

FEATURES OF CONVERTIBLE BONDS

Convertible bonds have many of the features that are common to both bonds and stocks. Investors buy bonds primarily for the regular payments of income that they pay and the return of principal at maturity, and investors invest in stocks primarily for capital appreciation and income generation if the stocks pay dividends. Convertible bonds provide income and capital appreciation if the stock of the company (issuing the convertible bonds) increases in value.

The downside to convertible bonds is that if both the bond and stock markets decline, convertible bonds are hit even harder in price than individual stocks and regular bonds. In the early 2000s,

AMR Corporation, the parent company of American Airlines, had to withdraw a $250 million 20-year convertible bond offering from the market because of a combination of a weak bond market and the company's poor credit quality.

So why do companies issue convertible bonds when they could raise money by issuing regular debt or equity? By issuing convertible bonds, companies can tap into the credit markets more easily. Because of the conversion feature, companies can issue convertible bonds with lower coupon rates than they would have to pay on regular bonds. Convertible bond issues are usually subordinated to the issuing company's other outstanding debt issues.

Why would investors want to invest in lower-quality, lower-yielding debt? Again, it is the conversion feature that makes the difference. Investors are willing to accept lower coupon rates and lower quality in return for the possible appreciation, if the stock price of the issuing company rises. In other words, investors are sacrificing current income for possible future capital gains. Convertible securities appeal to investors who prefer to receive regular interest payments while waiting for the potential appreciation when the issuing company's stock rises above the conversion price. In general, during down markets, convertible bond prices decline less than stock prices, and in rising markets, convertible bond prices appreciate less than stock prices.

The fact that convertibles are subordinated debenture issues does not mean that only weaker financially troubled companies issue them. Many financially weaker companies do issue convertibles because they can raise funds, which may not have been available through either ordinary debt or equity issues. However, in many cases, financially strong companies have also issued convertibles in order to lower their interest costs from issuing regular debt. Companies such as Anadarko Petroleum, Comcast, Tyco, and Ford Motor Company have issued convertible securities.

HOW DO CONVERTIBLES WORK?

A convertible bond is an unsecured corporate bond that can be converted at the convertible bondholder's option into a specified number of common shares of the issuing company. A convertible bond is a debenture bond with a conversion feature whereby the bond can be exchanged for a specified number of common shares of the issuing corporation at the option of the convertible bondholder. In a few cases, convertible bonds have been exchanged for preferred stock or other bond issues.

Suppose a corporation wanting to raise funds decides that it does not want to issue more common stock, because the market price of the stock is too low. To raise enough cash it would have to issue many more shares of common stock (at the low stock price), which would dilute earnings per share for existing shareholders. A straight debt issue would also be too costly because the company would have to match the coupon rate of comparable existing corporate debt issues with similar risks and maturities. Instead, the company can issue convertible bonds, and because of the conversion feature, investors would accept a lower coupon rate on the issue. The company would need to consider the current market price of its common stock to determine the number of shares that each bondholder would receive on conversion. For example, if the company's stock is currently trading at $18 per share, the company may decide on a conversion price of $25 to make the bonds more appealing to investors. The *conversion price* is the price of the underlying common stock at which the bond is exchanged. The *conversion ratio* is the number of common shares received for each bond, which in this example is 40 shares per bond (1,000/25). The conversion ratio is the face value of the bond divided by the conversion price. The *conversion value* is the market price of the underlying stock into which the convertible bond is exchanged multiplied by the conversion ratio ($25 × 40 shares, which equals $1,000). The following equations show the relationships among the defined terms.

$$\text{Conversion ratio} = \text{Number of common shares exchanged for each bond}$$

$$\text{Conversion ratio} = \frac{\text{Face value of bond}}{\text{Conversion price}}$$

$$\text{Conversion price} = \frac{\text{Face value of bond}}{\text{Conversion ratio}}$$

$$\text{Conversion value} = \text{Price per share of common stock} \times \text{Conversion ratio}$$

Convertible bonds are valued either in relation to the conversion value of the stock or as straight debt. In reality, both of these factors are taken into account in the valuation of the convertible security.

THE VALUE OF A CONVERTIBLE BOND AS STOCK

The value of a convertible security as stock depends on the market price of the common stock. Using the conversion equation, the value of the convertible bond is the number of shares into which the bond is convertible multiplied by the market price of the stock. In the example quoted, if the market price of the stock is $18, the convertible can be exchanged into 40 shares, which is then multiplied by $18, to equal the value of the convertible bond at $720.

The relationship between the value of the convertible bond as stock and the price of the common stock is illustrated in Table 12-1.

Table 12-1

Value of Convertible Bond as Stock

Conversion Ratio*	Market Price of Stock	Value of Convertible as Stock
40	$10	$ 400
40	18	720
40	25	1,000
40	30	1,200
40	35	1,400
40	40	1,600

* The number of shares the convertible is exchanged into.

From Table 12-1, as the market price of the stock rises (column 2), the value of the convertible as common stock increases. The value of the convertible is obtained by multiplying the conversion ratio by the market price of the stock. When the price of the common stock is below the conversion price of $25, the value of the convertible is less than the face amount of the bond ($1,000).

- When the stock price is greater than the conversion price ($25), the value of the convertible is greater than the face value of the bond. Thus, the conversion feature allows for the upside potential of capital gains through appreciation of the stock price.
- Moreover, there is a floor price below which the price of the convertible will not fall, and this is the straight value of the bond.

For example, assume that using the preceding illustration, the market price of the common stock falls to $10 per share. The conversion value is $400, but the market price will not fall below the value of the bond, owing to the value of the cash flows of the coupon interest payments on the bond. Similarly, the market price of the convertible will not be less than the conversion value of the security. This is due in part to the activity of arbitrageurs, who buy and sell the same security in two different markets to take advantage of price differentials. This concept is discussed in the next section. A graphical explanation of the dual pricing concepts of a convertible bond is shown in Figure 12-1.

FIGURE 12-1

Pricing of a Convertible Bond

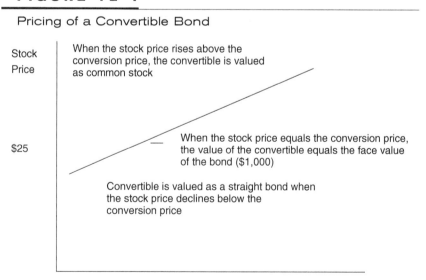

VALUE OF THE CONVERTIBLE BOND AS DEBT

The value of a convertible as debt is determined by the coupon rate, credit quality of the issuer, length of time to maturity, call provision, and market rates of interest. Most convertible bonds have call provisions. The investment value of the bond is determined by discounting both the coupon interest payments of the convertible and the face value of the bond at maturity (assuming that it is not converted) at a comparable rate of return used on similar debt. In other words, the value of the convertible bond is the present value of the cash flows of the coupon payments and the face value of the bond at maturity discounted at an interest rate that includes a risk premium for investing in the security.

As with regular bonds, the value of a convertible bond as debt fluctuates with changes in market rates of interest. When interest rates increase, the price of the convertible bond declines, and conversely, when interest rates decline, the price of the convertible rises. This inverse relationship occurs because the coupon rate on a convertible bond is fixed.

The value of a convertible as straight debt is important because it sets a floor price. When the stock price is trading below the conversion price, the straight bond value provides the floor value and the convertible bond will not fall below this value, because the convertible option is of no consequence at lower stock prices. When stock prices rise above the conversion price, the price of the convertible bond is the conversion value as stock. The convertible bond becomes equity in disguise.

VALUE OF THE CONVERTIBLE BOND AS A HYBRID SECURITY

At low stock prices (below the conversion price) the floor price of the convertible is no lower than its value as a straight bond, and at sufficiently high stock prices (above the conversion price), the price of the convertible is the same as the conversion value into stock. In between these extremes in stock prices, the convertible security generally trades at a premium price over its value as equity and over its value as debt.

These relationships are examined in Table 12-3 using the example of a 6 percent 20-year convertible bond with a conversion ratio of 40 shares. The market rate of interest (or required rate of return) used is 8 percent.

The price of the convertible bond is determined as follows:

$$\text{Convertible bond price} = \sum_{t=1}^{20} \frac{60}{(1+0.08)^{20}} + \frac{1000}{(1+0.08)^{20}}$$

$$= \$ 803.63$$

The price of a convertible bond can be determined using Excel software as illustrated in Table 12-2. Click on f* in one of the top rows of Excel's toolbar, highlight financial, and then click on PV to find the present value of the price of the bond. Enter the data as shown in Table 12-2.

The conversion value as stock is determined using the following equation:

$$\text{Conversion value} = \text{Price per share of common stock} \times$$
$$\text{Conversion ratio}$$

At low stock prices ($5 and $10 per share), the market price of the convertible bond is the same as its value as straight debt, and

Table 12-2

Determining the Present Value of a Bond using Microsoft's Excel Software

Rate	0.08	Rate = Interest rate per period
Pmt	20	Nper = Total number of payments
Pmt	60	Pmt = Payment (interest) each period
FV	1000	FV = Future value (face value) of bond
Type	0	Type = 1 for payments at the end of each period
Formula result (rate) = 803.63		Formula result = Present value of the bond

the premium over the stock price is large. At $25 per share, the conversion price, the market price for the convertible is $1,020, which exceeds both the value of the debt by $216.41 and the value as stock by $20. At a significantly high stock price of $40 for this company, the market price of the convertible is the same as the value as stock, and the premium over the value as debt is very high ($796.41).

This example illustrates that when the stock price rises, the premium paid over the value of the convertible bond as straight debt increases. This increase in premium is because of the importance of the conversion feature on the convertible and the fact that the straight debt becomes less important as the stock price increases.

There is also the probability that the bond could be called, which would force conversion when the stock price is greater than the conversion price. For example, suppose that the convertible bond was bought at $1,410 and the company calls in the bonds when the stock price is trading at $35. Convertible bondholders would not turn in their bonds for $1,000 per bond. Instead, they would convert their bonds into equity, receiving $1,400 per bond

Table 12-3

Premiums on Convertible Bonds

Market Price of Value	Premium of Bond	Premium of over Stock Bond	Convertible	Convertible bond as Stock Debt	Conversion Ratio of B over Share Price Value as ond straight Bond*	Value Non- convertible
$5	40	$200	$803.63	$803.59	$603.59	$0
10	40	400	803.63	803.59	403.59	0
18	40	720	803.63	820.00	100.00	16.41
25	40	1,000	803.63	1,020.00	20.00	216.41
35	40	1,400	803.63	1,410.00	10.00	606.41
40	40	1,600	803.63	1,600.00	0	796.41

* In reality, it is difficult to calculate the market price of the convertible security due to its hybrid nature and the many factors affecting the market price. Therefore, the market prices between the extremes in stock prices in this example are hypothetical and in reality fluctuate around these values.

(40 shares multiplied by $35), which results in a loss of $10 per bond for the bondholder. Thus, as the stock price rises, downward pressure is exerted on the premium over the stock price, and the market price for the convertible converges with the stock value of the convertible.

Most convertible securities trade at a premium over either the stock value or the value as a straight bond.

RISKS OF CONVERTIBLE BONDS

As with any debt security, the *risk of default* is a major concern. This is especially so for convertible bonds, because they are subordinate to the other debt issues of the issuing company. Consequently, convertible bonds are not as safe as the company's senior debt, and in the event of bankruptcy, convertible bondholders stand behind the other bondholders in the collection line. Hence, convertible bondholders might only receive a fraction of their invested principal at best.

Convertible bonds are affected by *interest rate risk*. Convertible bonds are fixed-income securities with coupon rates that tend to be lower than conventional debt issues. Consequently, an increase in market rates of interest causes a greater decline in the price of convertible issues than nonconvertible bonds. Generally, high interest rates tend to depress stock market prices, and a convertible bond is doubly cursed if the issuing company's stock price is depressed. Stock prices and stock markets are both uncertain and volatile, which does not ensure appreciation of the convertible. There is the risk that if the stock price never rises above the conversion value, the convertible bond is not converted, and the convertible bondholder then receives a lower return through the life of the bond than they would have on a regular bond. This lower return is due to the lower coupon yields of convertible bonds than those of comparable nonconvertible bonds.

Convertible bonds mostly have call provisions, and so there is always the *risk of call*. Corporations might call in bond issues when interest rates decline so that they can issue new bonds at lower coupon rates and save money.

PURCHASE AND SALE OF CONVERTIBLE BONDS

Convertible bonds are bought and sold in the same way as corporate bonds. New issues are bought through an underwriter or participating syndicate broker, where investors are not charged a fee or markup.

Convertible securities trading on the secondary market are purchased (sold) through full service brokerage firms, discount brokers, brokerage services offered by banks, and online brokers. Most of the convertible bonds are listed on the over-the-counter markets while convertible bonds of larger, well-known companies are listed on the New York Bond Exchange.

Brokerage fees for purchasing convertible bonds are similar to those charged for buying regular bonds. Markups charged per bond vary depending on several factors, such as the number of convertible bonds purchased, total value of the purchase, and type of broker (full service or discount). It is important to shop around to find the lowest markups and dealer spreads before buying. Investors have the same difficulties obtaining prices on convertible bonds as they do on other types of bonds, such as corporate, agency, and municipal bonds.

Fees for convertible preferred stock are similar to those when buying common stock.

THE ADVANTAGES OF CONVERTIBLE BONDS

- Convertible bonds offer upside potential through capital gains when the stock price of the underlying company rises above the conversion price, and downside protection when the market price of the stock falls below the conversion price since the convertible would be valued at no less than the value of the bond.
- Convertible bond prices generally rise when interest rates decline, which could also coincide with increasing stock prices. This action happened in 2003 and 2004 when convertible bonds outperformed the stock market indices. On an individual basis, much depends on the

fundamental financial factors of the issuing company and the features of the convertible bond. Generally, however, if the stock price of the issuing company keeps increasing, investors will not do as well with convertible bonds as they would have had they bought the common stock of the company instead of the company's convertible bonds.

- Some companies do not pay dividends, and by investing in the convertible bonds of these companies, investors receive a regular stream of income from the fixed-interest payments before conversion.

- Convertible securities offer some protection against inflation, since market prices of both common stocks and convertible bonds rise with inflation. However, if the market price of the common stock does not reach the conversion price and conversion never occurs, then investors receive no protection from inflation as the amount of the interest payments on bonds are fixed.

- Experienced investors can use convertible bonds to profit from diverging prices of the convertible in the bond and stock markets. This action involves the use of arbitrage activities: buying one security and simultaneously selling short the related security. For example, buying the convertible bond and selling short the related stock can result in profits when there are price discrepancies. A definition of arbitrage helps to understand the exploitation of the pricing of convertibles in two different markets. *Arbitrage* takes place when a similar security is bought and sold in different markets in order to exploit price differentials.

For example, if the market value of the convertible bond is $900 (same example used in the previous section), when the stock price moves to $24, arbitrageurs will exploit this price differential for their own profit. The conversion value is $960 (40 shares multiplied by $24 per share), and arbitrageurs would sell short the stock. To sell short is to borrow a security and sell it on the market. Arbitrageurs simultaneously buy the convertible bond for $900 while selling short 40 shares of the stock for $960. The conversion option on the convertible bond is exercised and the shares that were borrowed are tendered. The resulting profit is $60 per bond before taking into account commissions charged for buying and selling the securities. Through this action, arbitrageurs bid up the price of the bonds until there is no longer a price differential. In reality, the price of a convertible bond is rarely the same as its conversion value into stock. Mostly, the price of the convertible exceeds that of the conversion value due to the bond's value. In addition to the upside appreciation due to the conversion value, the value of the bond as debt provides a floor price for the convertible bond. See Table 12-4 for another arbitrage example.

TABLE 12-4

Convertible Bond Arbitrage

What would an arbitrageur do to exploit the differential in this situation?

Convertible bond price: $1,000

Conversion price: $35

Conversion ratio: 28.57 shares

Stock price: $37

1. Buy the convertible bond at $1,000 per bond.
2. Convert the bond into common stock worth $1,057.09 (28.57 × 37 = $1,057.09).
3. Sell the stock, which results in a profit of $57.09 per bond purchased ($1,057.09 – $1,000).
4. The greater the number of bonds purchased, the greater the total profit.

or

1. Sell the stock short (receive $1,057.09).
2. Buy the convertible bonds at $1,000 per bond.
3. Convert the bond into stock and then close out the short position.
4. Realize a profit of $57.09 for each convertible bond or batch of 28.57 shares of the stock.

This example ignores transaction costs.

DISADVANTAGES OF CONVERTIBLE SECURITIES

- In the event of liquidation or bankruptcy of the issuing company, convertible bondholders' claims to the assets are subordinate to the claims of the company's other holders of debt.

- Convertible securities, like all fixed-income securities, are sensitive to changes in interest rates. Convertible bonds generally have call provisions, and when market interest rates decline, there is an increased risk that the issuing company will call the convertible bonds. The issuing company can then refinance their convertible bonds with cheaper debt.

- Yields on convertible securities are generally lower than yields on straight bonds, which is advantageous for corporations looking for a cheaper source of funds than issuing straight bonds. If the bonds are never converted, investors would have received lower coupon yields for the life of the bonds than they would have had they had invested in comparable nonconvertible bonds.

- In the event that the company is bought out, the convertible bondholder is left holding a nonconvertible security that has a lower coupon than other bonds.

WHEN TO BUY CONVERTIBLE SECURITIES

Convertible securities offer the potential for both appreciation and a steady stream of income, but they may not be the best of both worlds. They certainly allow you to hedge your bets in both the debt and equities markets. However, under certain conditions, they might not be the best investments, and you would have been better off owning either regular debt or equity securities.

Generally, convertible securities do well when interest rates are falling and the stock market is rising. This was the case in 1992, 1999, 2003, and 2004 to 2006, when convertible securities outperformed the stock market indices. However, on an individual basis, much depends on the fundamentals of the issuing company of the convertible. If investors like the common stock of a particular company but they are not sure whether the stock market is going to go up, they could buy the company's convertible bonds, which would potentially be less volatile in price swings than the common stock, while receiving a regular stream of interest income. However, if the stock price of the company increases, investors would not do as well with convertibles as they would have had they bought the stock instead of the convertible.

The downside to convertible bonds is that they can be complicated in structure with call provisions, which could result in holders losing money if they had bought the convertible bonds at a premium price. Similarly, if convertible bonds are not converted into equity, investors generally would have been better off with regular bonds, which tend to pay higher coupons.

Convertible securities are suited to investors who have the knowledge of the workings and intricacies of these specialized securities who can hedge their bets in the bond and equity markets.

WHAT THE CONVERSION PREMIUM OR DISCOUNT MEANS

A *conversion premium* is the excess amount at which a convertible bond sells above its conversion value. A convertible bond generally sells at a premium price over its straight bond value and conversion value into equity. For example, Navistar International issued senior convertible bonds in a private placement in December 2002 at a conversion premium of 30 percent on a closing equity price of $26.70. The price of a convertible bond is usually quoted as a percentage of its conversion value, which is also known as the conversion premium. For example, a convertible bond selling at $1,000 with a straight bond value of $798 and a conversion value of $852 is trading at a conversion premium of 17.4 percent:

$$\text{Conversion premium} = \frac{\text{Price of the bond} - \text{Conversion value}}{\text{Conversion value}}$$

$$= \frac{\$1,000 - 852}{852}$$

$$= 17.4\%$$

In 1999, Amazon.com Inc. sold $1.25 billion convertible bonds at a 27 percent conversion premium. Several years ago, the 6 percent convertible bonds of Battle Mountain, a gold mining company, were trading at a 141% premium over its equity value, whereas the 7 percent convertible bonds of another mining company, Couer d'Alene, were trading at a 31 percent premium over the equity value. So, what does the conversion premium mean and how is it interpreted? In general, the higher the conversion premium, the more the convertible trades like a bond, and, conversely, the lower the conversion premium, the more it performs like a stock. Investors pay a premium for the convertible security's higher yield and reduced downside risk. The conversion premium is affected by several factors. A company with a volatile stock price has a greater conversion premium (due to the fact that conversion is more likely with a volatile stock). After a convertible is issued, the conversion premium decreases if the stock price rises. For example, Couer d'Alene's convertible bond, with a lower premium over its equity value, offers greater appreciation potential than Battle Mountain's higher conversion premium bonds. The length of time to maturity also affects the conversion premium. Convertible bonds with long maturities have higher conversion premiums, due to the greater likelihood of the stock price being able to rise above the conversion price. The shorter the time left to maturity, the smaller the conversion premium. See Table 12-5 for a discussion of the hazards of investing in convertible bonds and the downside risk of not being able to convert the bonds to equity.

CAVEATS

- Do not buy convertible securities unless you are willing to buy that company's common stock. If the convertible security is never converted to common stock, the interest received on the convertible will be less than if you had invested in a regular bond.
- Be wary of buying convertibles that are trading at high premiums over both the market values of the common stock and/or the callable price of the convertibles.
- Check the call and sinking fund provisions of the convertibles before you buy, because these allow the issuing company to redeem a specific number of convertible bonds each year.

TABLE 12-5
_____

The Hazards of Convertible Bonds

Convertible bonds offer potential capital appreciation in rising stock markets and protection of a portion of invested capital in down markets due to the underlying floor price of the straight value of the bond. However, investing in convertible bonds is not without risk.

At the peak of the stock market in 1999, many technology and Internet companies raised new sources of funds by issuing convertible bonds. In that year a record 144 convertible issues came to the market, with 25 of them over $500 million per issue. Amazon.com Inc. raised $1.25 billion with a convertible bond issue despite the fact that its bonds had a rating of CCC+. What was even more remarkable was that the coupon rate was only $4\frac{3}{4}\%$ and the issue sold at a 27% conversion premium to equity. This issue was priced when Amazon's stock was $61 per share and a conversion price of $78 per share. In the bear market that followed in 2000, the stock price of Amazon (and other Internet and technology companies) plummeted. When Amazon's stock price was $16 per share, the value of the straight bond was $530. Consequently, investors in this issue had little choice but to wait until maturity in 2009 to receive their invested principal. Some time later, Amazon's stock price slid into the single digits, when many investors feared that Amazon might default on its bond obligations. If a bankruptcy occurred, convertible bond holders would have received nothing. Convertible bonds don't offer the same protection in bankruptcy as straight bond issues, because convertible bonds are subordinate to regular bond issues of a company.

The choices for Amazon convertible bondholders were to sell their bonds at significant losses to their purchase prices (the convertibles were trading well below their straight bond values), or to hold them and hope that Amazon would not default on its debt obligations. Of course, there is always the hope with convertibles that the underlying stock price will rise above the conversion price, resulting in capital appreciation. In Amazon's case this would be a meteoric rise to above $78 per share. However, in 2007 the price of Amazon company's stock rose to a high of $101 per share, well above the conversion price, allowing significant appreciation for holders of the convertible bonds.

The hazards of convertible bonds are greater than straight debt if the underlying stock price never goes above the conversion price. In the event of bankruptcy, convertible bondholders are the last in the line of debt-holders to claim on assets. Secondly, if there is no conversion, convertible bondholders receive lower yields than they would have on comparable straight debt.

Source: Avital Louria Hahn, "'Tech-communica-dia' Propels Convertible Issuance to New Heights," June 10, 2000, www.findarticles.com/, and "No Protection on Converts. Moody's Says the Hot Hybrids Are Risky," July 23, 2001, www.findarticles.com/

THE DIFFERENT TYPES OF CONVERTIBLE SECURITIES

Convertible preferred stock is similar to convertible bonds. The convertible preferred stockholder has the option to convert each share of preferred stock into a fixed number of shares of common stock of the issuing company. Generally, the conversion ratio for convertible preferred securities is small. For example, it may be one share of preferred for one share of common stock.

Convertible preferred stock issues have many similar characteristics to convertible bonds. However, with convertible preferred stock, dividends are paid only if the board of directors of the company declares them. Dividends are not like interest payments on convertible bonds, in which a default in the interest payments can cause bondholders to bring action against the company. Although the number of convertible preferred stock issues has increased in the last few years, they are not as popular as convertible bonds.

Small, growing companies in need of cash have issued risky *convertible preferred securities with floating conversion ratios*, also known as *death spirals and toxic convertibles*. Many of these companies that have issued these securities have seen their stock prices fall due to dilution and an increase in short selling. When preferred stockholders convert their securities to common stock, there is a larger number of shares outstanding, which results in lower earnings per share. The conversion puts downward pressure on the price of the common stock. Short sellers also exacerbate the situation. Short sellers have jumped in when these securities have been issued as they are looked on as a type of financing of last resort for companies. Short sellers bet that the stock price will go down. They sell "borrowed" stock and then buy the stock back at a later stage when the stock price goes down. This puts further downward pressure on the stock price (Lucchetti and Scism, 1998).

There are many different *zero coupon convertible bonds*, one of which is Merrill Lynch's liquid yield option note (LYON). Zero coupon bonds are sold at a deep discount from their face value and do not pay yearly cash interest. Instead, the interest accrues and at maturity the bond is redeemed for its face value. However, these securities also have call provisions, which make their valuation more complex.

Zero coupon convertible bonds tend to be offered by companies that want to conserve their cash. Walt Disney Company issued zero coupon convertibles to raise funds for their European Disneyland in Paris. These securities were convertible into EuroDisney stock traded on the Bourse in Paris, which, unfortunately for its holders, had been declining in value. This example illustrates the disadvantage of this type of security. When the stock price is depressed and there is a call provision, the zero coupon convertible will trade close to its call price, which could be less than what investors paid for the security.

Another similar combination security is the *payment in kind* (PIK). PIKs are in some respects similar to zero coupon securities in that interest (or dividends in the case of preferred stock PIKs) is not paid out in cash in the early years. Instead interest (or dividends) is paid in the form of additional securities of the underlying issue. For bonds, interest will be in the form of more bonds; for preferred stock, dividends will be additional preferred shares.

PIKs tend to carry higher coupons to entice investors. However, investors need to examine the issuing company's financial status carefully to determine whether the company will be around in future years to be able to make the payoffs in cash. Again we are reminded that there are no free lunches on Wall Street—it is a high-yield security in return for high risk.

Step-up income redeemable equity notes (SIRENs) are intermediate convertible bonds with two coupons. The first coupon is below market rates of interest, and then after a few years the coupon increases to a higher rate until maturity. These securities have a convertible provision where holders can convert their notes into the common stock of the issuer at a price determined by the issuer (conversion price). As with all convertibles, if the price of the common stock goes up, holders stand to profit. If the price of the common stock goes down, holders of SIRENs have a floor price on their notes but they would earn less than they would on a similar conventional bond.

The clincher is that SIRENs are issued with call provisions, which allow the issuer to call the bond at the time of the step-up, by paying a slight premium over par. Thus, if the stock price has not risen above the conversion price, investors would not convert and they would have sacrificed a few years of below market rate yields on their SIRENs.

ARE CONVERTIBLE SECURITIES SUITABLE FOR YOU?

Convertible securities offer the potential for both appreciation and a steady stream of income, but they may not be the best of both worlds. They certainly allow investors to hedge their bets in both the debt and the equities markets. However, under certain conditions, they are not the best investments, and investors would be better off owning either regular debt or equity.

Generally, convertible securities do well when interest rates are falling and the stock market is rising. This was the case in 2005 to 2007 when convertible securities outperformed the stock market indices.

The downside of convertibles is that they can be complicated in structure, with call provisions, which can result in holders losing money if they had bought the convertibles at a premium. Similarly, if convertibles are not converted into equity, investors generally would have been better off with regular bonds, which tend to pay higher coupons.

Convertible securities are suited to investors who have the knowledge of the workings and intricacies of these specialized securities who can hedge their bets in the bond and equity markets.

CONVERTIBLE SECURITY MUTUAL FUNDS

Instead of investing in individual convertible bonds, investors can opt for convertible mutual funds. The choices of convertible security mutual funds are not as large as for corporate bond funds, for example. Most mutual fund families tend to offer only one convertible fund. Thus, investors would need to look at and compare the convertible security funds offered by several different fund families.

Since most convertible bonds issued by corporations are unsecured and subordinated debt, the credit quality and risk of default are of a greater concern than they would be for secured, better quality bonds. However, the diversification achieved by convertible security mutual funds tends to lessen the impact of loss from any potential downgrades in credit quality and the possible default of a few issues.

The risks of a convertible security fund depend on the holdings in the portfolio of investments, average length of time to maturity, market rates of interest, and state of the bond and stock markets. Because of the complexities of convertible securities, murky pricing, and the fact that their well-being is interdependent with many factors, investors might be better off in mutual funds, where professional managers can handle the complexities.

WHAT ARE THE RISKS OF CONVERTIBLE SECURITY MUTUAL FUNDS?

Owing to the *lower credit* quality of convertible bonds, investors in convertible security mutual funds need to have a long investment time horizon, at least five years. Share prices of convertible security mutual funds have the potential to be much more volatile than regular bond funds. When interest rates are low and the stock market is in bull mode, convertible security mutual funds can easily outperform many other types of bond funds. However, if the stock markets are in bear mode, and market rates of interest are moving up, convertible security mutual funds may very well underperform other conservative types of investments. Thus, investors in these funds are exposed to the *risk of loss of principal* due to the increased volatility of the underlying securities and the interdependence of the many other factors affecting their prices.

Convertible security mutual funds are subject to *interest rate risk*. Generally, a rise in market rates of interest not only depresses the prices of most fixed-income securities but also those of common stocks. This is the double whammy on convertible securities because the coupon yields on the bonds are lower than conventional bonds, which means that shareholders in these funds are likely to receive lower total returns than if they had invested in regular fixed-income mutual funds. This could prompt fund managers to invest in riskier securities to try and increase their overall returns, thereby increasing the overall risks of the fund.

HOW TO BUY AND SELL CONVERTIBLE SECURITY MUTUAL FUNDS

Convertible security mutual funds may be bought directly through mutual fund families or indirectly through brokers, financial planners, and banks. To save on sales commissions, you would be better off investing directly with the mutual fund family in no-load funds, especially in light of the increased potential share price volatility of convertible security mutual funds. Compare the expense ratio of several convertible funds. The lower the expense ratio, the less costly is the fund. For example, if a fund earns a yield of 5 percent per annum and the expense ratio is 1 percent, shareholders are essentially paying out 20 percent (0.01/0.05) of their earnings in fees. Look for low expense ratio funds.

A good starting point in determining which convertible security funds to consider is to look at the statistics published on a quarterly basis by the financial newspapers and magazines on the different types of mutual funds. From the total return history and expense ratios of the mutual funds listed, investors can determine which of the convertible security mutual funds would fit their criteria. By requesting a prospectus from each of the funds that you are interested in, you can compare them with regard to:

- The objectives of the fund and the degree of risk that the fund managers have in choosing lesser quality securities
- The types of securities in the fund
- Whether the fund charges a load (front end/back end)
- The expense ratios of each fund
- The total returns of the fund

You can obtain this information directly by downloading the prospectus from the fund's Web site. Table 12-6 illustrates comparison statistics of Fidelity's and Vanguard's convertible securities funds obtained from the fund family's Web sites.

Table 12-6

Comparison of Two Convertible Securities Mutual Funds

Fidelity Convertible Securities Fund		Vanguard Convertible Securities Fund
Expense ratio	0.83%	0.77%
Redemption fee	None	1% on sales of shares held less than one year
Total annual returns:*		
1-year	16.24%	10.61%
3-year	12.34	10.02
5-year	14.93	13.44
Beta Coefficient	0.88	1.01
Composition of Portfolio:*		
Convertible Securities 81.2%		81.15%
Equity	15.1%	12.28%
Cash & other	3.5%	6.57%

* as of 12/31/2007

Source: www.fidelity.com and www.vanguard.com

The beta coefficient of the Vanguard convertible securities fund was 1.01, indicating a positive correlation to the movements of the market. The market has a coefficient of 1. What this means is that the fund will rise and fall with the market. If the market goes down by 50 percent, the fund's portfolio should also decline by 50 percent. A beta coefficient greater than 1 indicates that the fund will increase by more than the market when the market goes up, and the fund will decrease by more than the market on the downside. A beta coefficient that is less than 1 indicates less volatility than the market on both the upside and downside of the market. The expense ratio of the Vanguard convertible securities fund was 0.77 percent versus a slightly greater expense ratio of 0.83 percent for the Fidelity convertible securities fund. The redemption fee of 1 percent ($10 per $1,000 invested) on sales of shares held less than one year is only significant if the investor intends to trade the securities on a short-term basis. In such a case, the Fidelity convertible fund would be the better choice. Fidelity's fund performed better than Vanguard's fund for all three years. The credit risk for each fund should be compared to determine your comfort level by examining the breakdown of the credit quality of the issues.

Interest rate risk can be gauged by examining the length of time to maturity of the issues. The greater the number of securities with longer maturities held in the fund, the greater is the impact of interest rate risk. The shorter the number of maturities in the fund, the lesser the impact that changes in market rates of interest will have on the fund.

The yield of the fund indicates what the portfolio earns as a percentage of the total net asset value of the fund. The greater the expense ratio, the lower the returns of the fund as expenses are paid out of the returns (interest and dividends) received by the fund.

When you have decided on a fund, to open the account, you just fill out an application form and send it with a check to the address on the form. Each fund offers several different types of account services, which can be chosen by ticking off the appropriate boxes on the application form. These include the payment options for dividends and capital gains (whether you want these sent to you every month or reinvested in the fund), redemption options (by wire or mail), purchase options, and so forth.

WHAT ARE THE ADVANTAGES OF CONVERTIBLE SECURITY MUTUAL FUNDS?

- Convertible security mutual funds offer shareholders the potential for higher returns than plain vanilla types of bond funds due to the potential appreciation of the common stock as well as the ability to receive income from the securities that have not been converted.
- Convertible security mutual funds offer shareholders an easy way to own complex securities.
- Because of their diversification, convertible security mutual funds offer shareholders protection against default and the risks of credit downgrades.
- Investing in convertible security mutual funds instead of individual convertible securities spares the investor from having to shop for the best prices.

WHAT ARE THE DISADVANTAGES OF CONVERTIBLE SECURITY MUTUAL FUNDS?

- If interest rates rise and the stock market turns down, the returns on these funds will be lower than regular bond funds.
- Share prices of convertible security mutual funds can experience volatile swings due to changes in interest rates and the status of the equity markets. Investors in these funds need long time horizons to weather these swings in share price.

CAVEATS

- If you invest in a convertible security mutual fund, invest in one with a low expense ratio.
- Because of the risks and potential volatility of the share price, only a portion of your total investment dollars should be invested in convertible security mutual funds.

SHOULD YOU INVEST IN INDIVIDUAL CONVERTIBLE SECURITIES OR CONVERTIBLE SECURITY MUTUAL FUNDS?

The benefits of investing in individual convertible securities over convertible security mutual funds are summarized in Table 12-7. As of January 2008, there are no convertible securities exchange-traded funds.

Table 12-7

Characteristics of Investing in Individual Convertible Securities versus Mutual Funds

	Individual Securities	Mutual funds
Ease of Buying or Selling	Difficult to buy and sell individual bonds. Easier to buy convertible preferred shares.	Easy to buy and sell shares. Trades are transacted at the closing price at the end of the day.
Costs to trade	Incur commissions to buy and sell bonds on the secondary market. Lack of transparent pricing of securities.	None when investing in no-load funds.
Income stream	Fixed for convertible bonds until conversion	Income stream varies from month to month
Management fees	None	Vary depending on the fund
Returns	Depend on the portfolio holdings, but returns are not diminished by fees.	Variable returns reduced by the total fees charged by the fund.
Tax planning	Easy to predict income and can plan capital gains and losses	Unpredictable distributions of income and capital gains that can upset careful tax planning.
Investment amounts	Requires a large investment to build a diversified portfolio	Required minimum amounts vary by fund and are relatively small.
Safety of Principal	If convertibles are not converted and held through maturity, principal is recovered	A chance that principal may not be recovered if share price is below the purchase price when shares are sold.
Holdings	Known	Not disclosed until the end of the quarter.
Diversification	Need a large amount of money to build a diversified portfolio.	Small investment buys a holding in a diversified portfolio.

With individual convertible securities you are in control. You know exactly how much interest you will receive and when. You can convert your bonds at your discretion when the stock price rises above the conversion price. This is not so with mutual funds. Also, the amount of the monthly dividend payments from mutual funds varies.

Barring any defaults, individual convertible securities are likely to yield higher returns than mutual funds, which typically can pay out a percentage point in total fees.

Investing in individual convertible securities over mutual funds gives investors greater control over their tax planning with regard to capital gains. Mutual funds do not pay taxes when they sell securities at higher prices than their purchase prices, and so these gains are passed through to the shareholders in the fund. An investor could conceivably buy into a convertible security mutual fund that had already realized substantial capital gains for the year, and that shareholder would be subject to taxes on those gains, even if they occurred before the investor was a shareholder. There is another tax problem that could affect convertible security mutual funds. With the raging bull market of the past three years, mutual fund managers may have bought convertible preferred stocks at higher prices than the current prices. The fall in equity prices will lower the net asset value of the fund, which may result in unrealized principal losses to shareholders. At the same time, the fund manager may have converted some of the convertible bonds to common stock, and then sold the common stock, which would result in capital gains. At the end of the tax year, investors in the fund could face potential capital gains for which they would have to pay the taxes at the same time as seeing paper losses in their principal investments due to share prices of the fund being lower than their purchase prices.

There is another side of the picture that better favors a mutual fund over individual securities. Mutual funds own a diversified portfolio of securities, which cushions the impact of defaults or credit rating downgrades. Investors in individual convertible securities, on the other hand, would have to invest substantial amounts of money to achieve the diversification offered by mutual funds. Therefore, the risk of loss may be greater for individual convertible securities than for mutual funds.

Convertible security mutual funds allow investors to invest with smaller amounts of capital, as opposed to the larger denominations needed to invest in individual convertible securities. Because of the murky pricing of individual convertible securities, investors would not be able to obtain favorable price spreads when buying and selling individual convertible securities.

Convertible bonds are complex in their make-up, which requires that investors have the time and knowledge to study the provisions of the indenture before they invest. Investing in convertible mutual funds shifts this focus to the professional managers of the funds who have the time, knowledge, and expertise to make the appropriate investment decisions.

REFERENCES

Bary, Andrew. "Trading Points," Barron's, February 8, 1993.

Lucchetti, Aaron and Leslie Scism, "Unusual Convertible Preferred Raises Needed Cash and Risks," *Wall Street Journal*, September 28, 1998, pp. C1, C7.

CHAPTER 13

Zero Coupon Bonds and Zero Coupon Mutual Funds

KEY CONCEPTS

- What are zero coupon bonds?
- The relationship influencing the price of zero coupon bonds
- The different types of zero coupon bonds
- The risks of zero coupon bonds
- How to buy and sell zero coupon bonds
- The advantages of zero coupon bonds
- The disadvantages of zero coupon bonds
- Caveats
- Zero coupon mutual funds

Zero coupon bonds are the most volatile of all the different types of bonds. Zero coupon bond prices are most sensitive to changes in interest rates and swing up and down, resembling a roller coaster ride. Zero coupon bonds are more complex than regular bonds, and you need to understand how they work.

WHAT ARE ZERO COUPON BONDS?

Zero coupon bonds are debt securities that are issued at deep discounts from their face values, pay no periodic interest, and are redeemed at face value ($1,000) at maturity. For example, a 10-year zero coupon bond (with a face value of $1,000) yielding 8 percent would cost about $463 at issuance. In other words, you would buy this zero coupon bond for $463, receive no interim interest payments, and at the end of the tenth year receive $1,000, the face value of the bond. Since zero coupon bonds do not pay interest, they do not have a current yield like regular bonds.

The price of a zero coupon bond is the present value of the face value of the bond at the maturity date discounted at its internal rate of return. In other words, the investor's funds grow from $463 to $1,000 in 10 years. The initial price is compounded at its internal rate of return to equal $1,000 in 10 years. The rate of return, or yield, on a zero coupon bond can be solved mathematically, using compound interest tables, or using a financial calculator.

The yield on a zero coupon bond also can be determined using Microsoft Excel software:

1. Click on the "f*" key on the toolbar.
2. Highlight "rate."
3. Fill in the information in the following box (Figure 13-1):

Knowing the yield on the bond is helpful not only for federal tax purposes but also for calculating the price of the bond. Even though zero coupon bondholders receive no interest payments, bondholders are required to pay federal income taxes on their accrued interest as if it had been paid. In the example used, the accrued interest for the first year is $37.04.

FIGURE 13-1

Using Microsoft Excel Software to Calculate the Yield on a Zero-Coupon Bond

Nper	10	Nper = total number of payments
Pmt	0	Pmt = payment (interest) each period
PV	−463	PV = present value of bond (needs a
FV	1,000	negative sign before the amount)
Type	1	FV = future value (face value) of bond
Formula result (rate)	0.08	Formula result = rate

$$\text{Interest} = \$463 \times 0.08$$
$$= \$37.04$$

The zero coupon bondholder pays taxes on this amount of $37.04 even though it has not been received, thereby creating a negative cash flow. The bondholder pays cash out of pocket for the taxes without receiving the $37.04. Instead, the interest is added to the principal price of the zero coupon bond so that at the end of the first year, the price of the bond increases to $500.04 ($463 + 37.04).

The accrued interest for year two is $40.00:

$$\text{Interest} = \$500.04 \times 0.08$$
$$= \$40.00$$

The price of the bond at the end of the second year is $540.04 ($500.04 + 40.00). Theoretically, the price rises with accrued interest until the price reaches $1,000 at maturity. This theoretical price structure is illustrated in the graph in Figure 13-2. There are factors besides accrued interest that affect the price of a zero coupon bond. For example, if interest rates increase, the price of the bond would fall below the theoretical prices shown in the graph.

Owing to negative cash flows from paying taxes on accrued (phantom) interest during the life of the bond, zero coupon bonds are best suited for investment accounts that are not subject to taxes. These are pension funds, individual retirement accounts (IRAs), 401(k)s, and simplified employee pension (SEP) accounts. In these plans, accrued interest is taxed only when the funds are withdrawn.

FIGURE 13-2

Price of a Zero Coupon Bond from Issue to Maturity

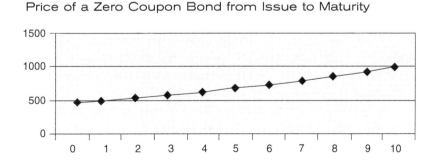

Investing in municipal zero coupon bonds can eliminate the phantom interest tax problem.

Do not be fooled by clever advertisements for zero coupon bonds that tout the wonderful growth aspects of investing small sums of money and then receiving larger amounts at maturity. This growth is due to the compounding of interest on interest and principal at the *yield to maturity rate,* 8% in the previous example. However, the tax disadvantages are not openly disclosed in these advertisements.

RELATIONSHIPS INFLUENCING THE PRICE OF ZERO COUPON BONDS

The price of a zero coupon bond is affected by the quality of the bond, length of time to maturity, call provision, market rates of interest, and yield. The *quality* of the zero coupon bond is important because the return depends on:

- The ability of the issuer to redeem the bonds at maturity.
- Whether the bondholder is able to sell them before maturity at a higher price than the purchase price.

A zero coupon bondholder has more to lose in the event of a default than a conventional bondholder because with the latter, bondholders receive some interest payments that reduce the original principal invested in the bonds.

The quality of a zero coupon bond is an assessment of the issuer's ability to pay off the bond at maturity. A good-quality zero coupon bond has less risk of default than a speculative, low-quality zero coupon bond. Investors are willing to pay more for a good quality bond. Thus, there is a positive relationship between *quality* and *price.*

Ratings assigned by ratings agencies such as Moody's and Standard & Poor's are yardsticks as to the credit quality, but you should always be aware that these ratings are subject to changes in the financial positions of the issuing entity.

The quality of a zero coupon bond is also related to its *yield.* A low-quality zero coupon bond offers a higher yield than a good-quality zero coupon bond to entice investors. The flip side of the coin is that investors pay less for a low-quality zero coupon bond than for a high-quality zero coupon bond. Price is therefore inversely related to yield.

However, the yield is also related to the *length of time to maturity*. The longer the maturity, the lower the price and the higher the yield. This is true because zero coupon bondholders only receive their interest payments at maturity (or an accrued amount built into the sale price before maturity).

Zero coupon prices are sensitive to *fluctuations in interest rates*. The purchase price of a zero coupon bond determines the yield over the life of the security because interest is only paid at maturity and interest accrues at that fixed yield. If market rates of interest rise above the fixed yield of the zero coupon bond, investors would want to sell the zero coupon bond and reinvest in a bond with a higher yield. This action has the effect of depressing the price of existing zero coupon bonds more than conventional type bonds, which pay interest annually or semiannually. Zero coupon bonds are more volatile in price than regular fixed-interest payment bonds because zero coupon bondholders do not receive any interest payments until the zero coupon bonds mature. Similarly, when interest rates fall, zero coupon bonds appreciate more than existing conventional bonds owing to the fixed yield on the zero coupon bond.

Zero coupon bonds have higher durations than conventional bonds of similar maturity and yield, because bondholders do not receive any interest payments until the zero coupon bond matures.

Market factors also have a bearing on price. An actively traded zero coupon bond is priced differently from an inactively traded zero coupon bond with the same maturity and yield.

TYPES OF ZERO COUPON BONDS

Besides conventional zero coupon bonds issued by corporations and government entities, there are different types of zero coupon bonds. Several brokerage houses introduced derivative zero coupon bonds during the early 1980s, primarily for use in retirement accounts. They are called derivative securities because these securities obtain their value based on another underlying security.

Stripped Government Securities

In 1982, Salomon Brothers and Merrill Lynch both created *zero coupon stripped Treasury securities*. To create their respective securities, the brokerage firms bought long-term U.S. Treasury bonds and held them in escrow. They then sold zero coupon bonds representing an ownership interest in the underlying Treasury bonds (held in escrow) and their interest payments. Stripping the coupon payments on the U.S. Treasury bonds created these securities with their own CUSIP numbers (the unique identification number assigned to a registered bond). An important distinction to make with stripped zero coupon securities is that they are not backed by the faith and credit of the U.S. Treasury. Treasury bonds are backed by the faith and credit of the U.S. government, but the zero coupon securities are merely the products of the brokerage houses.

Salomon's product was marketed under the name CATS (Certificates of Accrual on Treasury Securities) and Merrill Lynch's stripped zero coupon security went under the name TIGRs (Treasury Investment Growth Receipts). Other brokerage firms followed with their stripped zero coupon securities under other acronyms.

The major disadvantage to these stripped zero coupon securities of the brokerage firms is the lack of liquidity. Competing dealers did not trade the securities of other brokerage firms, so to improve liquidity of the stripped zero coupon bonds, a group of primary dealers in the Treasury bond market decided to issue generic securities. These securities were called "Treasury receipts," and they were not associated with any of the participating dealers (Fabozzi and Fabozzi, 1989).

In 1985, the U.S. Treasury announced its own Separate Trading of Registered Interest and Principal (STRIP) program. Designated Treasury bonds could be stripped to create zero coupon Treasury bonds. STRIPs are Treasury securities that have had their coupons and principal payments separated, which forms the basis for the creation of zero coupon bonds.

Since these securities are the direct obligations of the U.S. government, they tend to have slightly lower yields than brokerage firms' stripped zero coupon securities. Moreover, the Treasury's STRIP securities offer greater marketability than the generics offered by brokerage firms.

Salomon Brothers created stripped federal agency zero coupon bonds in the late 1980s. Salomon purchased $750 million Financing Corporation (FICO) bonds, stripped them of their interest, and sold them as zero coupon FICO strips. Congress had created FICO for the purpose of raising money for the financially strapped Federal Savings and Loan Insurance Corporation (FSLIC).

The FICO zeros were not assigned credit ratings by the rating companies but were believed to be relatively safe because of Congress' commitment to FICO and the FSLIC. Hence, yields on FICO zeros were slightly higher than those on Treasury STRIPS. Agency strips, such as FICO strips, can be bought through brokers and trade over the counter in the secondary market.

Mortgage-Backed Zero Coupon Bonds

Ginnie Mae, Fannie Mae, and Freddie Mac offer mortgage-backed zero coupon bonds that are fully backed by their issuers. However, owing to prepayment risk, investors may find that these zeros could be paid off before their stated maturities. Holders of this group of zero coupon bonds are taxed on imputed interest even though interest payments are not received before maturity or the sale of the securities.

Municipal Zero Coupon Bonds

These securities are issued by state and local governments and are advantageous in that the accrued interest is exempt from federal income taxes and generally from state taxes (if issued in the state of the taxpayer).

Municipal zero coupon bonds come in two types: *general obligation zero coupon bonds* issued by states and *project zero coupon bonds* issued by highway authorities for highway projects, public power projects for sewer systems, and other municipal projects. General obligation issues are backed by the taxing power of the states issuing them, whereas project securities are backed by the revenues generated from the projects. Hence, project zero coupon bonds are less secure.

The quality of a zero coupon bond issue is important for the reason stated earlier in the chapter, namely, that the holder receives no payments other than the payment of principal and interest at maturity. Consequently, you should not settle for lower-quality zero coupon municipal issues because there are so many good-quality issues. This point is especially relevant for long-term issues (over 15 years to maturity), where anything could happen to affect the issuer's ability to repay the bonds. For higher-quality zero coupon bond issues, you will sacrifice slightly on yields.

Many municipal zero coupon issues are callable, and you should check the call provisions before buying. If there is a choice between a callable and a noncallable issue of similar quality and maturity, avoid the callable issue.

Both the call price and the call date listed in the bond's indenture are important. The call price could be less than the market price, resulting in a loss if the issue is called, so it is wise to check out the call provision first. An issue might have a serial call, which means that some bonds in the issue could be called earlier than other bonds in the issue.

Although municipal zero coupon bonds are exempt from federal income taxes, investors might want to find out how their states tax the accrued interest on the securities. Some states tax the phantom interest as it accrues, and other states tax the interest at maturity or when the securities are sold. Investors can get the information from their state revenue offices. Before selling a zero coupon bond, you should consult with your tax advisor or accountant as to the tax consequences of gains and losses.

Zero Coupon Corporate Convertible Bonds

These securities are deeply discounted bonds with conversion provisions. The yields of these securities tend to be lower than those of conventional bonds, and they do not pay annual interest. Holders are required to accrue interest for federal tax purposes, and as with regular zero coupon bonds, they are suitable for tax-deferred accounts such as IRAs, 401(k)s, and pension plans.

Like convertible bonds, these securities can be exchanged into a predetermined number of the issuing corporation's common stock. ST Microelectronics NV, the largest European semiconductor maker, issued $1.2 billion in zero coupon convertible bonds in July 2003 due in 2010.

Some zero coupon convertibles have put options, which allow holders to sell their securities back to the issuer at the original issue price plus accrued interest after a certain date (usually 5 or 10 years). Call provisions on many zero coupon convertible securities have worked to the detriment of investors, as illustrated by the example of Walt Disney securities. Walt Disney issued zero coupon convertible securities that were scheduled to mature in 2005, but they were called several years after issuance at prices that were lower than what many investors had paid in the secondary market to purchase the zero coupon convertible securities. The conversion feature did not help the holders of those Disney zero coupon convertible bonds because the securities were tied to Euro Disney stock, traded on the Paris Exchange. The stock price was depressed and trading well below the conversion price.

The advantage of zero coupon convertible bonds is the upside potential of capital appreciation if the common stock rises above the conversion price. However, if the stock price never rises above the conversion price, the investor receives a lower return than similar maturity plain vanilla bonds (regular bonds) for the life of the bond.

To counter the disadvantage of negative cash flows from federal taxation of phantom interest, many municipalities have issued *zero coupon convertible municipal issues*. These have been sold under different acronyms: FIGS (future income and growth securities), BIGS (bond income and growth securities), PACS (principal appreciation conversion securities), and TEDIS (tax-exempt discount and income securities).

These securities are much the same as regular zero coupon convertible securities, except for the exemption of accrued interest from federal taxes. However, state taxes may be applicable on the accrued interest, and the quality of the issue is, of course, dependent on the financial position of the issuing municipality. These securities may also contain call provisions.

WHAT ARE THE RISKS OF ZERO COUPON BONDS?

The *risk of default* of an issue is directly related to the financial position of the issuer and is of great importance to the zero coupon bondholder because the interest and principal are paid in a single payment at maturity, and if the issuer is not able to make this single payment, the holder receives no payments. With regular bonds, the holder would have received some interest payments during the life of the bond before default. Consequently, the quality of the zero coupon bond is an assessment of the likelihood of the issuer's ability to be able to pay off the bondholder at maturity. The risk of default can be lessened by choosing high-quality zero coupon bond issues and/or government stripped bonds.

Interest rate risk has a greater impact on zero coupon bonds than on regular coupon bonds. The increased volatility of zero coupon bond prices to changes in interest rates is due to the fact that the entire amount that a zero coupon bondholder receives is a single payment at maturity, whereas for regular interest-bearing bonds the price is the discounted cash flows of the interest payments and principal at maturity. Generally, with coupon interest-paying bonds, the lower the coupon rate of the bond, the greater is the price volatility due to changes in market rates of interest. This explains the price volatility of zero coupon bonds, which have no coupon payments. Some zero coupon bonds are more volatile in price than other similar yielding zeros as a result of different trading activity, quality differences, call features, and length of time to maturity.

When interest rates decline, many outstanding bond issues are called, and zero coupon bonds are no exception. Zero coupon bonds also have call provisions, which is a lesson many zero coupon bondholders have learned the hard way. When interest rates decline, higher yielding zero coupon bonds appreciate significantly owing to the fact that these bonds are locked into an above market rate yield. However, issuers of these bonds are not thrilled at paying above market rates, and if their bonds have call provisions, they would call them.

Zero coupon bonds have no *reinvestment risk* because the yield is determined by the purchase price and then locked in over the life of the bond. With a regular coupon bond, the holder is faced with the uncertainty of having to reinvest the interest payments at fluctuating market rates of interest. A further disadvantage is that when interest rates rise, zero coupon bondholders are locked into their existing lower yields.

If zero coupon bonds are sold before maturity, there is always the risk of loss in principal due to the extreme volatility of zero coupon bonds. Zero coupon bonds are the most volatile of all bonds. In addition, markups in the pricing of zero coupon bonds are large and prices also vary from dealer to dealer, making zero coupon bonds expensive to buy and sell over short periods of time.

HOW TO BUY AND SELL ZERO COUPON BONDS

Zero coupon bonds can be purchased in the primary market at issue (in other words, a new issue to the market). Investors who buy these new issues from the brokerage firms underwriting the issue avoid paying commissions or fees.

Existing zero coupon bonds trading in the secondary markets can be bought through securities brokers, dealers, and banks, as well as through online brokers. Brokers charge fees, which can be relatively high for zero coupon securities, considering that investors are investing smaller amounts of money (due to the deep discounts) than they would for the same number of regular bonds. These markups vary considerably from broker to broker, and you should not be deceived if your broker announces that his or her firm does not charge a fee or commission. The commission is buried in the markup. Transaction fees for a small number of zero coupon bonds can be considerable.

Some brokerage firms make a market in certain zero coupon issues. The prices at which these are bought and sold are determined by the brokerage firm and on the conditions of the market. Consequently, the investor does not pay a commission, but the size of the markup determines whether the investor is getting a break.

It is important to shop around at different brokerage firms for the best prices when buying and selling zero coupon securities. Many brokerage firms have inventories of different zero coupon issues, and they may be more competitively priced. Compare the yield to maturity and ratings of similar bond issues, which gives you some indication of the markups charged (markups reduce the yield of a bond). The lack of pricing transparency is a problem for bond investors, and so it is important to compare the yield to maturity of similarly rated bonds with similar maturities.

You should be aware that when buying zero coupon issues from sponsoring brokerage houses at issue, these brokerage houses are not required or obligated to make a market in these issues.

The high transaction costs on zero coupon issues make them less liquid than other fixed-income securities, and, consequently, they are more suited to a buy and hold strategy. By holding zeros to maturity, investors improve their returns.

Rather than buy individual zero coupon issues, investors can choose to put their money into mutual funds that specialize in zero coupon bonds. As with all mutual funds, fees are deducted from the earnings (and/or the net assets) of the funds and can be quite high. As of February 2008, there are no zero coupon exchange-traded funds that are offered to investors. There are total bond exchange traded funds that hold zero coupon bonds as a part of their holdings, but they are not a pure play on zero coupon bonds

ADVANTAGES OF ZERO COUPON BONDS

- Zero coupon bonds appreciate more than conventional fixed-income securities when interest rates decline. The opposite is also true when market rates of interest rise. Prices of zero coupon bonds decline more than those of conventional bonds.

- Investments in zero coupon bonds require less of a capital outflow than other fixed-income securities, since they are purchased at a deep discount. For example, a purchase of 10 regular bonds at face value requires an outlay of $10,000, whereas 10 zero coupon bonds selling at $180 require $1,800.

- Investors are not concerned with reinvestment risk. With zero coupon bonds there is no coupon to reinvest at unpredictable market rates of interest.

- Zero coupon bonds have fixed yields when held to maturity and provide predictable returns. Zero coupon bonds have a maturity value of $1,000 per bond.

- There are so many existing zero coupon bond issues on the market to choose from that investors can easily ladder their maturities to provide regular cash flows.

- There are different types of zero coupon bonds with special features, which make them attractive investment vehicles for investors with specific needs.
- Zero coupon bonds are excellent investments for IRAs, 401(k)s, and pension plans due to their tax-deferred growth and predictable amounts at maturity.

DISADVANTAGES OF ZERO COUPON BONDS

- Paying taxes annually on accrued (phantom) interest that is not received until maturity creates a negative cash flow.
- Zero coupon bond prices are extremely volatile. When market rates of interest rise, zero coupon bond prices decline, which could result in capital losses should the investor be forced to sell.
- When interest rates rise, investors in zero coupon bondholders are doubly disadvantaged because they are locked into a lower yield, and they receive no coupon interest payments to reinvest.
- Many zero coupon bonds have call provisions, which allow the issuers to redeem them before maturity.
- If a zero coupon bond issuer defaults, investors have more to lose than on conventional bonds, because with the latter, they would have received some interest payments that could have been reinvested.
- Markups tend to be higher on zero coupon bonds (percentage wise), making them less liquid than other fixed-income securities.
- Certain zero coupon bonds are not as marketable as conventional fixed-income securities.

CAVEATS

When investing in zero coupon bonds, outside of tax-deferred accounts such as IRAs, 401(k)s, and pension accounts, investors should be aware of the tax consequences. They can be quite complicated, and it might be necessary to hire an accountant or tax professional to compute the tax liabilities. The Internal Revenue Service (IRS) publishes two free guides that are quite helpful in determining the tax liability on zero coupon bonds. These are IRS Publication 550 on "Investment Income and Expense," and IRS Publication 1212, "List of Original Issue Discount Obligations."

Zero coupon bonds are excellent investment vehicles for tax-deferred accounts in that they provide a lump sum of money at a future date. When used for investment purposes outside of tax-deferred accounts, investors face the disadvantage of negative cash flows due to the taxation of phantom interest. For some investors, this is not a serious disadvantage, and the other features of zero coupon bonds become more important. Because of their extreme volatility, zero coupon bonds can provide aggressive rates of growth when interest rates decline.

A good strategy for investing in zero coupon bonds is to buy good-quality bonds with different maturities, which will average the interest rate spread and hold them to maturity.

ZERO COUPON BOND MUTUAL FUNDS

Instead of investing in individual zero coupon securities, investors can invest in zero coupon mutual funds. Not every mutual fund family offers a zero coupon bond mutual fund. Zero coupon bond funds differ from other types of bond funds in that zero coupon funds buy zero coupon bonds with the same date. At this maturity date, the bonds reach their par values, allowing the fund to distribute the proceeds to their fund's shareholders. You can find zero coupon mutual funds with short-, intermediate-, and long-term maturities.

WHAT ARE THE RISKS OF ZERO COUPON MUTUAL FUNDS

The greatest risk facing zero coupon bond mutual funds is *interest rate risk*. Zero coupon bonds are much more volatile than other types of bonds when interest rates change. Consequently, even if you buy into a short-term or an intermediate term fund, the share price of your mutual fund can still be quite volatile when interest rates rise and fall.

With the extreme volatility of zero coupon bonds, there is always the *risk of loss in share price* should investors need to liquidate their zero coupon bond fund before maturity or at a time when the share price is lower than the purchase price. This risk of loss in share price is minimized if shareholders hold their positions through maturity.

Credit risk is a factor that affects the share price of the mutual fund. If any zero coupon bonds held in the mutual fund portfolio are downgraded, this action has a downward effect on the share price of the fund. However, with the diversification achieved by the fund, a few downgrades in issues would not have as great an effect as they would on an individual portfolio of zero coupon bonds.

HOW TO BUY AND SELL ZERO COUPON BOND MUTUAL FUNDS

Zero coupon bond mutual funds, which are also called target maturity funds, can be bought directly through mutual fund families or indirectly through brokers, financial planners, and banks. To save on sales commissions or loads, look for no-load zero coupon bond funds and buy directly from the mutual fund family. The American Century mutual fund family offers five zero coupon bond mutual funds that mature in five-year intervals from 2010 to 2030. This is not a recommendation for this fund, but merely to show that you can scan the mutual fund tables in the financial newspapers to find those families that offer zero coupon bond funds. In light of the increased potential share price volatility of zero coupon funds, you can increase your potential returns by investing in no-load funds. Similarly, when comparing the expense ratios of the different funds, look for the low expense ratio funds. The American Century target maturity funds invest in zero coupon Treasury securities and are no-load funds with low expense ratios (around 59 basis points).

Examine the prospectus for the objectives and the degree of risk of the fund, the types of zero coupon bonds held in the fund, its total returns, and its expense ratio.

ADVANTAGES OF ZERO COUPON BOND MUTUAL FUNDS

- If you hold zero coupon mutual funds to their maturity dates, you need not be concerned about interest rate risk, credit risk, and reinvestment risk.

- Holding zero coupon bond mutual funds to maturity provides known returns to shareholders (average yield to maturity of the bonds held in the fund minus the expenses of the fund).
- Zero coupon bond funds appreciate more than conventional bond mutual funds when interest rates decline. When interest rates rise, zero coupon bond mutual funds decline more than conventional bond mutual funds.
- Zero coupon bond mutual funds are suitable investments for IRAs, 401(k) accounts, and pension plans because of their tax-deferred growth and predictable amounts at maturity.
- Investing in zero coupon mutual bond funds over individual zero coupon bonds would likely result in lower transaction costs. Mutual funds pay lower transaction costs to buy zero coupon bonds than individual buyers.

WHAT ARE THE DISADVANTAGES OF ZERO COUPON BOND MUTUAL FUNDS

- There are tax consequences to owning zero coupon bond mutual funds. Shareholders would have to pay taxes on the accrued interest, which creates a negative cash flow.
- Share prices of zero coupon bond mutual funds can be extremely volatile when market rates of interest change.
- If you need to sell your shares before maturity, there is always the risk that you will lose money due to the extreme volatility of zero coupon bond mutual funds.

CAVEATS

Zero coupon bond mutual funds are ideal investments for tax-deferred pension and retirement accounts because of the negative cash flows due to phantom interest. For regular accounts, investors experience negative cash flows by paying taxes on interest payments that are accrued and not received until maturity.

Because of the volatility of zero coupon bond mutual funds, you should buy them to hold to maturity.

SHOULD YOU INVEST IN INDIVIDUAL ZERO COUPON BONDS OR ZERO COUPON BOND MUTUAL FUNDS?

The benefits of investing in zero coupon bond mutual funds over individual zero coupon bonds are summarized in Table 13-1.

Table 13.1

Characteristics of Investing in Individual Zero-Coupon Bonds versus Mutual Funds

	Individual Securities	Mutual funds
Ease of Buying or Selling	Difficult to buy and sell individual bonds.	Easy to buy and sell shares. Trades are transacted at the closing price at the end of the day.
Costs to trade	Incur commissions to buy and sell bonds on the secondary market. Lack of transparent pricing of securities.	None when investing in no-load funds.
Income	Can determine the exact amount of accrued interest for tax planning purposes.	Not able to determine the amount of accrued interest declared by the fund which can upset careful tax planning.
Management fees	None	Vary depending on the fund
Returns	Depend on the portfolio holdings, but returns are not diminished by fees.	Variable returns reduced by the total fees charged by the fund.
Tax planning	Easy to predict capital gains and losses	Unpredictable distributions of capital gains that can upset careful tax planning.
Investment amounts	Requires a large investment to build a diversified portfolio	Required minimum amounts vary by fund and are relatively small.
Safety of Principal	If zero-coupon bonds are held through maturity, principal is recovered	A chance that principal may not be recovered if share price is below the purchase price when shares are sold.
Holdings	Known	Not disclosed until the end of the quarter.
Diversification	Need a large amount of money to build a diversified portfolio.	Small investment buys a holding in a diversified portfolio.

Mutual funds own a diversified portfolio of zero coupon securities, which lessens the impact of a default or credit rating downgrade; whereas investors in individual zero coupon bonds would have to invest in many different issues to achieve similar diversification. Thus, the risks of loss may be greater for holders of individual zero coupon bonds than for mutual fund shareholders.

Zero coupon bonds are complex securities, and for individuals who do not have the time or expertise to examine their features, it is easier to invest in mutual funds that employ professional managers.

Zero coupon mutual funds provide tax information at the end of each year for their shareholders, whereas individual zero coupon bondholders would have to calculate their accrued interest for tax purposes.

Mutual funds purchase large numbers of bonds and pay lower markups than individual buyers. However, the downside to mutual funds is the annual expense ratio that shareholders must pay, which lowers their returns. Holders of individual zero coupon bonds avoid having to pay annual fees.

Holders of individual zero coupon bonds are in control not only of the securities that they choose, but also over their capital gains and losses. Individuals can sell their bonds when they want to, which gives them some control over their capital gains and losses for tax-planning purposes. Individual holders are also able to determine the exact amount of their accrued interest for the year, which is not true for mutual fund shareholders.

REFERENCE

Fabozzi, Frank J. and T. Dessa Fabozzi, "Survey of Bonds and Mortgage-Backed Securities," in *Portfolio and Investment Management*, edited by Frank J. Fabozzi, Chicago: McGraw-Hill Publishing Co., 1989.

CHAPTER 14

International and Emerging Market Debt

KEY CONCEPTS

- Types of international debt
- How to buy international bonds
- Risks of investing in international bonds
- Advantages of investing in international bonds
- Disadvantages of investing in international bonds
- International bond mutual funds
- International bond exchange-traded funds (ETFs)
- Should you invest in individual bonds, mutual funds, or ETFs?

The U.S. bond market accounts for almost 50 percent of the global debt market. The global bond market consists of foreign government and corporate issuers of bonds. There are established bond markets in developed countries such as Germany, the United Kingdom, Japan, and Italy, as well as growing emerging debt markets in developing countries, such as Brazil, Argentina, Turkey, Russia, and South Africa.

Bond investors search for higher returns from foreign bonds than they can obtain from U.S. bonds. With yields of less than 5 percent in February 2008 on 30-year U.S. Treasury bonds, the higher yields offered by some international bond issuers are quite appealing to investors seeking fixed-income investments.

TYPES OF INTERNATIONAL DEBT

International bonds can be divided into two categories based on their currency denominations: dollar-denominated and non-dollar-denominated bonds.

Dollar-Denominated Bonds

With dollar-denominated bonds, the purchase price of the bond, interest payments, and principal received at maturity are all in dollars, resulting in no currency risk for U.S. investors.

Yankee bonds are dollar-denominated bonds, issued by foreign governments or corporations and sold to investors in the United States. These bonds must be registered with the Securities and Exchange Commission and trade in the U.S. bond markets. Yankee bonds in general are high-quality bonds that have competitive yields. Interest on Yankee bonds is usually paid semiannually. Foreign governments and corporations are attracted to raising money through the issuance of Yankee bonds in the U.S. markets when interest rates are declining and the value of the dollar is strong, which is advantageous for them in providing them with lower cost funding and increasing value from an appreciating dollar.

Other countries allow foreign governments and corporations to issue debt in their home countries' currencies that are the equivalent to Yankee bonds. Examples of foreign governments and corporations that issue bonds in other countries with currency denominations linked to the country of issue are *bulldogs* for British pound-denominated bonds issued by foreign governments and corporations in the United Kingdom, *matadors* for euro-denominated bonds issued in Spain, and *samurais* for yen-denominated bonds issued in Japan.

Eurodollar bonds are also dollar denominated, but these bonds are issued outside the United States. Eurodollar bonds are Eurobonds that are traded throughout the world and are named after the currency in which they are denominated. For example, Euroyen bonds are denominated in Japanese yen and trade outside of Japan. In general, Eurobonds are bearer bonds with interest paid annually to the bearer. There are no withholding taxes and the majority of these bonds are traded electronically. There are various types of Eurobonds: fixed-rate bonds with fixed redemptions, or variable rate bonds, subordinate bonds, asset-backed issues, or convertible debt. One of the centers of the Eurobond market is London, although these bonds are issued and sold worldwide. These bonds are primarily sold to institutional investors and not individual investors.

Brady bonds are also dollar-denominated bonds issued mostly by emerging market countries and collateralized by U.S. Treasury zero coupon bonds. Brady bonds are named after Treasury Secretary Nicholas Brady and were created in 1989 to assist developing countries from defaulting on their debt. Defaulted loans were combined with commitments and obligations by foreign governments along with backing by U.S. zero coupon bonds to insure the repayment of principal. Principal repayments are guaranteed but generally the interest payments are not. If a country cannot make its interest payments, investors can still collect the entire amount of their principal when the bonds mature. Some Brady bonds guarantee both interest and principal.

The following two examples of Brady bonds illustrate the risk and reward relationship:

- Republic of Argentina bonds with a 10.25 percent coupon maturing on July 21, 2030
- Federative Republic of Brazil bonds with a 10.125 percent coupon maturing on May 15, 2027

In a low interest rate environment of less than 5 percent for U.S. Treasury securities in February 2008, a 10 percent coupon paid annually through 2027 seems more like a stock investment than a bond investment. Despite the stellar returns from some Brady bonds, they are not without risk. Brazil for example, has large amounts of external debt as a percentage of its gross domestic product, in addition to these bonds being extremely volatile in price owing to economic and political changes.

Non-Dollar-Denominated Bonds

Foreign pay bonds are issued and traded in a currency other than dollars. Examples of non-dollar-denominated bonds are French government bonds denominated in euros, Japanese corporate bonds issued and traded in yen, British corporate bonds traded in pounds, and so forth.

Returns from foreign pay bonds can be altered significantly owing to foreign currency changes. For example, British corporate bonds bought at par with a 6 percent coupon and held to maturity yield a 6 percent internal rate of return if the dollar-pound exchange rate remains the same at purchase and maturity. However, after purchase, if the British pound declines in value relative to the dollar, the total returns from the bond will be less than 6 percent. If, on the other hand, the British pound appreciates relative to the dollar, the returns from the bond will be greater than 6 percent.

BUYING INTERNATIONAL BONDS

Investors have three options for investing in international bonds: individual bonds, international mutual funds, or international exchange-traded funds. Buying and selling individual international debt is the most difficult of the three options for U.S. investors. Foreign governments do not make it easy for investors to buy their bonds like the U.S. government through its Treasury Direct program. Consequently, one of the few sources for U.S. investors to buy foreign government and corporate bonds is through large brokerage firms with international exposure. If these brokerage firms do indeed carry international bonds, they might have limited inventories, resulting in investors being charged large commissions or markups. Most online brokerage firms in the United States do not carry inventories of foreign bonds.

Interest rates differ from country to country, resulting in differences in the characteristics of the bond offerings. Before buying bonds from a particular country, you want to have a good idea of where interest rates are heading, the strength of that country's currency, and the relationship between that bond's coupon rate as compared with other countrys' bond coupon rates and their respective quality with regard to credit and default.

For example, the coupon rate of 4 percent offered by a German government obligation might be considered to be low when compared with bonds of 13 percent offered by emerging governments like Brazil or South Africa. However, if the currency of Brazil and South Africa declines in value relative to the dollar and the euro keeps appreciating, the German government bonds begin to look more attractive to U.S. investors. Similarly, if interest rates in the European Union decline, while interest rates in both Brazil and South Africa increase due to inflation and other economic reasons, then the German bond will increase in value while the emerging country bonds will decline in value. Foreign corporate bonds generally offer higher coupons than government bonds, but they can also carry greater credit and default risk.

RISKS OF INVESTING IN INTERNATIONAL BONDS

Foreign bonds are exposed to many more risks than domestic bonds. Foreign governments do not carry the same risk-free characteristics of U.S. government bonds. Some emerging country governments have defaulted on their debt, and so it is important to check on the ratings of foreign bonds before investing. Default risk on emerging government debt and foreign corporate debt is real. For example, political instability could result in a government being overthrown and causing the country to default on its existing debt obligations. Credit and default risks are much harder to determine on foreign bonds than on domestic issues.

Fluctuating currency can have a significant impact on foreign bond prices and returns. Exchange rate risk occurs when there is a change in value in the currency in which the bond is bought and issued, and the value received when the bond pays interest and the receipts from sale or maturity of the bond. For example, an investment in German bonds in 2005 through 2007 would have returned greater returns than the bond's internal rate of return because of the appreciating euro relative to the dollar. On the other hand, an investment during the same period in South African bonds would have resulted in returns that were less than the internal rate of return of the bonds because of the depreciating South African rand relative to the value of the dollar.

Looked at in another way, foreign-denominated bonds trade and pay interest in their local currency. Consequently, when you receive your interest payments and par value of your bond at maturity, you need to convert these receipts into U.S. dollars. When the foreign currency is weak relative to the dollar, you receive fewer dollars because it takes more of the foreign currency to buy a dollar in the conversion. Similarly, when the foreign currency appreciates relative to the dollar, in the conversion the foreign currency buys more dollars. Thus, a positive rate of return in a local currency can equal a loss in dollar terms and the opposite when there are large changes in currency values.

Interest rate risk affects the value of international bonds in the same manner as domestic bonds. When interest rates rise, prices of existing bonds decline, and when market rates of interest decline, prices of existing bond issues increase. Avoid investing in the bonds of countries that are expected to raise their interest rates.

Inflation or purchasing power risk erodes returns of bonds. Although coupon rates of bonds rise to accommodate rising inflation, existing bondholders suffer because their returns are fixed. High or increasing levels of inflation in a country is a double-edged sword for investors and is often a predictor of what is to follow from that country's central bank, which is to raise interest rates. Consequently, foreign investors' returns are eroded by inflation, which also decreases currency values, along with decreasing bond prices due to higher interest rates.

Foreign corporate bonds might not be as actively traded as domestic corporate bonds, thereby exposing holders to liquidity and marketability risk. In such cases, it might be difficult for investors to find buyers for thinly traded issues.

Investors should determine whether the foreign bond issue has a call provision, which subjects the bond issue to call risk. Compare the coupon yield of the bond issue with the call provision with a comparable issue that does not have a call provision. A bond issue with a call provision should have a higher coupon yield to compensate investors for the call risk. Be aware of the details in the call provision, namely the call date and the call price.

Investors should understand the different types of risk of foreign bonds before investing.

ADVANTAGES OF INVESTING IN FOREIGN BONDS

- Investing in international bonds offers investors the opportunity to obtain higher returns from their fixed-income investments.
- Investing in foreign bonds adds diversification to a bond portfolio, especially because historically, foreign bonds have had a low correlation with returns from U.S. bonds.
- Investors in foreign bonds receive increased returns when the dollar weakens relative to the invested currency.

DISADVANTAGES OF INVESTING IN FOREIGN BONDS

- Increased risk from investing in foreign bonds might not be worth the additional potential returns.
- It is difficult to obtain information on individual issues.
- Investors might not be able to buy and sell international bond issues at good prices.
- International bond markets are not as liquid as the U.S. bond markets.

INVESTING IN INTERNATIONAL BOND MUTUAL FUNDS

There are a number of reasons why investing in foreign bond mutual funds has become popular with many investors. In 2007, investment funds into foreign bond funds doubled to $19 billion (Anand, 2008). The factors that favor owning individual foreign bonds are the same for owning foreign bond mutual funds. These factors are:

- Historically low interest rates in the United States have prompted investors to look outside the United States for higher coupon payments.
- The declining value of the dollar against other currencies makes foreign bonds more valuable in dollar terms.

- Foreign governments are expected to cut interest rates as the global economy slows.

Mutual funds offer investors the advantage of diversification with a small investment, which is important when investing in emerging market debt owing to their increased credit and default risk.

There are many international bond funds, emerging market funds, and global funds to choose from. You should read the prospectus to determine what the expense ratios are, whether the fund charges load and redemption fees, whether the fund can hedge its currency exposure, whether the fund invests primarily in dollar-denominated bonds or non-dollar-denominated bonds, and whether the fund invests primarily in good-quality foreign government bonds or riskier corporate bond issues.

Oppenheimer's international bond fund charges a front-end load of 4.75 percent, whereas T. Rowe Price's International bond fund has no front-end load. Oppenheimer's fund has a one-year return of 17.6 percent versus T. Rowe Price's fund return of 10.05 percent. When the load is backed out, the returns become comparable. Pimco Developing Local Markets' fund has an expense ratio of 1.25 percent along with a load of 3.75 percent, which is steep when compared with T. Rowe Price's emerging markets bond fund, which has a 0.98 percent expense ratio and no load fees.

The holdings of an international bond fund impact the returns of the fund not only with regard to their coupon returns and quality of holdings but also whether the holdings are predominantly dollar denominated or non-dollar denominated. Funds that have invested primarily in dollar-denominated bonds have not fared as well as funds with non-dollar-denominated investments as a result of the declining value of the dollar during the past few years through June 2008. Funds that invested primarily in emerging market debt and riskier corporate bonds returned double-digit returns, around 10 percent, versus the more conservative funds that hold better quality debt, around 6.5 percent (Anand, 2008). Most of the returns came from currency conversions. To control some of the currency volatility, some funds use currency futures to hedge against currency risk.

WHAT ARE THE RISKS OF INTERNATIONAL BOND MUTUAL FUNDS?

In addition to the risks affecting domestic bond mutual funds, international bond mutual funds are exposed to additional risks, such as currency risk, global political risk, and economic risk.

Mutual fund shareholders are always exposed to the risk of loss of funds invested owing to the decline in the share price of the fund. Because share prices of international bond funds are more volatile than domestic bond funds, the risk of loss is much greater with international bond funds. Share prices of funds with lower quality bond holdings are also likely to be more volatile when interest rates in their respective countries change.

Another reason for the increased volatility in share price is that interest rates can fluctuate more widely in developing nations than developed nations.

Currency risk and default risk are the major concerns for shareholders in these funds. For example, an increase in the U.S. dollar would eat into the higher returns of foreign bond funds after conversion for a fund that has not hedged its currency. A mutual fund that hedges correctly against this occurrence would neutralize this risk.

Default risk is of concern to shareholders of funds that invest in lower quality debt, such as the bonds of emerging market governments experiencing political tensions and economic problems, and lower quality corporate debt. In general, higher-yielding, lower-rated bonds of foreign corporations and emerging market governments have a higher risk of default than higher-quality, lower-yielding bond issues of developed governments and blue chip companies. Pay attention to the quality of the bond issues of a fund's holdings to assess the risk of default of the fund.

Because foreign bond mutual funds have outperformed domestic bond funds for the past years in the mid 2000s, investors should not think that this is a permanent trend. Bond prices rise when interest rates fall, and when interest rates rise, bond prices fall. A slowdown in global economies with a rise in interest rates will expose emerging market debt to greater risk.

HOW TO BUY INTERNATIONAL
BOND MUTUAL FUNDS

Investing in international bond mutual funds is easier for investors than buying individual international bonds because investors do not have to sort out valuations, quality, and prices of individual issues, or face illiquid markets with little price transparency and fluctuating currency values. Of course, sophisticated investors can use currency ETFs to hedge their positions in foreign bonds so that they are not exposed to currency risk. For example, if an investor thinks that the euro is going to appreciate in value against the dollar, that investor could buy the Rydex Euro Currency Trust, ticker symbol FXE, which invests in euros in a money market fund in order to balance the depreciating currencies of emerging bond issues.

Look for funds that have low expense ratios, have no front-end or back-end (redemption) loads, and hold a predominance of issues with good-quality ratings. Determine also whether the fund hedges its currency positions.

International bond funds can be purchased directly from the investment companies that sponsor the funds. Download and read the prospectus of the fund before investing.

ADVANTAGES OF INVESTING
IN INTERNATIONAL BOND
MUTUAL FUNDS

- With a small investment, investors buy into a diversified portfolio of international bond holdings.
- Such an investment adds portfolio diversification to domestic bond holdings.
- Currency swings that are favorable to the holdings of a fund can increase returns on conversion to dollars.
- Investors have the potential to earn higher returns than those from domestic bonds.
- It is easier to invest in international bond mutual funds than in individual international bonds.

DISADVANTAGES OF INVESTING IN INTERNATIONAL BOND MUTUAL FUNDS

- Fees and expense ratios erode returns.
- Investors only get to know the fund's holdings after the end of the fund's accounting quarter.
- Investors have no control over the selection of the bond holdings in the fund.
- International bond mutual funds do not mature like individual bonds. As a result, investors might not receive the entire amount of their investments when they sell their shares.
- International bond funds carry more risk than domestic bond funds.
- Investors do not know the buying or selling price per share when they put in their orders to buy or sell shares (share price is calculated at the close of the day and this is the price used for purchase and sale transactions).

INTERNATIONAL BOND EXCHANGE-TRADED FUNDS

International bond ETFs present a third alternative form for investors to invest in international bonds. This is not quite so easy because as of February 2008, there is only one international bond ETF offered to investors in the U.S. market to choose from. There is a Hong Kong-based ETF that holds developing Asian country currency denominated bonds issued by governments and quasi-governments that is listed on the Hong Kong stock exchange (ticker symbol 2821). This ETF is difficult for American investors who do not have access to brokers in Hong Kong to buy and sell the shares.

The American international bond ETF was introduced to the market on October 5, 2007, by State Street, under the name SPDR Lehman International Treasury Bond, ticker symbol BWX, which trades on the American Stock Exchange. The objective stated by the fund on its Web site is to provide investment results before expenses and fees that correlate to the price and yield performance of the Lehman brothers Global Treasury ex U.S. Index.

The holdings of this ETF offer broad exposure to good-quality foreign government bond issues. To obtain the exact holdings of the fund, type in the ticker symbol BWX on Yahoo Finance. The average quality of the bond holdings in the fund as of February 27, 2008, was AA2, the yield to maturity 3.61 percent, and the gross expense ratio 0.50 percent. The yield to maturity might seem low when compared with some of the international bond mutual funds, particularly emerging debt mutual funds, which offer greater yields because the quality of most of their bond holdings are not as highly rated. Consequently, these emerging market bond funds carry greater credit and default risks.

The SPDR Lehman International Treasury Bond ETF trades like a common stock on the American Stock Exchange and can be bought and sold through regular and online brokers at any time during the trading day, including after hours.

THE RISKS OF INVESTING IN INTERNATIONAL BOND ETFS

Even though there has historically been a low correlation in returns between foreign bonds and U.S. bonds, if there is a global recession or worldwide inflation, then diversification into foreign bonds might not immunize U.S. investors' portfolio returns from an overall decline.

International bond ETFs trade like stocks and are subject to market risk. A sell-off in the market could affect this stock even though fundamentally there might not be a good reason for this stock to decline in price. Consequently, there is always the risk that investors could lose money when the share price falls below the price at which the investor purchased the shares.

The SPDR Lehman International Treasury Bond ETF invests in bond issues from at least 18 countries and has exposure to 11 different currencies. Consequently, the fund is exposed to currency risk. If the U.S. dollar appreciates significantly against the Japanese yen, the euro, and Canadian dollar, returns from this ETF are reduced when interest and principal are converted back into dollars.

International bond ETFs are also exposed to interest rate risk, credit and default risk, political risk, and economic risk, which is magnified if the holdings are primarily from emerging market countries.

ADVANTAGES OF INVESTING IN INTERNATIONAL BOND ETFS

- ETFs are transparent with regard to their disclosure of their holdings of international bond issues.
- ETFs generally are more cost efficient than bond funds.
- It is easy for investors to buy and sell shares of ETFs at any time during the trading day or during after hours trading when the stock exchanges close.
- Share prices of ETFs are transparent.

DISADVANTAGES OF INVESTING IN INTERNATIONAL BOND ETFS

- Actively managed mutual funds might have a better chance of outperforming indexed bond ETFs.
- Actively buying and selling shares of ETFs incur brokerage fees, which erode returns.
- Investors face the risk of losing part of their principal investment if share prices decline below their purchase price because of market risk and geopolitical and economic risk.
- There is only one international bond ETF as of February 2008 offered to U.S. investors.

SHOULD YOU INVEST IN INDIVIDUAL INTERNATIONAL BONDS, INTERNATIONAL MUTUAL FUNDS, OR INTERNATIONAL ETFS?

The advantages of investing in individual international bond issues over mutual funds and ETFs are that investors have greater control over their investment holdings. Investors investing in individual bonds are able to buy and sell bond issues of their choice, whereas with mutual funds there is no control over the holdings and the holdings are only disclosed to investors at the end of each quarter. ETF holders also cannot control the holdings of the fund, but ETFs provide disclosure of their holdings to potential investors.

However, individual investors need to have the expertise, time, and information to be able to carefully select and manage bond issues that match or exceed the returns of funds. Individual bonds offer predictable streams of income, whereas with mutual funds and ETFs the streams of interest income are not predictable. With individual bonds, principal is returned at the maturity or call date, whereas bond funds and ETFs do not have stated maturity dates. Individual bondholders know what their yield to maturity is for the bond issues in their holdings, whereas with mutual funds and ETFs, the yield to maturity cannot be known in advance.

As individual bonds near their maturity dates, their prices are impacted less by changes in interest rates, whereas bond mutual funds and ETFs are more vulnerable to changes in interest rates. Ongoing fees charged by mutual funds and ETFs eat into returns, whereas trading ETF shares incurs brokerage fees. However, ETFs are generally more cost efficient than mutual funds. Pricing of foreign bonds is not transparent, and so investors can never be sure that markups and commissions charged to trade individual bonds are reasonable.

Actively managed foreign bond mutual funds might have a better chance of outperforming indexed bond ETFs.

Despite the many advantages and disadvantages of individual international bonds, bond mutual funds, and ETFs, the question to start with is do you have the expertise, knowledge, and time to research the characteristics of the different bond issues and the geopolitical and economic risks pertaining to the foreign countries of the bonds? If not, then the easier choice is between bond mutual funds or ETFs. Table 14-1 summarizes the advantages and disadvantages of whether to invest in individual bonds, mutual funds. or ETFs.

Table 14-1

Characteristics of Individual International Bonds versus Mutual Funds and ETFs

	Individual Securities	Mutual Funds	ETFs
Ease of buying and selling	Difficult to buy and sell individual bonds.	Easy to buy and sell shares. Trades occur only at the closing price at the end of the day	Easy to buy and sell shares at real time prices during the trading day.
Costs to trade	Commission costs when buying and selling existing bonds on the secondary market. Lack of transparent pricing of bonds. Need access to brokers with inventories of foreign bonds.	None when investing in no-load mutual funds.	Commissions incurred for each trade. Transparent prices of shares.
Income stream	Income stream remains fixed for each bond until maturity or call.	Income stream varies from month to month.	Income stream varies.
Expense ratios	None	Vary depending on the fund.	Vary depending on the ETF (tend to be lower than mutual funds).
Returns	Return is not diminished by fees.	Variable return reduced by the total fees charged by the fund.	Variable return reduced by the total fees charged by the ETF.
Tax planning	Easy to predict income and plan capital gains and losses.	Unpredictable distributions of income and capital gains can upset careful tax planning.	More tax efficient than a mutual fund.
Investment amounts	Requires a minimum of $25,000- $50,000.	Required minimum investment amounts vary by fund (can be quite low).	Minimum purchase is a single share of stock.
Safety of principal	If good quality bonds are held through maturity, principal is recovered.	A chance that principal may not be fully recovered if share price falls below the purchase price when shares are sold.	Fluctuating share price could result in a loss of principal.
Holdings	Known	Not disclosed until the end of the quarter.	Known, although they can change over time.
Diversification	Need large amount of money to build a diversified portfolio	Small investment buys a holding in a diversified portfolio.	Small investment buys a holding in a diversified bond portfolio.

REFERENCE

Anand, Shefali, "Investors Flock to Foreign Bonds," *Wall Street Journal*, February 13, 2008, pp. D1, D3.

CHAPTER 15

Closed-End Funds

KEY CONCEPTS

- Closed-end funds
- Unit investment trusts
- The risks of closed-end funds and unit investment trusts
- Their advantages
- Their disadvantages
- Caveats
- Whether they are suitable investment vehicles for you

WHAT ARE CLOSED-END FUNDS?

Closed-end funds differ from open-end mutual funds, discussed in many of the preceding chapters in this book, but there are also some similarities. Table 15-1 summarizes the similarities and differences. An open-end mutual fund issues an unlimited number of shares, and the fund sells and redeems shares to and from shareholders. The fund can issue more shares when new investors buy more shares.

A closed-end fund issues a fixed number of shares, and when all the shares issued are sold, no more are issued. Shares of closed-end funds are traded on the stock exchanges or on the over-the-counter market where they can be bought and sold. Most closed-end funds are traded on the New York Stock Exchange with some on the American Stock Exchange and a few on the over-the-counter market.

Since there are a fixed number of shares in a closed-end fund, investors who want to invest in an existing fund (as opposed to a new fund) have to buy shares from shareholders who are willing to sell their shares on the market. Consequently, the share price of the closed-end bond fund fluctuates depending on the supply and demand for the shares, and on other factors, such as the return of the fund's investments, average maturity of the investment holdings, net asset value (NAV), and other fundamental factors affecting the share price.

Like open-end mutual funds, the NAV is important in the valuation of the share price. However, unlike open-end funds, share prices of closed-end funds can sell above or below their NAVs. Market factors affect share prices of closed-end funds. For example, when interest rates decline, prices of closed-end bond funds could increase above their NAVs. Hence, these funds would trade at a premium to their NAVs. Similarly, when interest rates increase, shares of closed-end bond funds could trade at significant discounts to their NAVs. For example, a closed-end bond fund could have a NAV of $9 per share and be selling at $7.50 per share (trading at a $1.50 discount per share). At times, the discounts to NAVs of closed-end funds can be as much as 20 to 30 percent. Table 15-2 lists two examples of funds trading at a discount and a premium to their NAVs, as well as how to calculate the premium or discount percentage. Prices of closed-end funds can be obtained from financial newspapers or from Web sites on the Internet.

The types of bonds held in the fund and their maturities also affect the share price. The longer the maturities are of the bond holdings, the greater is the volatility in the fund's share price.

Like open-end funds, there are many different closed-end funds. There are stock funds, bond funds, international funds, and specialized funds. In 2006 there were 444 closed-end bond funds, of which 135 were domestic taxable bond funds, 276 were municipal bond funds, and 33 were global and international bond funds (www.ici.org).

Closed-end funds have professional managers who assemble and manage the investment portfolios according to the goals and objectives of the funds. Existing bond issues can be sold and new ones bought for the portfolio. When bond issues mature, the

T a b l e 1 5 - 1

Closed-end Funds versus Open-end Funds

Closed-end Funds	Open-end Funds
1. Issue a fixed number of shares which are sold to original shareholders 2. Shares after issue are traded on the exchanges. 3. Shares can trade at, above or below net asset value. 4. Share prices depend not only on fundamentals but also on the supply of and demand for the shares. 5. Shareholders sell their shares to investors on the secondary market. 6. Closed-end funds do not mature; unit investment trusts do.	1. Issue an unlimited number of shares 2. Shares including new shares can be bought and sold from and to the fund. 3. Shares trade at net asset value. 4. Share prices depend on closing prices of the holdings of the fund's investment holdings. 5. Shareholders sell their shares to the investment company sponsoring the fund and the portfolio manager might be forced to sell bonds in the portfolio to raise cash. 6. Open-end funds do not mature except for zero-coupon bond funds.

T a b l e 1 5 - 2

Closed-end Fund Premiums and Discounts

Fund Name	Ticker Symbol	Net Asset Value	Market Price*	Premium/ (Discount)
Blackrock Ins Muni	BMT	10.58	10.10	(4.5)
PIMCO Corp. Inc.	PCN	13.43	14.78	10.1

* Prices as of January 28, 2008

How to Calculate the Discount or Premium

$$\text{Premium (Discount)} = \frac{(\text{market value} - \text{NAV})}{\text{NAV}}$$

$$\text{PIMCO Corp Income} = \frac{(14.78 - 13.43)}{13.43}$$

$$= 10.01\%$$

proceeds received are used to buy new issues. Closed-end funds, like open-end funds, do not mature. The basic advantage of closed-end funds over open-end funds is that closed-end fund managers do not have to sell any of their bond holdings when shareholders sell their shares because with closed-end funds shareholders sell their shares to investors on the exchanges.

NAVs for closed-end funds are calculated in much the same way as for open-end funds. The total assets minus any liabilities equal the net worth of the fund, which is divided by the fixed number of shares to give the NAV per share.

Shares of closed-end funds are bought and sold through brokers. You should be aware of the following facts about the purchase of closed-end funds:

- Brokerage firms underwrite and sell newly issued shares of closed-end funds.
- Brokerage fees on newly issued shares can be quite high, which then erodes the price of the shares when they trade on the market. For example, if a closed-end fund sells one million shares at $10 per share, and there is a brokerage commission of 6 percent, the fund receives $9.4 million to invest ($600,000 is deducted from the $10 million proceeds). The share price drops in value from the $10 originally paid and trades at a discount to the offer price.
- Another reason not to buy newly issued shares in a closed-end fund is that the portfolio has not yet been constituted, so investors do not know what the investment assets are and in the case of bond funds, the yields on those investments.

WHAT ARE UNIT INVESTMENT TRUSTS?

A unit investment trust (UIT) is a type of closed-end fund that also issues a fixed number of shares, which are sold originally by the sponsor of the trust. The proceeds from the sale are used to buy stocks or bonds for the trust, which are held to maturity. Unlike an open-end fund or regular closed-end fund, no active trading of the securities in the portfolio takes place. Consequently, no active management of the trust takes place, which should translate into lower management fees, although this is not always the case. A trust has a maturity date, and the proceeds are then returned to the shareholders of the trust. Consequently, these trusts are well suited to bonds, with their streams of income and maturity of principal. The majority of UITs sold consist of tax-exempt municipal bonds, followed by taxable bond trusts and then stock trusts.

UITs have been seductively marketed as an investment that earns high current income and returns investors' entire investments when the trust assets mature. Theoretically, this might be possible, but in practice this might not always be possible. By examining how unit trusts work, the difficulties of living up to these lofty promises become apparent.

A UIT, like a closed-end fund, sells a fixed number of shares. For instance, assume that the trust sells one million shares at $10 per share for a total of $10 million. A 5 percent sales commission of $500,000 would be deducted, leaving the unit trust (same for a closed-end bond fund) with $9.5 million to invest in different bond issues. The trust (closed-end fund) then remits the earnings on the investments after management fees to the shareholders. When the different investments mature, the trust then pays back the proceeds from the investments to shareholders. (Closed-end funds differ in that when issues mature, the proceeds are reinvested in other issues). Because $9.5 million is invested in bonds, the maturity value of the bonds would be $9.5 million, but investors invested $10 million. Similarly, if a bond issue defaults on its interest and principal obligations, shareholders might receive even less.

Generally, with UITs, the portfolios of investments do not change after they have been bought. In other words, no new bonds are bought and no existing bonds are sold. Theoretically, as the bond issues approach maturity, so the prices of the individual bonds rise towards their par prices. Again, theoretically, management fees should be lower on UITs than closed-end funds because the portfolio remains unmanaged. In fact, there should be no management fees on a UIT because the portfolio is unmanaged, but in most instances, this is not the case. With closed-end bond funds, the portfolio changes as issues are bought and sold.

Shares of closed-end bond funds trade on the secondary markets but UIT shares can be sold back to the sponsor of the trust. However, in certain conditions, shares in UITs can be illiquid. This happens when interest rates are rising and new investors would not want to buy into a trust with bond investments that are locked into lower yields. Hence, existing unit trust shareholders may have difficulty selling their shares due to illiquidity.

WHAT ARE THE RISKS OF CLOSED-END BOND FUNDS AND UNIT INVESTMENT TRUSTS?

Both closed-end bond funds and UITs are subject to *interest rate risk*. When market rates of interest increase, generally prices of bond issues held in both the portfolios of unit trusts and closed-end bond funds decline. This means lower share prices. Moreover, this is a double-edged sword in that if there is selling pressure on the fund's shares, the decline in share prices will be even greater than the decline in NAV. The opposite is true in that if interest rates decline, there will be appreciation in the assets and, of course, in the share price. For both closed-end funds and UITs, there is the risk that share prices will fall below NAVs owing to excess selling pressure in the stock markets. Then, of course, the danger arises of not being able to recoup the original price paid for the shares when selling. This is a common phenomenon experienced by closed-end funds and UITs.

For UIT shareholders, there is the added risk of not getting back the full amount of their original investments at maturity. This can be caused by a number of factors. The composition of the trust's assets, commissions, high management fees charged to the trust, and the use of leverage are all factors that can add to the risk of loss of principal. The managers of UITs and closed-end bond funds charge in many cases very generous annual fees, in addition to their up-front commissions on the original sale of the shares. This means that these funds have to earn spectacular returns in order for the managers of these funds to be able to collect their fees without eroding yields significantly. They also have to rake up some capital gains to be able to recoup the sales commissions in order to return to the shareholders their entire investments at maturity. This explains why many closed-end funds use leverage and resort to derivative securities as ways to try and boost their returns.

The types of investments that a fund or trust holds have a marked effect on the NAV, as well as the volatility of the share price. Unfortunately for the original shareholders of closed-end bond funds and UITs, there is no way of knowing the composition of the portfolio investments when they originally subscribe to the shares of the fund/trust. That's because only after the original shareholders invest their money to buy the shares do the managers of the fund or trust buy the investment assets. Thus, original shareholders might not be able to evaluate the levels of risk of the assets until the portfolio has been constituted. The composition may include the bonds of highly risky companies. Investors then trying to exit the fund or trust might experience losses from the decline in the share price. If there is an exodus of shareholders from UITs and closed-end funds, shareholders may find it difficult to sell their shares without taking large losses.

When interest rates decline, there is always the risk of bond issues being called, causing reinvestment rate risk. Shareholders of UITs receive part of their principal investment, which is then reinvested at lower rates of interest, reducing their overall returns.

Many closed-end funds use leverage to increase their yields. Leverage is where the funds use borrowed money to supplement amounts invested by shareholders to invest in portfolio assets. This strategy has worked well for many funds because of the yield curve, which shows the relationship between long-term and short-term rates. When short-term rates are lower than long-term interest rates, funds can borrow on a short-term basis and invest the funds in long-term issues, which yield higher returns. This strategy works well for funds as long as short-term rates are lower than long-term rates. However, this is a risky strategy because if interest rates bottom out and begin to rise, not only will borrowing costs climb, but the increased costs will cut into the yields paid to shareholders. Moreover, prices of the different bond securities held in the portfolio will decline, which, of course, translates into lower share prices. Thus, the use of leverage adds further risks when compounded with changes in interest rates.

HOW TO BUY AND SELL CLOSED-END FUNDS AND UNIT INVESTMENT TRUSTS

When closed-end funds and UITs are newly issued, the shares are underwritten by brokerage firms and sold by brokers. Brokerage fees can be as high as 8 percent, which means that the investor's investment is immediately reduced by 8 percent. For instance, if a fund or trust sells one million shares at $10 per share for $10 million, it will have only $9.2 million to invest after deducting

$800,000 (8 percent) for brokerage commissions. This means that after shareholders have paid $10 per share to invest in the new fund or trust, the shares will drop in value and trade at a discount. This is a quick erosion in capital and is a well-documented phenomenon for closed-end funds and UITs. This will not be a topic of conversation brought up by brokers, who stand to earn high commissions from the sale of these shares. Many brokers assert that closed-end funds are sold commission free. This is a play on words because it might be commission free, but in its place is a hefty underwriting charge that is absorbed by the shareholders. Investors would do better to wait until the funds are listed on the stock exchanges than to buy them at issue only to see the shares drop in price.

Another reason not to buy closed-end funds or UITs at issue is that the portfolio of assets has not been constituted, so investors do not know what they are getting and they most certainly won't know what the yields will be. UIT sponsors do not like to see the shares of their trusts fall to discounts, and so they often advertise above market yields to keep the shares from trading at discounts to their NAVs.

Common sense suggests that besides the attractiveness of buying into a fund when its shares are selling below their NAVs there are other factors to consider:

- The yield is important, particularly if investors are buying into the fund in order to get income. Examine the yield, total return, and expense ratios before investing.
- The frequency that dividends are paid—semiannually, quarterly, or monthly.
- The composition of the bonds and their credit quality.
- The average length of time to maturity of the portfolio investments.

Share prices of listed closed-end funds can be found in the stock exchange sections of daily financial newspapers and on financial Web sites on the Internet. Before buying closed-end funds or trusts, ask your broker or call the fund sponsor for the annual or quarterly report.

WHAT ARE THE ADVANTAGES OF CLOSED-END FUNDS AND UNIT INVESTMENT TRUSTS?

- Investors can sometimes purchase closed-end funds at discounts to their NAVs, which may offer the potential for capital gains and increased yields. The downside of this strategy is that it could lead to capital losses if the discount to the NAV widens.
- Investors can sometimes sell their closed-end fund shares at premiums to their NAVs.
- The shares of the larger actively traded closed-end funds can be bought and sold on the stock exchanges.
- For income-seeking investors, most UITs pay dividends on a monthly basis.
- UITs have maturities at which time investors will have all (or most) of their capital returned to them.

WHAT ARE THE DISADVANTAGES OF CLOSED END FUNDS AND UNIT INVESTMENT TRUSTS?

- Both closed-end funds and UITs are subject to interest rate risk. UITs have no protection against a rise in interest rates, because their portfolios of investments are fixed.
- There is the risk that the share prices of funds and trusts can move independently to the value of the securities that are held in the fund's portfolios. More investors exiting the fund than buying the fund have the effect of driving the price down despite the fact that the assets in the fund are doing well. This often represents a buying opportunity when the fund's shares trade at a deep discount to its NAV.
- Brokerage commissions along with management fees can be high, which reduce the yields of closed-end funds and UITs.
- Some of the shares of the smaller less actively traded funds and trusts can be illiquid.
- Buying into funds and trusts when they are first offered to shareholders means that these shareholders are investing

into an unknown portfolio of assets. This is of particular significance for UITs in that investors cannot gauge the level of risk in the composition of the assets and whether the fund uses leverage to try and increase yields.

- UITs offer no protection against the credit deterioration of their assets since their portfolios are fixed.

CAVEATS

- Investors should avoid investing in closed-end bond funds and UITs when they are first offered to the public because a percentage of their initial funds will go toward paying underwriting fees and selling commissions. For example, if investors pay $10 per share and $0.80 goes toward these expenses, NAVs will fall to $9.20 directly after issuance.
- Compare the long-term performance of closed-end funds and UITs before investing. Some have not performed well and investors may want to avoid those with poor long-term track records.
- Examine the fees charged before buying into closed-end funds and UITs. Fees can be high.
- When bonds are called or sold early in UITs, the principal and any interest is returned to investors. If this is spent, you are spending part of your principal investment.

ARE CLOSED-END FUNDS AND UNIT INVESTMENT TRUSTS FOR ME?

Under certain conditions, closed-end funds and UITs have provided investors with profitable returns in the past. Investors sometimes have an opportunity to buy bond funds at a discount to their NAVs. Some closed-end bond funds and UITs trade at premiums to their NAVs when the funds' coupon yields of their bond investment holdings are higher than current rates of interest. UITs, which do not buy and sell their bond issues, retain their higher yields to maturity as interest rates fall. If the bonds are called, the trust then returns the principal to shareholders. With closed-end bond funds, the manager of the fund uses the proceeds to invest in new bonds with lower coupon yields, thus lowering the average total yield of the fund.

It is often advantageous for investors to buy into closed-end funds and UITs when they are trading at discounts to their NAVs. In fact, many investment advisors recommend buying closed-end funds when they are trading at large discounts by historical standards to their NAVs and selling them when they have small discounts or premiums. The caution to this strategy is that these fixed-income closed-end funds and UITs are sensitive to changes in interest rates. When market rates of interest rise, prices of bond funds and trusts decline, which can push the discounts to NAVs even lower.

UITs need to be examined carefully before buying because of their inherent characteristics. Because UITs mature, investors have their principal returned to them at the maturity date. Whether they get all of their principal back is questionable. If interest rates continue to decline, UIT shareholders benefit from the higher coupon yields, but depending on the fees charged by the trust, shareholders might not receive all of their original principal back.

Fees charged by closed-end funds and UITs tend to be larger than those of open-end funds, and so investors should include mutual funds in their decision process.

SHOULD AN INVESTOR INVEST IN INDIVIDUAL SECURITIES OR USE FUNDS?

Bond closed-end funds offer investors the opportunity to invest in diversified portfolios of different types of bonds and international bond funds, just like mutual funds. The advantages of both closed-end funds and mutual funds are the use of professional management, diversification, freedom to invest small amounts of money, and ease of buying and selling. For many investors, these advantages far outweigh their disadvantages. Decisions of which individual bonds to invest in are avoided by choosing bond mutual funds and closed-end funds.

An advantage of a closed-end fund over a mutual fund is that closed-end funds can trade at a discount to their NAVs. This is akin to buying a dollar's worth of assets at less than a dollar. This strategy appeals to value investors, who have the patience to wait for the assets to rise in value.

Mutual fund managers can experience liquidity risk from excessive sales of shares by shareholders. Fund managers would have to sell some of their bond holdings to raise enough cash to be able to redeem the shares sold by shareholders. This does not happen in closed-end funds, allowing their managers to invest in less liquid bonds.

Investing in individual bonds and closed-end funds allows investors to choose their purchase and selling prices during the trading day. Mutual fund transactions are enacted at the NAV price as of the close of the trading day. Similarly, there are no minimum investment amounts stipulated with closed-end fund investments as there are with mutual funds. An investor can buy or sell a single share or in round lots of shares.

However, in certain cases, a strong argument exists for buying individual securities over mutual funds and closed-end funds. Returns on individual bonds could be greater than those earned from mutual funds and closed-end funds due to fees charged by the funds. This statement is true even for no-load funds because in place of sales commissions, other fees, such as 12 (b)–1 and management fees, reduce the returns of mutual funds. By investing in individual securities, you avoid these fees. Closed-end funds do not charge 12 (b)–1 fees, but management fees can be high.

Investing in mutual funds and closed-end funds is a good strategy if you do not have enough money to diversify your investments, and do not have the time, expertise, or inclination to select and manage individual bonds. In addition, a wide range of funds offers you the opportunity to invest in the types of securities that would be difficult to buy individually.

Table 15-3 compares some characteristics of investing in individual securities versus mutual funds and closed-end funds.

Table 15-3

Characteristics of Individual Securities versus Mutual Funds, and Closed-End Funds

	Individual Securities	Mutual Funds	Closed-End Funds
Diversification	Achieved only if a large number of securities is purchased	Achieved with a small investment	Achieved with a small investment
Ease of Buying and Selling	More difficult to buy bonds because of a lack of pricing transparency	Easy to buy and sell shares. Trades occur only at the closing price at the end of the day	Easy to buy and sell liquid closed-end funds
Professional Management	No	Yes	Yes
Expenses and costs to buy and sell	Brokerage fees to buy and sell	Low to high expenses depending on fund.	Low to high expenses depending on fund plus brokerage fees to buy and sell shares
Tax Planning	Easier to predict income and plan capital gains and losses	Can upset careful tax planning due to unpredictable distributions of income and capital gains	Can upset careful tax planning due to unpredictable distributions of income and capital gains

CHAPTER 16

Portfolio Management and Evaluation

KEY CONCEPTS

- Investor's objectives
- Asset allocation
- Selection of individual investments

INVESTOR'S OBJECTIVES

The aim of portfolio management is to assemble individual investment securities in a portfolio that conforms to the investor's level of risk and rate of return. The investor's objectives are the most important guidelines to managing an investment portfolio. The main types of objectives for a portfolio are preservation of principal, providing income, or seeking capital growth. An investor pursuing capital growth for a portfolio, for example, might allocate a greater portion of the portfolio's assets toward growth stocks, small-cap stocks, and real estate. From time to time the investor evaluates the performance of the portfolio investments with regard to risk and return and whether the portfolio is meeting his or her investment objectives.

An investor seeking income with some capital growth from a portfolio would allocate a greater portion of the portfolio to bonds along with some stock investments. For example, a total portfolio amount of $600,000 might be invested in the following manner: $500,000 in bonds yielding 6 percent, which would generate income of $30,000 per year, and $100,000 in 4 percent dividend-yielding stocks, which would bring in an additional $4,000 in income per year. By investing a small percentage of the portfolio in stocks rather than 100 percent in bonds, this investor is seeking potential capital growth to the portfolio and also minimizing the total risk of the portfolio. If large-cap stocks increase by 8 percent for the year, the value of the stock portfolio would grow to $108,000, which would more than offset the reduction in income from investing in lower-yielding stocks than bonds.

Investors should be aware that not only do their objectives and individual characteristics change over time, but their investments also must be monitored because of changing financial conditions and markets. Companies change and their securities might no longer fulfill the criteria for which they were purchased. Not all investments in the portfolio realize their projected returns, so investors managing their portfolios might need to sell and replace them with other investments. This does not mean that all or most of the investments in the portfolio should be continuously turned over. Only those investments that are unlikely to achieve the objectives specified should be liquidated.

ASSET ALLOCATION

Asset allocation is a plan to invest in different asset classes (stocks, bonds, and money market funds) so that the capital invested is protected against adverse factors in the market. This, in essence, is the opposite of an investor putting all his or her eggs in one basket. The first step is to decide what percentage of your investment money to put into money market investments, bonds, stocks, and any other asset classes.

Diversification is the other balancing tool for a portfolio. For example, a portfolio might have investments in different asset classes according to a well-balanced asset allocation plan, but all the stock and bonds might be invested in the investments of companies in the same economic sector, which would not insulate the portfolio from the risk of loss. By investing in the stocks of different companies in various sectors of the economy and different types of bonds, the portfolio would be better insulated against the risk of loss.

In other words, the risk of loss is spread over a number of stocks and different types of bonds. Increasing the number of stocks and bonds held in a portfolio decreases the volatility. However, by increasing the number of stocks and bonds held in a portfolio, investors are also reducing the potential performance of that portfolio. Diversification seeks a balance between the risk-return trade-off. The return on a portfolio is dependent on the types of investments held in the portfolio.

Classifying some of the different types of investments on a continuum of risk, common stocks are considered to be the most risky (in terms of variability in share price), followed by long-term junk bonds, with shorter maturity good-quality bonds on the low-risk end and money market investments with the least risk. Bear in mind that there are many other types of investments that are riskier than common stocks, such as commodities and futures contracts. Similarly, there is a great variation of quality among common stocks. Common stocks of well-established "blue chip" companies are considered to be less risky than the bonds of highly leveraged companies with suspect balance sheets.

Figure 16-1 shows the levels of risk of different fixed-income securities. Money market securities at the base of the triangle have the lowest risk. With each ascending level of investments to the apex of the triangle, the level of risk increases. The riskiest of the bond types are zero coupon bonds. However, high-yielding, low-rated (junk) bonds (both corporate and municipal issues) can be just as risky as zero coupon bonds. The risk levels for these categories are relative and depend on the quality of the issue as well as the type. For example, a corporate bond issue from an issuer that is in questionable financial condition is riskier than a good-quality zero coupon bond.

Common stocks are considered to be the most risky due to the volatility of stock prices. However, over long periods of time where the ups and downs of the stock market can be averaged out, stocks have provided higher returns. Common stocks provide the growth in a portfolio and should be included among the investment assets to accomplish long-term growth goals. The percentage allocated to common stocks depends on the investor's objectives and personal characteristics. A retired widow who is dependent on the income generated from the investments in the portfolio might not hold any common stocks in the portfolio. However, if the portfolio generates more than a sufficient level of income for the widow's current needs, a small portion of the portfolio could be invested in common stocks to provide some growth in the portfolio for later years.

There is not a rigid formula for asset allocation. Rather, it is a good idea to think about the concept as a guideline when investing money. Some investors might tilt towards an aggressive portfolio, while others require a conservative portfolio. The mix of investment assets depends primarily on the levels of risk that investors are willing to take and their time horizons. The percentage allocated to the different types of assets can always be changed depending on circumstances. As individual circumstances change, so do the investor's objectives. If the emphasis shifts, for example, to greater income generation and preservation of capital from capital growth, the percentage of the investments in the portfolio can be changed accordingly. The most important aspect of investing is having an asset allocation plan, which signifies the broad mix of assets to strive for. Once these broad categories are determined, the individual assets are purchased. When considering the different types of securities to choose for a portfolio, investors should weigh the characteristics of the type of investments along with the risks to assist them in their overall choice.

FIGURE 16-1

Fixed-Income Securities and Levels of Risk

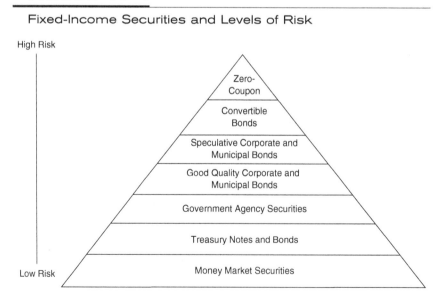

Investors need to revisit their asset allocation mix from time to time to determine whether to rebalance their mix and realign it to their investment objectives. The frequency with which the asset allocation plan is rebalanced also depends on the investor's portfolio management investment style. A *passive investment style* suggests leaving the portfolio alone. In other words, buying and holding the investments without regard for factors that affect the investments in the portfolio. An *active portfolio investment style* involves changing the investment assets within the portfolio whenever external circumstances have the potential to influence performance. The management of bond portfolios is very different from the management of stock portfolios. Bonds provide regular flows of income and have fixed lives, whereas stocks do not mature, might not provide regular flows of income if the stocks do not pay dividends, and do not have maturity dates, which means uncertainty with regard to future stock prices. This means that in the management of stock portfolios there is a greater emphasis on stock selection (buying those stocks that will appreciate the most).

Table 16-1 illustrates the need for rebalancing a portfolio. If the investor's objectives and personal characteristics have not changed one year later, the asset allocation mix should be realigned to the original mix. Both advantages and disadvantages arise from rebalancing a portfolio. The advantages are:

- The relative weighting of the portfolio assets are aligned with the individual's objectives, personal characteristics, risk tolerance, and rate of return.
- The risk of loss is reduced by selling appreciated assets to realize capital gains.

The disadvantages of rebalancing a portfolio are:

- Rebalancing a portfolio incurs trading costs (commissions) and advisory fees.
- Investors run the potential risk of loss that comes from selling the winners in the portfolio to buy more of the losing assets.
- Selling securities involves tax implications in taxable accounts.

Table 16-1

Rebalancing a Portfolio

1. *Begin with an asset allocation plan.*
The investor started with the following asset allocation as illustrated in Figure 16-2.

FIGURE 16-2

Original Asset Allocation Mix

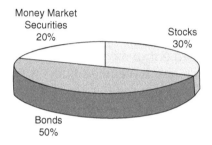

2. *Revisit the asset allocation plan after a period of time.*
One year later, with the rapid appreciation of the equity portfolio, the asset allocation mix has changed to the percentages shown in Figure 16-3.

FIGURE 16-3

Asset Allocation Mix One Year Later

3. *If necessary, rebalance the portfolio.*
The investor needs to determine whether this new asset allocation mix is consistent with his or her objectives, personal circumstances, and risk tolerance. With the appreciation of the equity assets, the new equity mix is now 50% of the total portfolio value and the bond mix has dropped from 50% to 35%. This may not be suitable for an investor who relies more on income-generating assets than growth assets. Rebalancing requires selling off some stocks and buying more bonds with the proceeds in order to realign the asset allocation mix closer to an acceptable asset allocation mix.

4. *Proposed asset allocation plan after rebalancing.*

Figure 16-4 shows the rebalancing of the current asset allocation mix back to a new asset allocation mix.

FIGURE 16-4

Current and Proposed Asset Allocation Mixes

Current Asset Allocation Mix

Rebalanced Allocation Mix

Current Asset Allocation Mix		Proposed Asset Allocation Mix	
Money market securities	15%	Money market securities	15%
Money market mutual fund	$45,000	Money market mutual funds	$45,000
Stocks	50%	Stocks	35%
Large-cap stocks	$150,000	Large-cap stocks	$52,500
Bonds	35%	Mid-cap stocks	$52,500
Individual bonds	$105,000	Bonds	50%
		Intermediate municipal bonds	$50,000
		Long-term Treasury bonds	$25,000
		Intermediate-term agency bonds	$35,000
		AAA corporate bonds	$40,000
Total	$300,000	Total	$300,000
Before-tax return	5.10%	Before-tax return	6.15%
After-tax return	3.15%	After-tax return	4.5%
Risk (standard deviation)	9.00%	Risk (standard deviation)	7.65%

Source: Esmé Faerber. "Fundamentals of the Bond Market." McGraw-Hill, New York, 2001, p168.

The most important aspect of investing is having an asset allocation plan that signifies the broad mix of assets to strive for. Once these broad categories are determined, the individual assets are purchased. Table 16-2 illustrates examples of different asset allocation plans for investors with different investment objectives.

Table 16-2

Asset Allocation Models for Different Investment Objectives

A *conservative portfolio* is where the investment goals are to preserve capital allowing for some growth to the portfolio. The weighting is geared toward high-quality bonds, and some common stocks for growth. An example of a conservative portfolio asset allocation is illustrated in Figure 16-5.

FIGURE 16-5

Conservative Portfolio

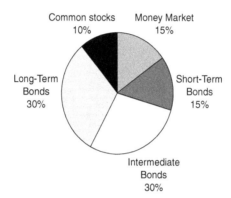

A *balanced portfolio* includes a greater percentage of common stocks, which provides capital growth for the portfolio, as well as keeping a large percentage of assets in fixed-income securities, which provide the income. Figure 16-6 provides an example of a balanced portfolio asset allocation.

FIGURE 16-6

Balanced Portfolio

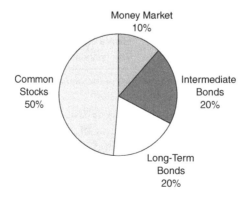

An *aggressive portfolio* is weighted more toward common stocks, which provide capital growth. Figure 16-7 illustrates an aggressive portfolio asset allocation plan (Faerber 2008, p.298).

FIGURE 16-7

Asset Allocation for an Aggressive Portfolio

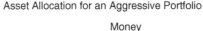

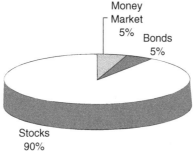

SELECTION OF INDIVIDUAL INVESTMENTS

In order to match your objectives with specific investments, you need to identify the characteristics of the different investments and their risks. Funds for immediate needs and emergency purposes should be liquid; in other words, one should be able to convert them easily into cash without incurring a loss in principal. Such investments are money market mutual funds, checking accounts, and savings accounts. These are readily convertible into cash. By increasing the time horizon from immediate needs to short-term needs, investors could increase marginally their rates of return by investing in certificates of deposit, Treasury bills, and commercial paper. However, of these, only Treasury bills are marketable, meaning that they can be sold on the secondary market before maturity.

Savings accounts, certificates of deposit, money market mutual funds, Treasury bills, and commercial paper provide some taxable income, are liquid, but do not offer the possibilities of capital gains or losses. Although investors might not lose any of their principal by investing in this group of investments, there is a risk that the returns from these investments might not keep up with inflation.

The financing of intermediate-term objectives that stretch several years into the future—such as the purchase of a car, house, or appliance, and the funding of a child's education—requires investments that generate income and the return of principal. These investments need to produce a greater rate of return than a savings account or short-term money market securities. Short-term to intermediate-term bonds offer increased rates of return over money market securities as well as the possibility of capital gains or losses if the investor needs the money before maturity. Although investors receive increased rates of return from intermediate-term securities over money market securities, investors need to be aware that their principal invested in intermediate-term bonds is not as liquid as in short-term securities.

An investment plan to finance a child's education in five years requires a relatively safe investment, which would not include investing in stocks. Most people would not gamble with the money earmarked for their children's education in the event of a declining stock market when the money would be needed.

Long-term objectives such as saving for retirement or for an infant's college education in 18 years require investments that offer long-term growth prospects as well as greater long-term returns. Stocks provide larger long-term returns than bonds or money market securities, but stock prices are more volatile. The level of risk that can be withstood on stock investments depends on the individual investor's circumstances.

A more conservative long-term portfolio might consist of long-term bonds, blue chip stocks, and conservative-growth stocks. The emphasis of this strategy is to invest in good-quality bonds and the stocks of established companies that pay dividends and offer the prospect of steady growth over a long period of time. Securities offering capital growth are important even for conservative portfolios in order to provide some cover against any potential erosion in future purchasing power from inflation.

A growth-oriented part of a portfolio seeks the generation of long-term capital gains and the monetary growth in value of the stocks in the portfolio. A more speculative portfolio, where an investor can absorb greater levels of risk to strive for greater growth and returns, would include growth stocks, stocks of emerging companies, foreign stocks, emerging market stocks, convertible bonds, junk bonds, real estate, options, commodities, and futures. Bear in mind that including the last three types of investments—options, commodities, and futures—is not an endorsement that these securities should play a major role in a portfolio. For a speculative investor who understands the nuances of these investments, these securities could account for no more than 5 percent of the total portfolio. The other assets mentioned offer investors the opportunity for large gains, but the risks of loss are also greater. Foreign bonds and stocks should also be considered, but investors should do their homework first so that they understand the risks fully. International mutual funds might be more helpful to spread some of the risks, although in the short-term there is always currency risk when investing in off-shore investments. Over the long term, however, exchange fluctuations tend to even out and are not a significant factor.

Investors who are not comfortable buying individual bonds and stocks could choose mutual funds, exchange-traded funds, or closed-end funds. Investors willing to make their own investment decisions on individual securities can eliminate the fees and expenses charged by mutual funds and closed-end funds. When considering the different types of securities to choose for a portfolio, investors should weigh the characteristics of the type of investment along with the risks. (See Table 16-3 for a summary of the strategies to reduce the different types of risks.)

MANAGEMENT OF A BOND PORTFOLIO

Passive Investment Strategy

Investors who do not believe that they can time the markets in order to benefit from increasing and decreasing yields generally follow a passive investment strategy. The philosophies of such investors are to buy and hold bonds through maturity. Bonds are bought with maturities or durations that match their time horizons. With this strategy, investors need to pay attention to the quality of the bond issues, call provisions, and coupon yields. Investors can ladder the maturities of their bonds or use bullet or barbell strategies discussed later in this chapter.

A second passive investment strategy is to build a bond portfolio based on an index such as, for example, the Merrill Lynch

Table 16-3

Summary of Strategies to Manage Risk

Investment	Risk	Strategy
Common Stock	Market Risk	Invest for a long period of time.
	Financial Risk	Diversification: Invest in companies with low leverage.
	Interest Rate Risk	Active or passive strategy, depending on the investor's time horizon.
	Declining Market Rates of Interest	Increase the percentage of the portfolio allocated to stocks.
	Increasing Market Rates	Decrease the percentage of the portfolio allocated to stocks.
	Credit Risk	Invest in good-quality stocks.
	Purchasing Power Risk	Requires active portfolio management. Invest in stocks that (when inflation increases) will weather the effects of inflation better, such as gold stocks, oil and commodity stocks.
Bonds	Interest rate risk	Interest rate management strategies
	Declining market rates	Increase maturities of bond issues
	Rising market rates	Shorten maturities and ladder bond portfolio
	Credit risk	Invest in higher quality issues and shorter maturities
	Inflation risk	Shorten maturities
		Invest in Treasury Inflation Protection Securities

Index or the Shearson Lehman Government or Corporate Bond Index. The latter index owns more than 4,000 bond issues in its corporate bond index, which makes it difficult for individual investors to be able to afford to replicate.

The overall advantage of a passive bond management portfolio strategy is lower transaction costs over an active investment strategy, but a passive strategy also makes fluctuations in the value of the bond issue before maturity meaningless. However, if the investor needs the money for any reason before maturity, the current market value would be important.

Active Investment Strategy

Active investment strategies involve bond swapping, anticipating changes in interest rates, analysis of bond values, credit, and yield analyses. Table 16-4 summarizes what strategies you can pursue to increase your rate of return.

Bond swapping involves replacing existing bonds in the portfolio with new bonds. This strategy may be used for tax purposes in order to reduce capital gains taxes. At the end of the tax year, if an investor has capital gains from other transactions, he or she can sell some bonds, whose prices have declined, for a loss to offset some or all of the capital gains. (If the investor has bonds in the portfolio that have not declined in price, this strategy cannot be used.) The proceeds from the sale of the bonds are used to buy similar type bonds (same maturity and quality). By swapping one set of bonds for another set of similar bonds, the investor has benefited by generating a tax loss, which brings about tax savings.

Table 16-4

Strategies to Increase Returns

Increase the income received from bond investments:

Increase the *maturities* of your bonds, particularly if the yield curve indicates that long-term rates will remain higher than intermediate-term and short-term bond rates. Bear in mind that the longer the maturity of the bond, the greater the potential volatility.

Increase your holdings of *lower-quality* bonds. Before doing so you should examine the spread between the yields of good-quality bonds and lower-quality bonds to see if the returns are worth the risks. Moving from Treasuries to good-quality corporate bonds with higher yields may give you fewer sleepless nights than a move from Treasuries to corporate junk bonds. If junk bonds are too risky, move up the spectrum to medium-quality bonds. The move to lower-quality bonds comes with the prerequisite that you can tolerate the increased risks.

If you are in the higher tax brackets, consider municipal bonds to increase *after-tax returns.* Calculate the taxable yields of municipal bonds so that they can be compared with the equivalent taxable bond yield. This can be done by dividing the tax-free yield of a municipal bond by 1 minus the marginal tax rate. For example, a 4.5% yield on a municipal bond is equivalent to a 6.92% taxable yield for an investor in the 35% tax bracket. If the after-tax yields are greater than what you can get from taxable bonds, you should consider municipal bonds.

Other reasons for swapping bonds are to improve yields (a lower yielding bond swapped for a higher yielding bond) or to take advantage of price differentials between different types of bonds. For example, selling agency bonds and replacing them with higher yielding corporate bonds.

Anticipation of *changes in interest rates* could prompt investors to swap bonds with different maturities. If higher market rates of interest are anticipated, the investor would swap existing bonds for shorter maturities. Anticipation of lower rates of interest would lead to swapping bonds for longer maturities.

Instead of trying to anticipate market rates of interest, investors could pursue a number of strategies that allow for changes in interest rates.

Using a *matching strategy*, an investor determines the holding period or time frame for the investments, and then selects a bond portfolio duration equal to the holding period. For instance, if the holding period is seven years, a bond portfolio duration equal to seven years is selected. Duration is a measure of the weighted average time that it takes for the bondholder to receive the cash flows from the bond to equal the investment in the bond.

The duration value is determined by three factors:

1. Maturity of the bond
2. Market rates of interest
3. Coupon rate

Duration has a positive correlation with maturity (the longer the maturity, the greater the duration) and a negative correlation with coupon rates and market rates of interest (the larger the coupon rate, the lower the duration, and similarly duration moves in the opposite direction to interest rates). By matching the duration to the time period when the funds will be needed, interest rate risk is minimized. If interest rates rise, the value of the bonds in the portfolio decline, but the interest payments received are reinvested at higher rates of interest. Similarly, if interest rates decline, the bonds in the portfolio increase in price, and the interest payments are reinvested at lower interest rates. Through the use of duration, a portfolio can be protected against the changes in market rates of interest.

Active bond portfolio management involves anticipating future interest rates and using the information to position the portfolio to benefit from the changes. One approach is to anticipate future rates and predict the future shape of the yield curve, which forms the basis for the choice of maturities for the bond portfolio.

There are three yield curve strategies that can be used for choosing bond maturities for a portfolio. These are:

1. Ladder strategy
2. Barbell strategy
3. Bullet strategy

A *ladder strategy* is another method to cope with changes in market rates of interest. It is a passive strategy that does not attempt to forecast future interest rates. Generally, long-term maturity bonds have the highest yields to maturity, but they also carry the highest interest rate risk, which means that a laddered strategy spreads the maturities uniformly over the investment period. Instead of pursuing the highest yields to maturity, a laddered strategy consists of choosing bonds with short-, medium-, and long-term maturities over a period of time. This strategy is illustrated in Figure 16-8 with a 10-year laddered portfolio that has 10 percent of the bond issues with a maturity of one year, another 10 percent of

FIGURE 16-8

Ladder Strategy

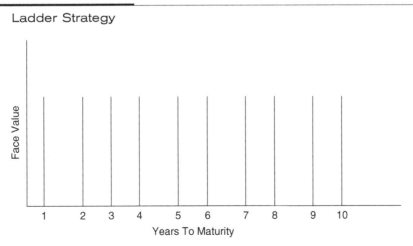

the bond issues with a maturity of two years, and so on. When the first year's bonds mature, the investor reinvests the funds (particularly if they are not needed by the investor) in issues with a 10-year maturity to maintain the original laddering structure. The time span chosen can fit the investor's needs (1 to 5 years for short-term frames or 1 to 20 years for a longer time frame).

The advantages of laddering are:

- Ten percent of bonds mature on a yearly basis to provide for short-term needs.
- Short-term bonds generally earn more than leaving funds in money market securities.
- The impact on valuations of the bonds in the portfolio is reduced when interest rates fluctuate.

The disadvantage of laddering is that if the investor anticipates a change in interest rates, the investor would have to sell most of the bond issues in the portfolio to react fully to the anticipated changes. For instance, in the 10-year laddering example, if interest rates increase, the investor would want to replace nine tenths of the portfolio with higher coupon, shorter maturity investments. The same would be true for lower anticipated interest rates. The investor would want to replace most of the short-term maturities with longer-term, higher-yielding coupon issues.

The *barbell or dumbbell strategy,* shown in Figure 16-9, is used to counter the major disadvantage of laddering (having to liquidate a large percentage of the portfolio to take advantage of anticipated or actual changes in interest rates). A barbell strategy involves using only short-term and long-term bonds. Figure 16-9 shows a concentration of bond investments maturing in the 5th and 15th years. By eliminating intermediate-term bonds from the portfolio, the investor is better positioned to take advantage of anticipated changes in interest rates. If half the portfolio is invested in short-term bonds and lower rates are anticipated, the investor would sell the short-term bonds and reinvest in long-term bond issues. The opposite occurs when higher market rates are anticipated; long-term bonds are swapped for short-term bonds.

The advantages of the barbell strategy are:

- By eliminating intermediate-term bonds from the portfolio, investors will get increased liquidity from the

FIGURE 16-9

Barbell Strategy

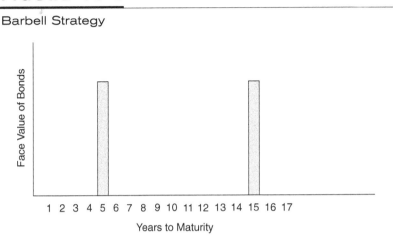

short-term bonds and increased returns from holding long-term issues.

- Only half the issues need to be swapped in the event of anticipated changes in interest rates.
- If market rates of interest are correctly anticipated, the impact of the changes will be reduced.

However, the major disadvantage is that if interest rates are incorrectly anticipated, the investor could experience greater losses.

A *bullet strategy* is a concentration of maturities at one point on the yield curve. An example is illustrated in Figure 16-10, where there is a concentration of bonds with 10-year maturities in the portfolio. Such a decision is usually based on anticipated interest rates or specific cash needs on the time horizon.

The advantage of a bullet strategy is:

- If cash is needed at a specific point in time in the future, a bullet strategy allows for that concentration of maturities.

The major disadvantage is that an adverse swing in interest rates could affect the entire portfolio.

These strategies (ladder, barbell, and bullet) are attempts to eliminate the effects of changes in interest rates on a portfolio. However, a key ingredient for the successful active management of a bond portfolio is accurate forecasting of interest rates.

FIGURE 16-10

Bullet Strategy

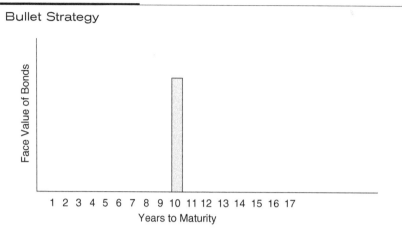

Active management involves monitoring the *credit risk* of bonds in a portfolio. Ideally, the aim is to sell bonds before they are downgraded by the ratings services, because once bonds are downgraded, their prices decline rapidly. Most investors, however, are not clairvoyant, and so credit analysis requires fundamental analysis of the financial condition of corporations (for corporate bonds), municipalities, and agencies, along with the external economic factors that affect bonds in order to determine which bonds to hold and which to sell.

Another active management tool is *yield spread analysis*, which involves comparing the yield-to-maturity (YTM) rates of bonds to the benchmark U.S. Treasury bond. Generally when YTM rate spreads widen between different quality bonds, the market is forecasting slower economic growth and expecting greater default risk on lower grade bonds. A narrowing of YTM rate spreads of different quality bonds indicates an economy with faster economic growth and lower risk of default on lower grade bonds. In March 2008, the credit markets reflected the risk of mortgage-backed bond defaults through yield spreads of more than 2.17 percentage points over comparable U.S. Treasury bonds. The spread on corporate junk bonds increased from 2.4 percent over the summer of 2007 to 8 percentage points over comparable maturity Treasury bonds (Rappaport, 2008).

Investors look to take advantage of changes in the yield relationships. If, for example, the risk of default is not perceived to be high on government-backed mortgage bonds, investors might feel comfortable swapping their U.S. Treasury bonds for government-backed mortgage bonds earning the additional yield spread. Investors should always question whether the additional returns are worth the additional risk from the move to swap into riskier securities.

CONCLUSION

Portfolio management begins with clear objectives as to what is expected from the portfolio. With careful analysis of personal and financial characteristics, an asset allocation plan of the categories of investments for the portfolio is made. The next step is the choice of the individual investments and the extent of the diversification among these investments. Finally, the management of the portfolio will be guided by the investment objectives. Managing a successful portfolio is more than selecting good investments.

The different types of investment assets can be complex. Investors should invest in only those investments that they fully understand. If the investor does not follow or fully understand the nuances of investing in individual stocks or bonds, he or she should stick with mutual funds or exchange-traded funds.

Even a passively managed portfolio should be examined at various intervals with regard to returns on different investments as well as the changing economic conditions. Not all investments achieve their anticipated returns, and if they turn out to be poor performers, they might need to be liquidated.

Investors who do not have the knowledge and skills to manage their portfolios might turn to professional advisors. Financial planners and accountants offer advice on the planning and management of portfolios. For investors who do not wish to be involved in the management of their assets, there are professional money managers and trust departments of various institutions. Their fees are often a stated percentage of the total dollar amount of the portfolio, which often requires that the portfolio be substantial in dollar terms.

The key to long-term successful investing is to allocate investments into bonds, stocks, and money market securities suited to
the investor's particular objectives and circumstances.

REFERENCES

Faerber, Esmé, *All About Stocks,* New York: McGraw-Hill, 2008.

Faerber, Esmé, *Fundamentals of the Bond Market,* New York: McGraw-Hill, 2001.

Rappaport, Liz, "Bond, Loan Markets Remain Wary," *Wall Street Journal,* March 27, 2008, pp. C1, C2.

INDEX